Prague

city guide

John King

Richard Nebeský

Prague – city guide
1st edition
Published by
Lonely Planet Publications
Head Office: PO Box 617, Hawthorn, Vic 3122, Australia
Branches: PO Box 2001A, Berkeley, CA 94702, USA
10 Barley Mow Passage, Chiswick,
London W4 4PH, UK
71 bis rue du Cardinal Lemoine,
75005 Paris, France

Printed by
Colorcraft Ltd, Hong Kong

Photographs by
John King (JK), Richard Nebeský (RN),
Rob van Driesum(RvD)

Front cover: The Astronomical Clock (RN)
Front cover gatefold: Top: National Theatre (RN)
Bottom: Basilica of St George (RN)
Back cover: Charles Bridge & Prague Castle (RN)
Back cover gatefold: Top: Týn Church (RN)
Bottom: St Nicholas Church,
Old Town Square (RN)

First Published
June 1994

National Library of Australia Cataloguing in Publication Data

King, John (John S.).
Prague city guide.

Includes index.
ISBN 0 86442 212 1.
1. Prague (Czech Republic) – Guidebooks. I. Nebesky, Richard. II. Title. (Series : Lonely Planet city guide)

914.37120443

John King

John grew up in the USA, destined for the academic life, but in a rash moment in 1984 he took off to China for a year, teaching English and travelling. Since then he has squeezed out a living as a travel writer and photographer, encouraged by his wife, Julia Wilkinson, who does the same. Together they split their time at 'home' between south-west England and remoter parts of Hong Kong. John is also author of LP's Karakoram Highway, co-author of Pakistan and of USSR, and has helped update West Asia on a Shoestring.

For this book, John concentrated his efforts east of the Vltava and on excursions outside Prague, and put together the Facts for the Visitor chapter.

Richard Nebeský

Richard was born in Prague but left with his family after the Soviet-led invasion in 1968 and settled in Australia. He has a BA in politics and history, and has travelled and worked in Europe, Asia, North America and Africa. He joined Lonely Planet in 1987, and since then he has been co-author of LP's Eastern Europe Phrasebook and has helped to update the travel survival kits to Australia and Indonesia; he is currently helping to update Thailand.

For this book, Richard climbed up and down the hills west of the Vltava, and put together most of the Facts about Prague chapter as well as the all-important Czech food notes in the Places to Eat chapter.

From the Authors

John wishes to thank Richard Bradley, vice-consul at the British Embassy in Prague; Ludmila Martinková for excellent help in Kutná Hora; Sara Meaker and Jon Giddings, who wrote from Poland with good advice; and the Čedok and PIS staffers whom he pestered to the point of madness. Thanks to Luděk Bartoš and Jiří Tuček for their good hospitality. Most importantly, *mokrát děkuji* to Richard for enduring John's questions and graceless meddling.

Richard would like to thank his father for help and invaluable advice, and of course also his mother. In Prague, a very special thanks for priceless information, help and generosity to Luděk Bartoš, including his family Zdena and Míša, and to Blanka & Olín Vala, all of whom put up with his intrusions and constant questions. Other people he would like to thank are Lucka & Martin Měkota, Lenka & Jaroslav Průcha, Petr Mařík, Aleš Krejčí, and Zdena Li for an interesting and different insight into her Prague. Also a special thanks to Růžena Bartošová and Vašíček Podhorský, as well as Tomáš & Mařena Bartoš.

John and Richard both owe great thanks to Rob van Driesum and Sally Woodward for heroic work under trying circumstances!

From the Publisher

This book was edited at the Lonely Planet head office in Melbourne, Australia, by Rob van Driesum, with help from Kristin Odijk and Simone Calderwood. The maps were drawn by Sally Woodward who also designed the book; Tamsin Wilson designed the cover. Rowan McKinnon produced the index, and LP's computer supremo, Dan Levin, made light work of the potentially crippling Czech accents.

Warning & Request

Things change – prices go up, schedules change, good places go bad and bad places go bankrupt. This is particularly true of Prague, where an explosion of tourism and the development of free enterprise combine to produce rapid changes in tourist facilities. So if you find things better or worse, recently opened or long since closed, please write and tell us and help make the next edition better.

Your letters will be used to help update future editions and, where possible, important changes will also be included in a Stop Press section in reprints. We greatly appreciate all information that is sent to us by travellers. Back at Lonely Planet we employ a hard-working readers' letters team to sort through the many letters we receive. The best ones will be rewarded with a free copy of the next edition or another Lonely Planet guide if you prefer. We give away lots of books, but, unfortunately, not every letter/postcard receives one.

Contents

Maps

Maps 5-18 appear at the back of the book

Introduction

As central Europe's Communist regimes fell like dominoes in 1989, Czechoslovakia's 'Velvet Revolution' stood out for its swiftness and dignity. The Czechs had already captured our imaginations in the aborted 'Prague Spring' of 1968 and, we felt, they'd make a good job of liberation. They confirmed it by choosing a playwright and moral philosopher as their new president.

At the centre of the drama was *Praha*, historic heart of Bohemia and one of Europe's most beautiful cities – kidnapped by neo-Stalinism but now 'home' again. This romantic image refuses to go away, in spite of the gloomy 'Velvet Divorce' that later split the country into Czech and Slovak republics, and the excesses that now accompany Prague's rise to the top of the tourism charts.

As many as 100 million people may have visited the two republics in 1993, and most of them spent some time in Prague. In summer the hotels of this former Eastern-bloc backwater are now stretched to breaking point, and its narrow lanes are choked with Dutch tour groups, German weekenders and Italian school children. The city has discovered shifty waiters, crooked cabbies, pick-pockets and other flotsam that collects in the wake of tourism. Prices keep rising, and the owners of newly privatised buildings scramble to repair them before they fall down.

View of Malá Strana from St Vitus Cathedral (RN)

And yet Prague remains for most of us a fairy tale come true – the 'city of 100 spires', its compact medieval centre a web of cobbled lanes, ancient courtyards, dark passages and churches beyond number, an architectural smorgasbord of Romanesque, Gothic, Baroque and Art Nouveau – all watched over by an 1100-year-old castle with liveried guards. Veteran travellers lament not having it to themselves any more, and of course it must have been a delight before 1989 – no crowds, no billboards, nobody shooting Audi commercials in the backstreets.

But there's a different kind of fizz here now. Prague is incredibly youthful: thousands of twentysomething Westerners have settled down here as artists, consultants and entrepreneurs, leading journalists to effuse about a 'new Left Bank'. Known already for its musical and literary life, and in this century for ground-breaking visual arts and cinema, the city has also become a magnet for top-flight jazz, rock and post-rock.

Meanwhile, from the open door of a backstreet pub comes the sound of Czechs enjoying the best beer in the world, and from the open window of a recreation centre the strains of an out-of-tune amateur string quartet. In some ways Prague carries on as it always has, and Czechs welcome visitors with grace and 'Praguematism', not only for their money but as new neighbours.

Facts about Prague

HISTORY

The oldest evidence of human habitation in the Prague valley dates from 600,000 BC, with more numerous clues left by mammoth-hunters during the last Ice Age, about 25,000 years ago. Permanent farming communities were established around 4000 BC in the north-western parts of Prague, and the area was inhabited continuously by various Germanic and Celtic tribes before the arrival of the Slavs in the 6th century. It was from a Celtic tribe named the Boii that Bohemia got its name, a name still used today for the western part of the Czech Republic.

Přemysl Dynasty

Prague Castle was established in the 870s by Prince Bořivoj as the main seat of the Přemysl dynasty, with Vyšehrad sometimes serving as an alternative in the 10th and 11th centuries (see the Vyšehrad section in the Things to See & Do chapter for notes on the mythical founding of this dynasty).

In 950, the German King Otto I conquered Bohemia and incorporated it into the Holy Roman Empire. It was ruled on the Germans' behalf by Přemysl princes until 1212, when the pope granted Otakar I the right to rule as king. Otakar bestowed royal privileges on the Old Town, and Malá Strana was established in 1257 by Přemysl Otakar II.

Prague's Golden Age

Wenceslas (Václav) III's murder in 1306 left no male heir to the Přemysl throne. Two Habsburg monarchs ruled Bohemia, and in 1310 John of Luxembourg (Jan Lucemburský to Czechs) became king. During the reign of his son, Charles (Karel) IV (1346-78), as king of Bohemia and Holy Roman emperor, Prague experienced its so-called Golden Age and grew into one of the largest cities on the continent. It acquired its fine Gothic face, and landmarks including Charles University, Charles Bridge and St Vitus Cathedral.

The Hussite Revolution

The late 14th and early 15th centuries witnessed the Church-reform movement led by Jan Hus (1372-1415), who was inspired by the English reformist theologian John Wycliffe. Hus preached in Czech (sermons had previously only been in Latin) against the corruptness of the Catholic Church, a century before Martin Luther espoused similar ideas in Germany. Hus was tried at the Council of Constance for heresy and burned at the stake in 1415, sparking a nationalist rebellion in Bohemia led by the Hussite preacher Jan Želivský.

After the death of Holy Roman Emperor and King of Bohemia Wenceslas IV in 1419, Prague was ruled by various Hussite committees. In the 1420s a split developed in their ranks between the radical Taborites who advocated total war on the Catholics, and the moderate Utraquists who consisted mainly of nobles and were more concerned with transforming the Church.

In 1420, the combined Hussite forces led by General Jan Žižka successfully defended Prague against the first anti-Hussite crusade launched by Sigismund, the Holy Roman Emperor. In 1434 the Utraquists agreed to accept Sigismund's rule in return for religious tolerance; the Taborites kept fighting, only to de defeated in the same year at the Battle of Lipany.

The Hussite George of Poděbrady (Jiří z Poděbrad) ruled as Bohemia's only Hussite king from 1452 to 1471, with the backing of Utraquist forces. He was centuries ahead of his time in suggesting a European council to

Statue of Jan Hus, Old Town Square (RN)

solve international problems by diplomacy rather than war, but he couldn't convince the major European rulers or the pope. After his death, two weak kings from the Polish Jagiellonian dynasty ruled Bohemia, though real power lay with the Utraquist nobles, the so-called Bohemian Estates.

Habsburg Rule

In 1526 the Catholic Habsburgs were again elected to rule Bohemia. After an unsuccessful Utraquist uprising, Prague lost its royal privileges, though it remained the Bohemian capital.

In the second half of the 16th century the city experienced great prosperity under Emperor Rudolf II, and was made the seat of the Habsburg Empire. Rudolf established great art collections, and renowned artists and scholars were invited to his court.

A blow to Czech fortunes for the next 300 years was an ill-fated uprising of the Bohemian Estates in 1618, which began when two Habsburg councillors were flung from an upper window in Prague Castle (thus introducing the word 'defenestration' into political vocabulary). This sparked off the Thirty Years' War, which was to devastate much of Europe and Bohemia in particular; a quarter of the Bohemian population perished.

The Bohemian Estates elected Frederick of the Palatinate, the so-called 'Winter King', as their ruler. Because of ineffective leadership and low troop morale, the crucial Battle of the White Mountain in 1620 was lost almost before the first shots were fired, and the Winter King fled. The 27 nobles who had instigated the revolt were executed in Old Town Square.

The Czechs lost their privileges, rights and property, and nearly even their national identity through forced Catholicisation and Germanisation. Saxons occupied Prague in 1631-32, and the Swedes seized Hradčany and Malá Strana in 1648. The (unconquered) Old Town suffered months of bombardment. The population of Prague declined from 60,000 in 1620 to 24,600 in 1648. The Habsburgs moved their throne back to Vienna and Prague was reduced to a provincial town, although it did get a major Baroque face-lift over the next century, particularly after a great fire in 1689.

Prague again suffered extensive damage during the War of the Austrian Succession (1740-48) and the Seven Years' War (1756-63), which pitted the armies of Habsburg Empress Maria Theresa against those of Frederick II 'the Great' of Prussia. Bohemia and Moravia were the scene of much of the fighting, and Prague was attacked three times between 1741 and 1757.

But the city continued to evolve economically, and architecturally. The four towns of Prague (Staré Město, Nové Město, Malá Strana and Hradčany) were joined into a single, strong unit by imperial decree in 1784.

The Czech National Revival

In the 19th century, Prague became the centre of the so-called Czech National Revival (České národní obrození), which found its initial expression in literature, journalism and theatre. Prague also joined in the 1848 revolutions that swept Europe, and the city was the first in the Austrian Empire to rise in favour of reform. Like most of the others, however, Prague's uprising was soon crushed.

Prague landmarks of this period include the National Theatre, National Museum and the New Town Hall. In 1861, Czechs defeated Germans in Prague council elections and edged them out of power forever, though the shrinking German minority still wielded substantial influence well into the 1880s.

Independence

As WW I drew to a close, Czechoslovakia declared its independence with Allied support on 28 October 1918. Prague became the capital, and the popular Tomáš Garrigue Masaryk became the republic's first president.

On 1 January 1922, Greater Prague was established by the absorption of several surrounding towns and villages, growing to a city of 677,000. Like the rest of the country, Prague experienced an industrial boom until the Great Depression of the 1930s. By 1938 the population had grown to one million.

WW II

Unfortunately the new country was not left to live in peace. Most of Bohemia's three million German-speakers wished to join greater Germany, and in October 1938 the Nazis occupied the Sudetenland with the acquiescence of Britain and France after the infamous Munich Agreement; the Poles took part of northern Moravia, and the Hungarians seized Ruthenia and the southern areas of Slovakia. On 15 March 1939, Germany occupied Bohemia and Moravia, declaring the region a 'protectorate', while Slovakia proclaimed independence as a Nazi puppet state.

Prague suffered little physical damage during the war. The Germans destroyed the Czech underground – and hundreds of innocent villagers in Lidice – in retaliation for the assassination in Prague of Reichsprotektor Reinhard Heydrich by Czechoslovak parachutists trained in Britain. The assassins were betrayed in their hiding place in the Church of SS Cyril & Methodius, and eventually committed suicide with their last bullets.

On 5 May 1945 the population of Prague rose against the German forces as the Red Army approached from the east. US troops had reached Plzeň, but held back in deference to their Soviet allies. Many people died before the Germans began pulling out on 8 May, having been granted free passage out of the city by the Czech resistance movement. Most of Prague was thus liberated by its residents before Soviet forces finally arrived the following day. Liberation Day is now celebrated on 8 May; under Communism it was 9 May.

Communism

In 1945 Czechoslovakia was re-established as an independent state. In the 1946 elections, the Communists – who had played a leading role in the anti-German resistance – became the largest party with 36% of the popular vote, and formed a coalition government with other socialist parties.

Tension grew between socialists and non-socialists, and in February 1948 the Communists staged a coup d'état with the backing of the Soviet Union. A new constitution established the Party's dominance, and government was organised along Soviet lines. Thousands of non-Communists fled the country.

The 1950s were an era of harsh repression and decline as Communist economic policies nearly bankrupted the country. Many people were imprisoned, and hundreds were executed or died in labour camps, often for little more than a belief in democracy.

1968

In the 1960s Czechoslovakia enjoyed a gradual liberalisation under the reformist general secretary of the Czechoslovak Communist party, Alexander Dubček. But the short-lived 'Prague Spring' of 1968 was crushed by a Soviet-led invasion by Warsaw Pact troops on the night of 20-21 August. Prague was one of their first objectives, as Soviet special forces with help from the Czech secret service, the StB, secured Ruzyně Airport for Soviet transport planes.

At the end of the first day, 58 people had died. Passive resistance followed; street signs and numbers were removed from buildings throughout the country to disorient the invaders.

In 1969, Dubček was replaced by the orthodox Gustav Husák and exiled to the Slovak forestry department. Around 14,000 Party functionaries and 280,000 members who refused to renounce their belief in 'socialism with a human face' were expelled from the Party and lost their jobs. Many other educated professionals became street cleaners and manual labourers.

In 1977, a group of 243 writers, artists and intellectuals signed a public demand for basic human rights, *Charta 77* (Charter 77), which became a focus for opponents of the regime. Prominent among them was the playwright Václav Havel.

The 'Velvet Revolution'

The regime remained in control until the opening of the Berlin Wall in November 1989. On 17 November, Prague's Communist youth movement organised an officially sanctioned demonstration in memory of nine students executed by the Nazis in 1939. But the peaceful crowd of 50,000 was cornered in Národní street, where some 500 were beaten by the police and about 100 were arrested.

The following days saw constant demonstrations by students, artists and finally most of the populace, peaking in a rally on Letná by some 750,000 people. Leading dissidents, with Havel at the forefront, formed an anti-Communist coalition which negotiated the government's resignation on 3 December. A 'Government of National Understanding' was formed, with the Communists as a minority member. Havel was elected president of the republic by the federal assembly on 29 December.

The days following the 17 November demonstration have become known as the 'Velvet Revolution' *(Sametová revoluce)* because there were no casualties.

The 'Velvet Divorce'

Free elections to the federal assembly in June 1990 were won by Občanské hnutí (OH, Civic Forum) and its Slovak counterpart, Verejnosť Proti Násilu (VPN, People Against Violence). But Civic Forum soon split into two factions over differences on economic policy: the right-of-centre Občanská demokratická strana (ODS, Civic Democratic Party) led by Václav Klaus, and the left-of-

Summer 1990: Trabant on legs on Old Town Square (top) and graffiti-covered Russian tank on its side at the bottom end of Wenceslas Square (note the 'no tanks' traffic sign). Both works of art have since been removed (RvD)

centre Civic Forum led by Jiří Dienstbier. Klaus forced through some tough economic policies, whose success gave the ODS a slim victory in the June 1992 elections.

Meanwhile, separatists headed by Vladimir Mečiar won the 1992 elections in Slovakia, depriving the ODS of a parliamentary majority. Mečiar's and Klaus' very different economic positions made compromise almost impossible, with Mečiar favouring slow economic transformation and gradual independence for Slovakia.

The two leaders decided that splitting the country might be the best solution. A referendum on the issue would almost certainly have been defeated, and thus was not held, though Havel wanted one. In the end Havel resigned rather than preside over the inevitable split.

On 1 January 1993, Czechoslovakia ceased to exist for the second time this century. Prague became the capital of the new Czech Republic, and Havel was elected as its first president.

Thanks to Klaus' economic policies, booming tourism and a solid industrial base, the Czech Republic is so far undergoing a strong economic recovery. Unemployment in Prague is negligible, shops are full, and many buildings are getting facelifts. The picture is not all roses, however, with an acute shortage of affordable housing, steeply rising crime, severe pollution and a deteriorating health system. But the newly founded democracy and its radical economic transformation seem to be working.

GOVERNMENT

Prague is the capital of the Czech Republic and the seat of government, parliament and the president. The city itself is governed separately from other regions of the country, by the Local Government of the Capital City of Prague, headed by a council and a mayor. The acting body of this government is the municipal office together with the council. Prague is divided into 10 districts and 57 suburbs, governed by district and local governments.

ECONOMY

Since the Industrial Revolution, Bohemia and Moravia have specialised in light industry, and in central Europe their combined industrial output was second only to Germany's. During Communist rule, industry and agriculture were nationalised, and heavy industry was introduced along Soviet lines, mainly in steel and machinery. Other important industries include vehicles, armaments, cement, plastics, cotton, ceramics and beer.

Agricultural products include sugar beets, wheat, potatoes, corn, barley, rye, hops, lumber, cattle, pigs, chickens, horses and carp. The country lacks natural energy sources apart from large deposits of low-quality brown coal in North Bohemia and North Moravia, which generate most of the country's electricity and are a major source of pollution.

About 9% of Prague's population is employed in manufacturing, making it the largest manufacturing centre in the republic. Major industries are textiles, machinery and food; Karlín and Smíchov are the two major industrial suburbs. Most of the population is employed in service industries and of course touristm.

Since 1990, the government has embarked on an ambitious privatisation scheme in two phases. The 'small-privatisation' phase has included the return of property to pre-1948 owners or their descendants, and the sale of enterprises through auctions or straight to foreign buyers. Prague's hotels and restaurants are now all privately owned, though the government still holds most theatres and museums.

The 'large-privatisation' phase concentrated on large-scale industries and small enterprises that had not yet found buyers. Sales were conducted mainly through a coupon system by which every citizen had a chance to become a shareholder. An important element was the April 1993 reopening of the Prague stock exchange. This phase is now focusing on the return of Church property, implementation of a bankruptcy law, and privatisation of agriculture and health care.

Despite the setback of the split with Slovakia, the Czech economy is doing well. Inflation was managable at 16% in 1993. The Czech currency and its government-controlled exchange rates have been stable for three years. Unemployment is 3.2%, while in Prague it is under 1%.

The average wage is just over 7000 Kč a month, enough for a reasonably comfortable life. The exceptions are Prague residents who live in the central tourist zones, where many costs have gone through the roof.

ORIENTATION

Prague sits within the gentle landscape of the Bohemian plateau, straddling the Czech Republic's longest river, the Vltava (pronounced Vl-TA-va, Moldau in German). Thirty km downstream (north), the Vltava enters the

Labe, which drains northern Bohemia and then crosses Germany (as the Elbe) to the North Sea.

The centre of Prague consists of five historical towns. On a hill above the west bank is **Hradčany**, the castle district, with Prague Castle and St Vitus Cathedral giving the city its trademark skyline. Beneath this, climbing up from the river, is **Malá Strana**, the 13th century 'Lesser Quarter', marked by the dome of St Nicholas Church; from Petřín Hill, south and behind Malá Strana, are the finest panoramic views of the city.

On the Vltava's east bank is **Staré Město**, the 'Old Town', a Gothic and Baroque landscape surrounding an immense central square, Staroměstké náměstí (Old Town Square). Frozen in time in one corner of Staré Město is **Josefov**, the former Jewish ghetto, now riven by the Art-Nouveau bravado of Pařížská street. **Nové Město**, the 'New Town' (new in the 14th century), cradling the Old Town to the south and east, includes Václavské náměstí or Wenceslas Square, symbol of Bohemia's ancient aspirations and of the 'Velvet Revolution'.

Within these historical districts – linked by the landmark Charles Bridge over the Vltava – are most of the city's attractions. The whole compact maze is best appreciated on foot, aided by good public transport. Beyond the centre is 19th and 20th century Prague, many of whose districts began as remote towns.

Prague is divided into 10 districts, often quoted in addresses (see the Greater Prague map). Prague 1 and parts of Prague 2 to the south cover the historical centre.

Points of Arrival & Departure

See the Getting There & Away and Getting Around chapters for more information about the following gateways:

Air Ruzyně Airport is 17 km west of the centre, a 40-minute ride by bus.

Train The main train station, Praha hlavní nádraží (also called Wilsonovo nádraží), is three blocks from Wenceslas Square in the north-east of Nové Město. Other stations served by some international trains are Praha-Holešovice, north of the centre, and Praha-Smíchov in the south-west. All three are beside metro stations of the same name.

The most likely stations for long-distance domestic trains are the main station and Masarykovo nádraží, two blocks north of it. Others where you might end up are

Praha-Dejvice (two blocks to/from metro station Hradčanská), Praha-Smíchov, Praha-Vysočany north-east of the centre (bus No 185, 209, 259 or 278 to/from metro station Českomoravská), and Praha-Vršovice (tram No 24 to/from Wenceslas Square).

Bus Nearly all international and long-distance buses use Praha-Florenc station, also on the east side of Nové Město, beside metro station Florenc. Regional buses – eg for excursions out of Prague – go from here and, depending on the destination, from one of the stands near metro stations Anděl, Hradčanská, Nádraží Holešovice, Palmovka, Radlická, Roztyly, Smíchovské nádraží and Želivského.

Place Names

In this book we tend to use the Czech names for districts, squares, streets and some buildings; this will certainly make it easier for Czechs to understand your queries. Where useful, they're accompanied by English translations when they first appear.

A few places have become well known among Western tourists (and Czech tour guides!) by their English names – eg Charles Bridge, Old Town Square, Wenceslas Square – and for these we tend to use the English names.

Addresses

Numbers apply to buildings rather than premises. Confusingly, most buildings have *two* numbers. The one on a blue sign is its position on the street, sequentially with odd numbers on one side and even on the other. The one on a red sign is its number in the district, and usually bears no relation to its neighbours.

In this book we use 'blue' numbers if there's a choice. Older buildings may have only 'red' ones. Sometimes both numbers are given in an address, separated by a slash (/).

CLIMATE & WHEN TO GO

The Czech Republic has a transitional climate between maritime and continental, characterised by hot, showery summers, cold, snowy winters and generally changeable conditions. A typical day in Prague during June to August sees the mercury range from about 12°C to 22°C. Temperatures from December to February push below

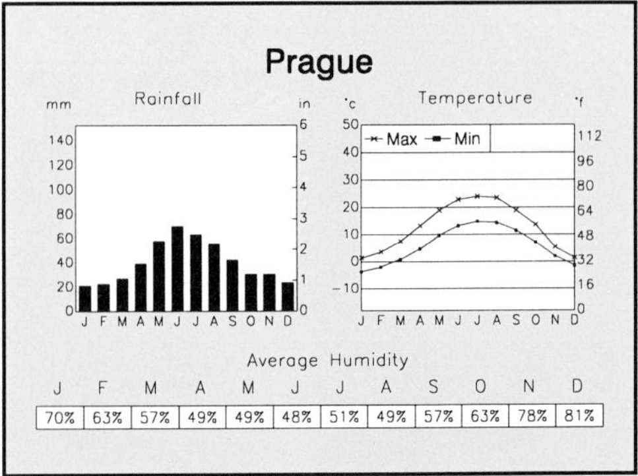

freezing. Wide variations are common, sometimes surpassing 35°C in summer and -20°C in winter.

The closest thing to a 'dry season' is January through March, when total precipitation (mostly as snow at that time) is less than a third of that during the wettest months, June through August. And yet January averages as many 'wet' days (about two out of five) as do the summer months. Summer's long, sunny hot spells tend to be broken by sudden, heavy thunderstorms. May and September have the finest weather, with April and October as somewhat cooler alternatives.

While attractions across much of the Czech Republic close or keep limited hours outside the summer season, Prague caters to visitors throughout the year. Certain periods, when the tourist crush is especially oppressive, are worth avoiding. Over the Easter and Christmas/New Year holidays, hordes of German, Austrian and Italian revellers descend on the city. European tourists' favourite season for Prague is May/June. Czechs themselves tend to go on holiday in July and August – during which time the supply of bottom-end accommodation actually increases, as student hostels are opened to visitors.

If you can stand the winter cold, hotel space is plentiful then (outside Christmas/New Year), and Prague is gorgeous under a mantle of snow.

Air Pollution

During most of the year, or after a long weekend or in windy weather, Prague's air is fairly breathable. But in mid-winter when everyone is burning coal for heating and the streets are jammed full of cars, the air can be thick and foul, especially when an inversion layer occurs (a meteorological phenomenon whereby the air temperature increases with altitude, causing very stable conditions). If you are just visiting for a few days, there is little to fear, but Prague residents suffer from a high rate of respiratory ailments.

Radio and TV stations provide bulletins about pollution levels, or the Prague Information Service (PIS, see the Facts for the Visitor chapter) should be able to tell you whether there is any risk.

POPULATION & PEOPLE

Czechs are West Slavs, as are Poles, Slovaks and Lusatians (Sorbs). According to the latest census, in 1991, the population of Prague was 1,215,000, or 2434 people per sq km. Roughly one out of 13 Czech citizens lives in Prague. In addition to Slovak and Romany (Gypsy) minorities, there are significant numbers of expatriate foreigners living and working in the city, especially Americans and Germans; conservative estimates put the number of Americans at around 10,000.

ARTS

Architecture

The earliest Slavic buildings in Bohemia were wooden and have not survived. The earliest non-perishable structures were stone Romanesque rotunda-churches, though most have since been incorporated into larger churches. Prague's finest rotunda is the Basilica of St George in Prague Castle.

The 13th century saw the appearance of the Gothic style in buildings and entire town centres, with arcaded houses built around a central square. Czech Gothic architecture flourished during the rule of Charles IV, especially in the works of Peter Parler. Prominent late-Gothic architects were Benedikt Rejt and Matěj Rejsek.

Renaissance architecture appeared in the early 16th century with Italian designers invited to Prague by Habsburg rulers. The emphasis was more on chateaux and merchant houses than on churches. The mixture of Italian and local styles gave rise to the unique 'Czech Renaissance' style, featuring heavy ornamental stucco decorations and paintings of historical or mythical scenes.

Re-Catholicisation and reconstruction after the Thirty Years' War introduced the Baroque style in Habsburg

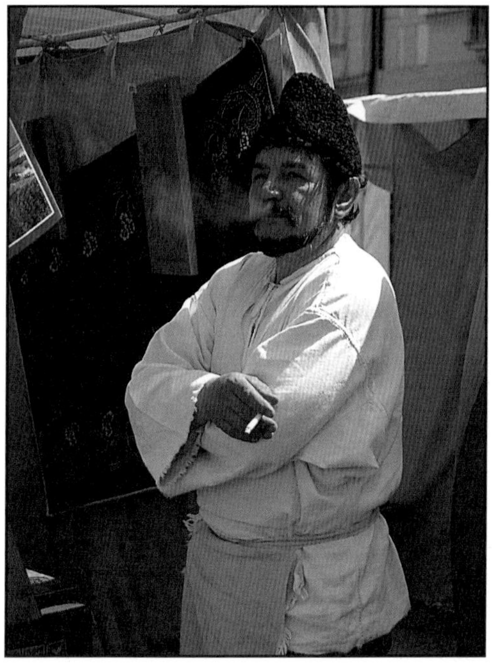

Souvenir salesman (RN)

palaces, residences and new churches. This was the grandest period in Bohemian architecture, responsible for the Baroque 'face' of Prague today. In the early 18th century a Czech Baroque style emerged. Its best-known practitioners were the Bavarian father and son Kristof and Kilian Ignatz Dientzenhofer, the Italian Giovanni Santini and the Bohemian František Kaňka. The best example among many is the Dientzenhofers' St Nicholas Church in Malá Strana.

The 19th century saw numerous revival movements – neo-Classical, neo-Gothic, neo-Renaissance – which in the mid-19th century coincided with the Czech National Revival in Czech and Slovak art. One of the finest works of this period is the neo-Renaissance National Theatre (1883) by Josef Zítek.

As in the rest of Europe, Czech architecture in the early 20th century was under the spell of Art Nouveau,

Top : Art-Nouveau façade of the Obecní dům (JK)
Bottom : Romanesque Rotunda of the Holy Cross (JK)

with its sinuous, 'botanical' lines. The term came from the French *l'art nouveau* and was known as *secese* in Bohemia, *Sezessionstil* in Austria and *Jugendstil* in Germany. The most visible Art-Nouveau works in Prague are the Municipal House (Obecní dům), the main train station, and structures built for the Terrestrial Jubilee Exposition of 1891 in Holešovice.

Cubism had a strong influence on architecture before WW I, developing into a striking local style. Some of Prague's finest Cubist façades were designed by Josef Chochol in the neighbourhood just below Vyšehrad.

The post-WW I era was a period of avant-garde architecture, most notably that of Jan Kotěra. Much of it was functional, such as the creation for the Baťa shoe industry of the town of Zlín, where Kotěra designed many buildings.

Architectural Styles

Romanesque This style dates from the 10th to 13th centuries. A typical Romanesque church has thick walls, closely spaced columns and heavy, rounded arches. Of the surviving Romanesque structures in Prague and the Czech Republic, many are simple circular (rotunda) chapels.

Gothic The Gothic style predominated in the Czech Lands in the 13th to 16th centuries. It represented not just a new aesthetic but new engineering that permitted thinner walls and – in churches – taller, more delicate columns and great expanses of stained glass. Distinctive features included pointed arches and ribbed roof-vaults, external 'flying buttresses' to support the thinner walls, and elaborate carved doorway columns.

Renaissance The 16th century saw a new enthusiasm for classical forms and an obsession with grace and symmetry. Czech versions, especially in houses and chateaux, featured elaborate gables and rooftops, and exterior walls covered with sgraffito – in which designs such as mythical scenes are cut through the plaster into deeper, darker coloured layers.

Baroque This resplendent, triumphal style is closely associated with the rebuilding (and re-imposition of Catholicism) in the region after the Thirty Years' War. Emotional sculpture and painting, and rich, gilded ornamentation, seem designed to awe. Prague is dominated by Baroque façades now.

Rococo This is essentially late, over-the-top Baroque. Florid in the extreme, elaborate and 'lightweight', it was popular with architects in the late 18th century.

Revivalist Styles Neo-Classical, neo-Gothic and neo-Renaissance styles appeared in the late 1700s and 1800s. Neo-Classicism favoured grand colonnades and pediments, and often huge, simple, symmetrical buildings. Renaissance and Gothic revival styles played a part in the so-called National Revival movements in the Czech and Slovak lands.

Modern At the turn of the century, the decorative and sensual style called Art Nouveau, *secese, Sezessionstil* or *Jugendstil* produced some of the country's most striking buildings, in particular Prague's Obecní dům. Unique to Czechoslovakia was the fruitful development of Cubist architecture; Prague has some surprisingly simple and elegant examples. ■

Communist-era architecture was heavy-handed and Stalinist. In the 1960s, prefabricated concrete panels came into use as building materials in huge housing estates. This era has produced many eyesores and little style or quality. Restoration concentrated on prime tourist sights, neglecting other buildings.

Restoration work, both state-funded and private, has gone into high gear since 1989, though much remains to be done, and some structures are beyond help.

Painting

Gothic influences appear in the 14th century. Some of this era's finest work is by Master Theodoric, in the Chapel of the Holy Cross at Karlštejn Castle and the Chapel of St Wenceslas in St Vitus Cathedral. Master Theodoric's work had an unusually realistic style and influenced art throughout central Europe. The gem of Czech Gothic Art is an altar panel painted towards the end of the 14th century by an artist known only as the Master of the Třeboň Altar; what remains of it is in the Convent of St George in Prague Castle.

Czech painting broke away from Italian influences in the 15th century and developed a local style. The Baroque era saw a strong development of Catholic religious art, and Czech artists again began producing outstanding paintings.

In the late 18th and early 19th centuries a Czech style of Realism arose as part of the Czech National Revival. Famous artists include Antonín Machek, the father and son Antonín and Josef Mánes, Mikuláš Aleš, Václav Brožík and Vojtěch Hynais. Alfons Mucha is well known for his Art-Nouveau posters in the late 19th century. Czech landscape art developed in the works of A Kosárek and Julius Mařák, followed by a wave of Impressionism and Symbolism with artists like Antonín Slavíček and Max Švabinský.

In the early 20th century, Prague developed as a centre of avant-garde art, centred on a group of artists called *Osma* (The Eight). Prague was also a leading centre of Cubism with painters like Josef Čapek and Emil Filla. The Functionalist movement flourished between WW I and WW II in a group called Devětsil, led by the adaptable Karel Teige, followed by the Surrealists, including artists like Zdenek Rykr, Josef Šíma and Jindřich Štýrský.

After WW II, 40 years of Communism brought little art of interest through official channels, but several underground artists are worth mentioning. Mikuláš Medek's abstract and surrealist art was occasionally exhibited in out-of-the-way galleries. Jiří Kolář was an outstanding graphic artist and poet. Some never-exhibited artists of the postwar years have begun surfacing since 1989.

Sculpture

Medieval sculpture, like medieval painting, served religious ends. In the 12th and 13th centuries, sculpture evolved from ornamentation into realism. The 14th century saw further realist tendencies, represented by the portraits of royal and noble figures in St Vitus Cathedral. Soon a more decorative style took over, best exemplified by the unknown artist in the *Krumlov Virgin* in the Convent of St George in Prague Castle.

Religious sculpture continued to dominate in this period. Gothic Realism in the latter 15th century brought more lively forms, culminating in masterpieces such as the sculpture by the Master of Sorrows from Zěbrák, in the Convent of St George in Prague Castle.

During the Baroque era, religious sculpture sprouted in public places, including Marian columns erected out of gratitude to the Virgin for protection against the plague. Two outstanding Baroque sculptors were Matthias Braun and Ferdinand Maximilian Brokoff. An important figure at the end of the 18th century was Ignác František Platzer, whose decorative statues are all over Prague.

Bohemian sculpture then declined until a revival in the mid-19th century, a principal figure of that time being Václav Levý. Josef Václav Myslbek dominated sculpture in the latter 19th century with his Romantic

Art-Nouveau doorway ornament (JK)

Slavic style. His students, including Stanislav Sucharda, produced some brilliant Symbolist pieces. Other sculptors were the impressionists Ladislav Šaloun and Josef Mařatka.

One of the best known Cubist sculptors was Otto Gutfreund. In the 1920s he switched to Realism and influenced the next wave of sculptors like Jan Lauda, Karel Pokorný and Karel Dvořák. Surrealism followed, one of its best known figures being Ladislav Zívr.

Literature

The earliest literary works were hymns and religious texts in Old Church Slavonic, replaced by Latin during the late 11th century. The 14th and 15th centuries saw the appearance of reformist theological texts, mostly in Czech, by Jan Hus and others.

Czech literature entered a dark age after the Thirty Years' War with the imposition of German, but re-emerged in the late 18th century when Josef Dobrovský and Josef Jungmann began writing in Czech. In the mid-1800s, František Palacký published a huge history of Bohemia and Moravia. Karel Hynek Mácha, possibly the greatest of all Czech poets, was the leading representative of Romanticism in the early 19th century; his most famous lyrical work is *Máj* (May).

Mid-19th century Romanticism produced outstanding pieces about life in the country – especially *Babička* (Grandmother) by Božena Němcová (the first major female Czech writer), and Karel Erben's *Kytice*. The radical political journalist Karel Havlíček Borovský criticised the Habsburg elite and wrote excellent satirical poems. Jan Neruda and Svatopluk Čech were two great poets who derived inspiration from Czech history.

At the end of the 19th century, Alois Jirásek wrote *Staré pověsti české* (Old Czech Legends), an interpretation of Czech legends from the arrival of the Czechs in Bohemia to the Middle Ages, and nationalistic historical novels, his best being *Temno* (Darkness). A major political philosopher and writer of his time was Tomáš Garrigue Masaryk, who went on to become the Czechoslovak Republic's first president.

One of the best known writers of all was Franz Kafka, who with a circle of other German-speaking Jewish writers in Prague played a major role in the literary scene at the beginning of this century. Others were the dramatist Franz Werfel, the critic Max Brod and the journalist Egon Erwin Kisch. Among their Czech-speaking contemporaries was Jaroslav Hašek, now most famous for his *Good Soldier Švejk*.

Karel Čapek is one of the best known post-WW I Czech authors, for his science-fiction play *Rossum's Universal Robots*, through which the word 'robot' entered the English language. A contemporary was the playwright František Langer. Well-known poets from the interwar years were Jaroslav Seifert (awarded the Nobel Prize for Literature in 1984) and Vítěslav Nezval.

The early Communist period produced little of literary value, though the 1960s saw a resurgence as controls were relaxed. Writers like Václav Havel, Josef Škvorecký, Milan Kundera, Miroslav Hrabal and Ivan Klíma wrote their first masterpieces during the years before the Soviet-led invasion of 1968. Some writers left, others stayed and wrote for the underground *samizdat* press, or had manuscripts smuggled to the West – Havel wrote his plays at home, while Kundera and Škvorecký wrote their novels in exile. Other important figures from this time are the philosopher Jan Patočka and the poet Jiří Kolář.

Theatre

Czech-language theatre did not develop fully until the 16th century. Themes were mostly Biblical and the intent was to moralise. At Prague's Charles University, Latin drama was used for teaching. The best plays were written by Jan Ámos Komenský (John Comenius) in the years before the Thirty Years' War, after which plays in Czech were banned. German drama and Italian opera were popular during the 17th and 18th centuries, when many theatres were built.

In 1785, Czech drama reappeared at the Nostitz (now Stavovské or Estates) Theatre, and Prague became the centre of Czech-language theatre. Major 19th century playwrights were Josef Kajetán Tyl and Ján Kolár. Drama, historical plays and fairy tales flourished as part of the Czech National Revival. In 1862 the first independent theatre opened: Prague's Prozatimní divadlo (Temporary Theatre).

Drama in the early years of the First Republic was led by Karel and Josef Čapek and František Langer. Later, E F Burian, an actor and playwright, became known for his performances of experimental drama.

During the years of Communism, classical theatre performances were of a high quality, but the modern scene was stifled. There were exceptions such as the excellent pantomime of the Black Theatre (Černé Divadlo) and the ultra-modern Laterná Magika, founded by Alfréd Radok.

Some excellent plays, including those by Václav Havel, went unperformed locally due to their anti-government point of view, but appeared in the West. In the mid-1960s, free expression was explored in Prague's Zábradlí divadlo (Theatre on the Balustrade), with works by Ladislav Fialka, Havel and Milan Uhde, and performances by the comedy duo of Jiří Suchý and Jiří Šlitr.

Marionette & Puppet Theatre Marionette performances have been popular since the 16th century. A major figure of this art form was Matěj Kopecký (1775-1847). The composer Bedřich Smetana wrote two plays for marionettes.

Marionette theatres opened in Prague and Plzeň in the early 1900s, with Josef Skupa's legendary Špejbl & Hurvínek (the Czech 'Punch & Judy') attracting large crowds; they still do.

Even during Communism, puppet and marionette theatre was officially approved and popular, and Czech performances ranked among the best in the world, especially in the films of Jiří Trnka.

Cinema

The pioneer of Czech cinema was the architect Jan Kříženecký, who made three comedies in American slapstick style that were shown at the 1898 Exhibition of Architecture and Engineering.

The domestic film industry took off in the early years of this century, and Czechs were leading innovators. The first film ever to show full frontal nudity was Gustaf Machatý's *Extase* (Ecstasy) in 1932, a hit (and a scandal) at the 1934 Venice Festival. Revealing all was one Hedvige Kiesler, who went on to Hollywood as Hedy Lamarr. Hugo Haas directed an excellent adaptation of Karel Čapek's anti-Nazi science fiction novel *Bílá smrt* (White Death) in 1937. Fear of persecution drove him to Hollywood where he made and starred in many films.

The Nazis limited the movie industry to nationalistic comedies, and under Communism the focus was on low-quality propaganda films. A 'new wave' of Czech cinema rose between 1963 and the Soviet-led invasion in 1968. Its young directors escaped censorship because they were among the first graduates of the Communist-supervised Academy of Film. It was from this time that Czech films began to win international awards.

Among the earliest outstanding works was *Černý Petr* (known in the USA as *Peter & Paula*, 1963) by Miloš Forman, who fled after 1968 and became a successful

Puppets for sale on Charles Bridge (JK)

Hollywood director with films like *One Flew Over the Cuckoo's Nest* and *Amadeus*. Other prominent directors were Jan Němec, Jiří Menzel, Věra Chytilová and Ivan Passer.

Some 1969-70 films critical of the post-invasion regime were banned or their production stopped. Probably the best film in the following two decades was Jiří Menzel's internationally screened 1985 comedy *Vesničko má středisková* (My Sweet Little Village), a subtle look at the workings and failings of Socialism in a village cooperative.

The Czech studios in Barrandov in south-west Prague are known for their world-class animated and puppet

Top : Musician on Charles Bridge (RN)
Bottom : Peruvian buskers (RN)

films, many from the 1950s to 1980s. The best of the puppet films, *Sen noci svatijánské* (A Midsummer Night's Dream), was produced by the talented Jiří Trnka.

Music

Before the advent of Christianity, folk songs and dances were the main form of music in the Czech Lands. The Church tried to replace these with Christian songs, and introduced Gregorian plainsong. Hussite reformers promoted hymns in Czech and drew on popular folk melodies, providing fertile ground for the future development of Czech music. Remnants of old Czech tunes can still be found in Protestant German hymns.

The Counter-Reformation put a lid on Czech musical culture until the mid-19th century, when several great composers arose in the early stages of the National Revival. Bedřich Smetana (1824-84), the first great Czech composer, incorporated Czech folk music into his classical compositions. His best known works are the *Bartered Bride*, *Dalibor & Libuše* and *My Country*.

Antonín Dvořák (1841-1904) spent four years in the USA where he lectured on music and composed the symphony *From the New World*. Among his other well-known works are the two *Slavonic Dances* (1878 and 1881), the operas *The Devil & Kate* and *Rusalka*, and his religious masterpiece, *Stabat Mater*. Another prominent composer of this generation was Zdeňek Fibich (1850-1900).

Moravian-born Leoš Janáček (1854-1928) also incorporated folk elements into his music and is one of the leading Czech composers of the 20th century. Never as popular as Smetana or Dvořák in his native country, his better known compositions include the opera *Jenůfa*, the *Glagolithic Mass* and *Taras Bulba*, while one of his finest pieces is *Stories of Liška Bystrouška*. Other well-known composers were Josef Suk (1874-1935) and Bohuslav Martinů (1890-1959).

Jazz Jazz has a grip on Czech cultural life that is unmatched almost anywhere else in Europe. It was already being played by amateurs and professionals in the mid-1930s, mostly for dancing. Czech musicians remained at the forefront of the European jazz scene until the Communist takeover in 1948. In the late 1950s, Prague Radio had a permanent jazz orchestra led by Karel Krautgartner, who also led several other orchestras in the 1960s.

Restrictions were gradually lifted in the 1960s. One of the top bands in this period was the SH Quartet, playing for three years at Reduta in Prague, the first Czech professional jazz club. Another was the Junior Trio, with Jan Hamr and the brothers Miroslav and Allan Vitouš, who all escaped to the USA after 1968. Jan Hamr (keyboards) became prominent in 1970s American jazz-rock as Jan Hammer, while Miroslav Vitouš (bass) rose to fame in several American jazz-rock bands.

Rock & Pop Rock was often banned by Communist authorities because of its 'corrupting influence', although certain local bands, and innocuous Western groups like Abba, were allowed. Karel Gott and Helena Vondráčková were the two most popular Czech pop stars.

Rock remained an underground movement, with a handful of bands playing to small audiences in obscure pubs and country houses. Raids and arrests were common. The music found fans among political dissidents like Václav Havel. The band Plastic People of the Universe achieved international fame by being imprisoned after a 1970s show trial intended to discourage underground music.

Since 1989, rock has become legitimate and bands have proliferated – so far without any genuine stars or unique styles. But the rock-club scene in Prague is booming. Well-established bands on the home front include pop-oriented Jerusalem, hard-rock Tři sestry, and Precedens, fusing classical and rock elements. Newer talent includes Lucie Bílá, who sounds like a toned-down Nina Hagen, and the thrash band Support Lesbiens.

AVOIDING OFFENCE

Czechs tend to be polite, mild-mannered people with a good sense of humour, not inclined to argue or fight. They can be quite conservative socially. If you are invited into someone's home, you'll find them very hospitable. Do at least bring flowers for your host, and remember to remove your shoes when you enter the house.

It is customary to say *dobrý den* (good day) when entering a shop, café or quiet bar, and to say *na shledanou* (goodbye) when you leave. On public transport, most younger people will give up their seat for the elderly, the sick and pregnant women.

When attending a classical concert, opera, ballet or a play in one of the traditional theatres, men should wear a suit and tie, and women an evening dress; foreigners tend to be the only ones who don't, and they're frowned upon by Czechs. Casual dress is fine at performances of modern music, plays etc.

RELIGION

Many Czechs were converted to Christianity by the 'Apostles of the Slavs', the Greek monks Cyril and Methodius, in the 9th century. It became the state religion under St Wenceslas ('Good King Wenceslas'), Duke of Bohemia from 925 to 929 and patron saint of the Czech Republic.

The Church remained loyal to Rome until the end of the 14th century, when reformers led by Jan Hus began to argue for the simpler and more accessible practices of early Christianity. Hussites preached in Czech, not Latin, and gave wine as well as bread in the Holy Communion, enraging their conservative colleagues. Hus was excommunicated in 1411 and burned at the stake in 1415, and Bohemia became a hotbed of anti-Catholic nationalism.

Although Hussitism eventually lost its military edge, Bohemia remained a Protestant and independent-minded part of the Holy Roman Empire for two more centuries, until the Czechs were decisively defeated at the Battle of the White Mountainwest of Prague in 1620. Bohemia was pulled into the Thirty Years' War and the Counter-Reformation, losing both its political and religious independence. The Habsburgs re-Catholicised the nation, though the Czechs never took to Catholicism as they had to Protestantism.

After 1948, Communism brought state atheism and the systematic oppression of all religion. Most religious institutions were closed and the clergy were imprisoned. Religion was never stamped out, and there was an underground religious network which included priests who secretely performed rites. But full religious freedom returned with the 'Velvet Revolution' of 1989, and churches locked up since 1948 have reopened.

The largest church in the country is the Roman Catholic Church, though only about two out of every five Czechs call themselves Catholic. Next-largest is the reconstituted Hussite Church, with 400,000 members. There are half a dozen Protestant Churches with small memberships, the largest of which is the Evangelical Church of Czech Brethren with about 180,000 members.

The majority of the population, however, seems to maintain a modest and personal religious faith. Though Church membership is not as strong as in many other European countries, there has been a slight rise in recent

St Agatha holding her severed breasts,
Convent of St Ursula (RN)

years, and a significant rise in the numbers of children attending religious education.

Since WW II the Jewish community in the Czech Republic has shrunk from a prewar number of 120,000 to only about 6000.

LANGUAGE

Czech is the main language in the Czech Republic. It belongs to the West Slavonic group of Indo-European languages, along with Slovak, Polish and Lusatian.

Geographical terms you'll encounter on maps and throughout this book include:

dům – house
galérie – gallery, arcade
hora – mountain
hrad – castle
hřbitov – cemetery
kaple – chapel
kopec – hill
kostel – church
most – bridge
nábřezí (abbreviated *nábř)* – embankment
náměstí (abbreviated *nám)* – square
ostrov – island
palác – palace
potok – stream
řeka – river
sad(y) – orchards, park
silnice – road
třída – avenue
ulice – street
ulička – lane
zahrada – gardens, park
zámek – chateau (live-in castle, manor)

Pronunciation

It's not easy to learn Czech pronunciation by reading it. However, it is spelt as it is spoken and once you become familiar with the sounds, it is easy to read.

Vowels

There are short and long vowels and the only difference is that long vowels take longer to say. Long vowels are indicated by an acute accent. The following approximations follow British pronunciation:

a as the 'ah' sound in 'cut'
á as the 'a' in 'father'
e as the 'eh' sound in 'bet'
é as the word 'air'
i or **y** as the 'u' in 'busy'
í or **ý** as the 'ee' in 'see'
o as the 'o' in 'pot'
ó as the 'aw' in 'saw'
u as the 'u' in 'pull'
ú or **ů** as the 'oo' in 'zoo'

Diphthongs

aj as the 'i' in 'ice'
áj as the word 'eye'
au an 'ow' sound as in 'out'
ej as the 'ay' in 'day'
ij, **yj** (short), **íj** or **ýj**(long) an 'eey' sound
oj as the 'oi' in 'void'
ou as the 'o' in 'note', but both the 'o' and 'u' are more strongly pronounced than in English
uj (short)or **ůj**(long) a short 'u' sound as in 'pull', followed by 'y'

Consonants

c as the 'ts' in 'lets'
č as the 'ch' in 'chew'
ch a 'kh' sound, as in the Scottish 'loch', or German 'ich'
f as the 'f' in 'fever', not as in 'of'
g a hard sound like the 'g' in 'get'
h as the 'h' in 'hand'
j as the 'y' in 'year'
r a rolled 'r', made by the tip of the tongue
ř a rolled sound, 'rzh', that has no English equivalent.
s as the 's' in 'sit', not as in 'rose'
š as the 'sh' in 'ship'
ž a 'zh' sound, as in 'treasure'
ď, **ň** or **ť** are very soft palatal sounds, ie consonants followed by a momentary contact between the tongue and the hard palate, as if a 'y' sound is added, as in the 'ny' in canyon. The same sound occurs with d, n and t followed by i, í or ě.

All other consonants are similar to English, although k, p and t are unaspirated, ie they're pronounced without a following puff of breath.

Stress

In Czech the first syllable is usually stressed, though it's often hard to discern any stress at all.

Greetings & Civilities

Hello.	*Dobrý den* (informal: *ahoj*).
Goodbye.	*Na shledanou* (informal: *ahoj*).
Yes.	*Ano* (informal: *jo*).
No.	*Ne.*
Excuse me. Pardon.	*S dovolením.*
May I? Do you mind?	*Dovolte mi?*
Sorry. (Excuse me. Forgive me)	*Promiňte.*
Please.	*Prosím.*
Thank you.	*Děkuji.*
You're welcome.	*Není zač.*
Good morning.	*Dobré jitro*, or *dobre ráno.*
Good afternoon.	*Dobré odpoledne.*
Good evening.	*Dobrý večer.*
Good night.	*Dobrou noc.*
How are you?	*Jak se máte?*
Well, thanks.	*Děkuji, dobře.*

Useful Phrases

Do you speak English?	*Mluvíte anglicky?*
Does anyone speak English?	*Mluví někdo anglicky?*
I speak a little ...	*Mluvím trochu ...*
I don't speak ...	*Nemluvím ...*
I understand.	*Rozumím.*
I don't understand.	*Nerozumím.*
Could you write that down?	*Napište mi to, prosím?*

Emergencies

Help!	*Pomoc!*
Please, call a doctor/ambulance/police!	*Prosím, zavolejte doktora/sanitku/policii!*
I am ill.	*Jsem nemocný* (m)/*nemocná* (f).
Where is the police station?	*Kde je policejní stanice?*
Where are the toilets?	*Kde jsou záchody?*
Could you help me please?	*Prosím, můžete mi pomoci?*

I wish to contact my embassy/consulate.	*Přeju si mluvit s mým velvyslanectvím/konzulátem*
dentist	*zubní lékař*, or *zubař*
doctor	*doktor*
hospital	*nemocnice*

Getting Around

What time does the train/bus leave?	*Kdy odjíždí vlak/autobus?*
What time does the train/bus arrive?	*Kdy přijíždí vlak/autobus?*
Where is ...?	*Kde je ...?*
Go straight ahead.	*Jděte přímo.*
Turn left ...	*Zatočte vlevo ...*
Turn right ...	*Zatočte vpravo ...*
address	*adresa*
entry	*vstup*
no entry	*vstup zakázán*
entrance	*vchod*
exit	*východ*
behind	*za*
in front of	*před*
far	*daleko*
near	*blízko*
opposite	*naproti*
Excuse me, where is the ticket office?	*Prosím, kde je pokladna?*
I want to go to ...	*Chci jet do ...*
I would like ...	*Rád bych ...*
a one-way ticket	*jednosměrnou jízdenku*
a return ticket	*zpáteční jízdenku*
two tickets	*dvě jízdenky*
a student's fare	*studentskou jízdenku*
1st class	*první třídu*
2nd class	*druhou třídu*
dining car	*jídelní vůz*
express	*rychlík*
local	*místní*
sleeping car	*spací vůz*

Accommodation

Do you have any rooms available?	*Máte volné pokoje?*
I would like ...	*Přál bych si ...*
a single room	*jednolůžkový pokoj*
a double room	*dvoulůžkový pokoj*
a room with a bathroom	*pokoj s koupelnou*
How much is it per night?	*Kolik stojí jedna noc?*
cheap hotel	*levný hotel*
good hotel	*dobrý hotel*
nearby hotel	*blízký hotel*
bathroom	*koupelna*
room number	*císlo pokoje*
key	*klíč*
shower	*sprcha*
soap	*mýdlo*
toilet	*záchod/WC*
toilet paper	*toaletní papír*
towel	*ručník*
blanket	*pokrývka*
cold/hot water	*studená/teplá voda*
clean/dirty	*čistý/špinavý*
dark/light	*tmavý/světlý*
quiet/noisy	*ticho/hlučný*
cheap/expensive	*levný/drahý*
cold/hot	*studená/horká*

Around Town

I'm looking for ...	*Hledám ...*
the art gallery	*uměleckou galérii*
a bank	*banku*
the church	*kostel*
the city centre	*střed města*
the embassy	*velvyslanectví*
my hotel	*muj hotel*
the market	*tržiště*
the museum	*muzeum*
the police	*policii*
the post office	*poštu*
a public toilet	*veřejné záchody*
the telephone centre	*telefonní ústřednu*
the tourist information office	*informační kancelář pro turisty*

building	*budova*
castle	*hrad*
cathedral	*katedrála*
chateau	*zámek*
church	*kostel*
concert hall	*koncertní síň*
main square	*hlavní náměstí*
market	*trh*
monastery	*klášter*
monument	*pamatník/pomník*
old city/town	*staré město*
palace	*palác*
opera house	*opera*
stadium	*stadión*
statue	*socha*
synagogue	*synagóga*
university	*universita*
cinema	*kino*
concert	*koncert*
discotheque	*diskotéka*
theatre	*divadlo*

Food & Drink

For food and drink terms, see the Places to Eat chapter.

Time & Dates

What time is it?	*Kolik je hodin?*
When?	*Kdy?*
in the morning	*ráno*
in the afternoon	*odpoledne*
in the evening	*večer*
today	*dnes*
now	*teď*
yesterday	*včera*
tomorrow	*zítra*
next week	*příští týden*
day	*den*
night	*noc*

Days of the Week *(Dny Týdne)*

Monday	*pondělí*
Tuesday	*úterý*
Wednesday	*středa*
Thursday	*čtvrtek*
Friday	*pátek*

Saturday	*sobota*
Sunday	*neděle*

Months *(Měsíce)*

January	*leden*
February	*únor*
March	*březen*
April	*duben*
May	*květen*
June	*červen*
July	*červenec*
August	*srpen*
September	*září*
October	*říjen*
November	*listopad*
December	*prosinec*

Seasons *(Sezóny)*

summer	*léto*
autumn	*podzim*
winter	*zima*
spring	*jaro*

Dates in Museums

year	*rok*
century	*století*
millennia	*milénium* or *tisíciletí*
beginning of ...	*začátek ...*
first half of ...	*první polovina ...*
middle of ...	*polovina ...*
second half of ...	*druhá polovina ...*
end of ...	*konec ...*
around ...	*kolem ...*

Numbers

0	*nula*
1	*jeden*
2	*dva*
3	*tři*
4	*čtyři*
5	*pět*
6	*šest*
7	*sedm*
8	*osm*
9	*devět*
10	*deset*
11	*jedenáct*

12	*dvanáct*
13	*třináct*
14	*čtrnáct*
15	*patnáct*
16	*šestnáct*
17	*sedmnáct*
18	*osmnáct*
19	*devatenáct*
20	*dvacet*
21	*dvacet jedna*
22	*dvacet dva*
23	*dvacet tři*
30	*třicet*
40	*čtyřicet*
50	*padesát*
60	*šedesát*
70	*sedmdesát*
80	*osmdesát*
90	*devadesát*
100	*sto*

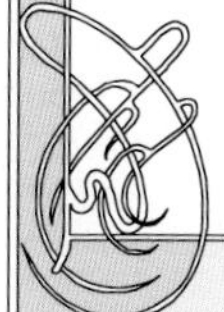

Facts for the Visitor

VISAS & EMBASSIES

Nationals of all Western European countries can visit the Czech Republic without a visa for up to 90 days, and Britons for up to 180 days. Nationals of the USA can stay for 30 days without a visa. Nationals of all other countries including Canada, Australia, New Zealand and South Africa must obtain a visa, good for a stay of up to 30 days. Multiple-entry visas are also available.

When applying, you'll need one or two passport-size photos, and cash or a money order for the fee which varies according to your nationality. Most Czech embassies in Western capitals will accept applications by post if you include a self-addressed envelope with return certified postage, and payment by postal money order; get forms from the embassy or a travel agent. Processing is usually immediate for applications in person, and mail applications take about two working days.

At the time of writing, there were only a few Czech border points issuing on-the-spot tourist visas, and border facilities between the Czech and Slovak republics were still being sorted out; see Car & Motorbike in the Getting There & Away chapter for details.

Visas are also issued at the arrivals hall at Prague's Ruzyně Airport.

Registration & Visa Extension

If you plan to stay longer than your visa (or visa-free) period, you're expected to register within two or three working days of your arrival, and apply for a visa extension, at the Foreigners' Police & Passport Office (Úřadovna cizinecké policie a pasové služby, ☎ 27 95 43) at Olšanská 2, Žižkov, Prague 3 (tram No 9 from Wenceslas Square).

Enter around the right side and queue up at any door inside. The desk in the corner sells the duty stamps you'll need for the application – about 100 Kč for a normal 180-day extension, or a heady 900 Kč if you've already overstayed. The office is open from 8 am to 3 pm on Monday, Tuesday and Thursday, 9 am to 5 pm on Wednesday, and 8 am to 2 pm on Friday.

See Work at the end of this chapter if you intend to stay for more than six months.

Czech Embassies Abroad

Following are addresses of some Czech embassies and consulates abroad:

Australia
47 Culgoa Circuit, O'Malley, Canberra, ACT 2606 (☎ 06-290 1386)
Consulate: 169 Military Rd, Dover Heights, Sydney, NSW 2030 (☎ 02-371 8877, visa info 371 8878); visas are normally issued only from the Sydney consulate.

Austria
Penzinger Strasse 11-13, 1140 Vienna (☎ 82 26 20)

Belgium & Luxembourg
152 Avenue A Buyl, 1050 Brussels (☎ 647 5898)

Canada
50 Rideau Terrace, Ottawa, Ontario K1M 2A1 (☎ 794 4442); only visa applications in person are accepted.
Consulate: 1305 Pine Avenue West, Montreal, Quebec H3G 1B2 (☎ 514-849-4495); applications in person or by post are accepted.

France
15 Avenue Charles Floquet, 75 007 Paris (☎ 47 34 29 10)

Germany
Ferdinandstrasse 27, 5300 Bonn (☎ 28 50 81)
Consulate: Otto-Grotewohl-Strasse 21, 108 Berlin (☎ 229 40 27)
Consulate: Herzog-Rudolf-Strasse 4, 8000 Munich 22 (☎ 226 63)

Hungary
Stefánia út 22-24, Budapest XIV (☎ 251 1700)

Ireland – see UK

Italy
Via dei Colli della Farnesina, 144 Lotto VI, 00194 Rome (☎ 327 8741)

Netherlands
Parkweg 1, The Hague (☎ 070-355 80 97)

New Zealand
12 Anne St, Wadestown, Wellington (☎ 72 3142); visa applications must be made to the Czech Consulate in Sydney, Australia.

Poland
Koszykowa 18, 00-555 Warsaw (☎ 287 221/5)

Switzerland
Muristrasse 53, 3000 Bern 16 (☎ 44 56 81)

UK & Irish Republic
30 (visa office: 28) Kensington Palace Gardens, London W8 4QY (☎ 071-229 1255)

Ukraine
Yaroslavov val 34, Kiev (☎ 212 19 12 or 224 61 80)

USA
3900 Spring of Freedom St NW, Washington, DC 20008 (☎ 202-363 6315)

Foreign Embassies in Prague

Most embassies are in or around Malá Strana and Hradčany and are open for visa-related business only until about 1 pm.

Australia
The Australian embassy has closed down, though Australians can get emergency help at the UK Embassy; the nearest Australian embassies are in Warsaw and Vienna.

Austria
Viktora Huga 10, Prague 5 (☎ 54 65 57)

Belgium & Luxembourg
Valdštejnská 6, Prague 1 (Consulate, ☎ 53 40 51) and Pod Kaštany 3 (Embassy, ☎ 37 07 47)

Bulgaria
Krakovská 6, Prague 1

Canada
Mickiewiczova 6, Prague 6 (☎ 312 01 51, after hours 312 02 51/2)

France
Velkopřevorské náměstí 2, Prague 1 (☎ 53 30 42/4)

Germany
Vlašská 21 (visas), Prague 1 (☎ 53 23 51/6)

Hungary
Badeního 1, Prague 1 (☎ 36 50 41/4); closed Thursdays

Italy
Nerudova 20, Prague 1 (☎ 53 14 33)

Netherlands
Maltézské náměstí 1, Prague 1 (☎ 53 13 78)

New Zealand
There is no NZ Embassy, but for emergency help go to the UK Embassy; the nearest NZ embassy is in Bonn

Poland
Václavské náměstí 49, Prague 1 (☎ 26 54 41)

Russia
Korunovační 34, Prague 6 (☎ 37 43 66); closed Tuesday and Thursday

Slovakia
Pod hradbami 1, Prague 6

Switzerland
Pevnostní 7, Prague 6 (☎ 32 04 06)

UK & Irish Republic
Thunovská 14, Prague 1 (☎ 53 33 40, 53 33 47/9, 24 hours)

Ukraine
Schwaigerova 2, Bubeneč, Prague 6 (☎ 32 29 66)

USA
Tržiště 15, Prague 1 (☎ 53 66 41/9)

Buggy driver on Old Town Square (RN)

CUSTOMS

You can import a reasonable amount of personal effects and up to 3000 Kč (about US$100) worth of gifts and other 'non-commercial' goods. If you're aged over 18, you can bring in two litres of wine, a litre of spirits and 250 cigarettes (or equivalent other tobacco products).

Before you make any major purchase in Prague, find out how much it will cost to get it out of the country. Consumer goods exceeding the value of 500 Kč are dutiable at 20%. Fuel (except in your car's tank), food products, and most gold and silver items face 150% duties and you'll need an export licence. Nearly everything from Tuzex shops is duty-free, though you'll need to show purchase receipts.

You cannot export genuine antiques. If you have any doubt about what you're taking out, talk to curatorial staff at the National Museum on Wenceslas Square or the Museum of Decorative Arts on 17.listopadu, or go to the customs post office (Celnice-pošta, ☎ 232 22 70) at Plzeňská 139, Smíchov, Monday to Friday between 7 am and 3 pm (take tram No 4, 7 or 9 to the Klamovka stop). Inspectors from the National Museum and then from customs will look it over. If it passes both inspections, you're free to mail or take it out of the country.

You can't import or export more than 100 Kč in Czech currency, though there is no limit on the amount of foreign currency that can be taken in or out of the country. Visitors are no longer obliged to change a minimum daily amount into crowns. Arriving visitors may occasionally be asked to prove that they have the equivalent of at least US$600 in convertible currency.

MONEY

The unit of Czech money is the *koruna* or crown, abbreviated Kč (for *Koruna česká)*. A crown is divided into 100 *haléřů* or heller (h). Notes come in 1000, 500, 200, 100 and 50-crown denominations, and coins in 50, 20, 10, 5, 2 and 1-crown and 50, 20 and 10-heller sizes.

All old notes and coins from the days of united Czechoslovakia (identifiable by the words *Korun československých)* ceased to be legal tender in the Czech Republic in October 1993. They have been replaced by new Czech versions. Beware of being offered old Czechoslovak currency.

Exchange Rates

The crown is not yet freely convertible on world currency markets. Exchange rates are determined by the government, and the fairly high inflation (16% in 1993) tends to flow through to tourists. If all goes to plan, the crown will be 'freed' in 1995. When this book went to press, the exchange rates were:

A$1	=	19.8 Kč
C$1	=	20.8 Kč
DM1	=	16.8 Kč
FFr1	=	4.9 Kč
UK£1	=	42.8 Kč
US$1	=	29.3 Kč

The conversion rate for Slovak crowns (Sk) is about 80 Kč to Sk 100, though by the time you read this, the Sk will probably be worth less.

US dollars and Deutschmarks are as welcome as crowns in the touristy parts of Prague, and are the most sensible currencies to pack. You cannot import or export more than 100 Kč in Czech currency, but if you've saved your encashment receipts, you can sell unused crowns at your port of exit (or at Komerční banka).

Banks & Exchange Offices

The city's main foreign-exchange banks are:

American Express (☎ 26 17 47), Wenceslas Square 56, Monday to Friday from 9 am to 6 pm (to 7 pm in summer), Saturday to noon (Saturday and Sunday to 3 pm in summer)
Česká obchodní banka, Na příkopě 14, Monday to Friday from 7.30 am to noon and 1 to 3.30 pm; another branch is due to open on Wenceslas Square, at Vodičkova 41
Komerční banka, Na příkopě 28, Monday to Friday from 8 am to 7 pm, Saturday from 9 am to 2 pm; other branches around town are open Monday to Friday from 8 am to 5 pm
Thomas Cook (☎ 26 31 06, 26 66 11), Wenceslas Square 47, Monday to Friday from 9 am to 5 pm (to 7 pm and on weekends in summer), exchange office to 7 pm daily
Všeobecná Úvěrová banka, Celetná 31, from 8 am to noon and 12.30 to 4 pm Monday, to 3 pm Tuesday and Thursday, to 5 pm Wednesday, to 2 pm Friday
Živnostenská banka, corner exchange office at Na příkopě 20, Monday to Friday from 8 am to 6 pm

Živnostenská is foreigner-friendly (and even if you have no business, it's worth looking in at the lavish Art-Nouveau interior). Komercní has the best hours and the most branches.

Good for late-night transactions is the 24-hour exchange at the Hotel Jalta, Wenceslas Square 45. There are 24-hour private exchanges at Old Town Square 21 and 28.října 13.

Travellers' Cheques

The easiest, cheapest option is American Express or Thomas Cook travellers' cheques, which can be converted to crowns, at bank rates and free of charge, at the American Express and Thomas Cook offices.

Czech banks have reasonable rates and charges. Komercní cashes up to about US$200 in Eurocheques at no charge. Živnostenská charges nothing for up to about

US$20 of Eurocheques, and 1% for other cheques. Most hotel exchange desks charge about 5%.

Private exchanges (a growing plague) are convenient but take the biggest cuts; some advertise low commissions but invent their own lopsided rates. The exchange desks at PIS charge almost 8%!

Converting Cash to Crowns

Bank rates for cash are a bit lower than for travellers' cheques. Česká obchodní's electronic exchange machine charges 1% for any amount of foreign currency. Živnostenská charges 1% for up to about US$20. American Express charges 2% for any amount, Komercní 2% up to about US$100. The Bank of Austria on the corner of Melantrichova and Havelská has a 24-hour machine charging 3%.

Selling or Buying Other Currencies

Živnostenská cashes Eurocheques into US dollars at no charge, and other cheques into US dollars for 2% commission. Most other banks charge at least 4%. Komercní buys Slovak crowns, but only Všeobecná Úverová sells them too.

Black Market

Avoid it. Not only is the usual black-market rate barely above the bank rate, but it's common to get fleeced with discontinued crown notes or worthless Polish and Yugoslav notes. The Czech Republic also has a problem with counterfeit currencies, especially US dollars and Deutschmarks.

Credit Cards

In Prague, upper-end hotels and restaurants accept certain cards, usually American Express, Visa or MasterCard, and sometimes Eurocard, Diner's Club, Access or JCB. Čedok and most travel agents accept all of these cards. A few tourist shops accept cards.

Cash Advances American Express and Thomas Cook card-holders can get commission-free cash advances from those offices; American Express also has an electronic teller at the airport. Živnostenská charges nothing for crowns or US dollars from Visa or MasterCard. MasterCard and Eurocard can be used in machines at Česká obchodní banka (for 1.5%) and Komerční (for 2%).

Lost Travellers' Cheques & Cards

If your cheques or cards are lost or stolen, the best way to freeze the accounts and get replacements is to call your home office (or the Prague office in the case of American Express or Thomas Cook).

Živnostenská can also help, at its office or via its credit-card hotline (☎ 236 66 88). It may also let you draw emergency cash on a lost Visa card or MasterCard if you have your account number and passport.

Studying at the foot of the František Palacký monument (JK)

If you're not an American Express or Thomas Cook customer, the fastest way to get emergency money from home is through Western Union at the office of Sport Turist, Národní 33, although you will only be paid in crowns. A funds transfer to a Prague bank can take up to 10 working days.

Costs

Things are still fairly cheap in Prague for Western visitors (though not for Praguers). The big exception is accommodation, where tourist prices are in line with Western Europe.

By staying at cheap hostels or campsites, sticking to self-catering and stand-up cafeterias, and going easy on the beer, you might get away with US$15 per person a day in summer. If you stay in private homes or up-market hostels away from the city centre, eat at cheap restaurants and use public transport, you can get by on US$20 to US$30. Sharing a double room with bath in a mid-range hotel or pension, and eating in good Czech or Western restaurants, will cost US$40 to US$60. These costs don't include extras like souvenirs, postage and tours.

Eating and sleeping near the city centre will cost more, as will having a room to yourself. Rates may drop if you take a room for more than one or two nights. Except for the Christmas/New Year and Easter periods, some lower-end hotels drop their prices outside the summer season. In nearby towns, such as those described in the Excursions chapter, prices are lower.

Some restaurants have separate prices for foreigners and Czechs, but with enough charm and enough Czech you can pay local prices by steering clear of 'tourist' rooms and by ordering from the Czech-language menu. Naturally, Bohemia's splendid beer will increase your costs: half a litre ranges from about 30 US cents in local shops to US$2 or more in posh restaurants.

Public transport is a bargain, and if you stay in Prague for more than a few days you'll do even better with a multi-day travel pass (see the Getting Around chapter).

Tipping

A tip of 5% to 10% is appreciated in any restaurant offering table service. The usual protocol is for them to show you the bill and for you, as you hand over the money, to say how much you are paying with the tip included.

Youth, Student & Senior-Citizen Discounts

Lots of discounts – for transport, tourist attractions, in hotels and in some restaurants – are available to full-time students and people aged under 26 or over 59, and sometimes to their spouses and children. Many bargains are not advertised, and the best way to find them is to wave an identity card at every opportunity.

Apply at your student union or student travel agency for an ISIC student card. CKM (☎ 26 85 07), at Jindřišská 28, also sells them. You'll need a passport-size photo and proof of student status. If you aren't a student but are aged under 26, ask at your student travel agency. For senior citizens, Rail Europe Senior is British Rail International's name for its discount card, and there are equivalents in other Western European countries.

TOURIST OFFICES & INFORMATION

Čedok

Čedok (*Č*eská *do*pravní *k*ancelář, or Czech Transport Office) is the state-run tour operator and travel agency. It's not a tourism-promotion office, but makes money by organising things for tourists (whether Czech or foreign), so don't expect a lot of advice on doing things independently.

That said, the main office at Na příkopě 18 is a pretty good one-stop shop for maps, excursions, concert/theatre tickets and travel bookings. Following is a list of the Prague offices; all but the Panská office are open Monday to Friday from 8.30 am to 6 pm, Saturday to 12.30 pm:

Main Office, Na příkopě 18 (☎ 212 73 50, 212 76 42): excursions, tickets, and air, train, bus and boat bookings
Bílková 6 (☎ 231 82 55, 231 66 19): mainly tours and excursions, concert and theatre tickets
Rytířská 16 (☎ 26 36 97): mainly tours and excursions, concert and theatre tickets
Panská 5 (☎ 22 56 57, 22 70 04), Monday to Friday from 9 am to 8 pm (to 9 pm in summer), Saturday to 4 pm, Sunday to 2 pm: accommodation only

Čedok Offices Abroad Representative offices include:

Austria
Parkring 10, A-1010 Vienna (☎ 01-512 43 72, fax 512 43 72 85)
France
32 ave de l'Opéra, 75002 Paris (☎ 01-47 42 74 87)
Germany
Strausbergerplatz 8/9, 1017 Berlin-Friedrichshain (☎ 030-429 41 43, fax 427 47 56)
Kaiserstrasse 54, 6 Frankfurt am Main (☎ 069-27 40 17, fax 23 58 90)
Prof Messershmidtstrasse 17b, 8900 Augsburg (☎ 0821-59 31 75, fax 59 32 86)
Hungary
Kossuth tér 18, 1055 Budapest (☎ 01-112 82 45, fax 153 23 35)
Netherlands
Leidsestraat 4, 1017 PA Amsterdam (☎ 020-622 01 01, fax 638 54 41)
Poland
ul Nowogrodzka 31, 00 511 Warsaw (☎ 022-267 076, fax 217 955)
Russia
Tversko-Yamska ul 35/39, vkhod 7, kv 136, 125 047 Moscow (☎ 095-2258 89 32, fax 258 99 22)
UK
49 Southwark St, London SE1 1RU (☎ 071-378 6009, fax 403 2321)
USA
Suite 1902, 10 East 40th St, New York, NY 10016 (☎ 212-689 9720, fax 481 0597).

Prague Information Service (PIS)

PIS (Pražská informacní služba) is a municipal bureau with more city information and entertainment listings than Čedok. It also has guided tours, an information-by-telephone number (☎ 54 44 44) and a monthly what's-on booklet with classical music, opera, theatre and exhibitions.

Offices are at Old Town Square 22 (including accommodation service and concert/theatre tickets), Na příkopě 20, Panská 4 (☎ 22 43 11, city tours), and the main train station. Summer hours are Monday to Friday from 8 am to 8 pm, Saturday and Sunday from 9 am to 6 pm.

CKM

CKM (Cestovní *k*ancelář *m*ládeže, or Youth Travel Office) is the youth-travel equivalent of Čedok. It's a good place to get a student card or arrange cheap accommodation, though its transportation office isn't very switched-on. Addresses and opening times are:

Jindřišská 28 (☎ 26 85 07), Monday to Friday from 9 am to 1 pm and 2 to 5 pm, Saturday to noon: accommodation, ISIC and IYHF (HI) cards
Žitná 12 (☎ 20 54 46), Monday to Friday from 9 am to noon and 1 to 6 pm: accommodation only
Žitná 9 (☎ 20 33 80), Monday to Friday from 9 am to noon and 1 to 6 pm: international bus & train bookings.

American Hospitality Center

This cheerful private outfit (☎ 26 15 74) at Na můstku 7 at the bottom of Wenceslas Square has maps, books, entertainment listings and a good information desk, plus snacks and nonstop CNN TV. It's also a good source of help with official matters and emergencies.

Other Information Sources

Prague's English-language papers, the weekly *Prague Post* and bi-weekly *Prognosis*, list concert venues, galleries, museums, cinemas, theatres, clubs and restaurants, along with restaurant reviews and excursion ideas. Their day-by-day events calendars are very thorough.

Several advertiser-supported tourist handbooks are sold at travel agencies and newsstands. Best of the lot is the *Prague Guide*, with useful numbers, transport, banks, embassies, travel agents, clubs, and up-scale shops and restaurants.

If you're staying longer and looking for flatmates, Czech lessons, work, a haircut etc, check the notice boards at Laundry Kings, Dejvická 16 near Hradčanská metro station (open from 8 am to 10 pm daily), and at New York Pizza, Na perštýně 4.

CULTURAL CENTRES

If you're looking for newspapers or information about other cultures, try these centres:

France
Institut Français de Prague (☎ 235 20 58), Štěpánská 35
Germany
Goethe Institute (☎ 29 95 51/4), Masarykovo nábřeží 32
Hungary
Hungarian Cultural Centre, Rytířská 25, Monday to Friday from 8 am to 6 pm
Poland
Polish Cultural Centre (☎ 22 80 58), Wenceslas Square 49, Monday to Friday from 9 am to 5 pm, Saturday to noon

UK
: The British Council (☎ 20 37 51/5), Národní 10, Monday to Friday from 9 am to 4 pm: British newspapers and magazines and satellite Sky TV news; the British Embassy, at Thunovská 14 in Malá Strana, also has a reading room

USA
: American Center for Culture and Commerce (USIS, ☎ 236 42 48), Hybernská 7a: US newspapers, magazines, and reference books, plus a business reference service and occasional events.

BUSINESS HOURS

Shops tend to open from 9 am to 5 pm on weekdays and to midday on Saturday, closing on Sunday. Department stores may close later, and some are open on Thursday evening. Some small food shops open as early as 7 am.

Restaurant hours vary, but most places operate from at least 11 am to 11 pm daily (some close on Monday).

Banking hours vary, but the major banks are open Monday to Friday at least from 9 am to 5 pm. Many money-exchange offices carry on daily until 11 pm or later (see the earlier Money section).

Government office hours are Monday to Friday from 8.30 am to 5 pm, though some tourist offices operate later and on weekends. The main post office at Jindřišská 14 is open 24 hours a day, though the hours for services like poste restante are more limited (see Post & Telecommunications). Other post offices are open from 8 am to 6 pm weekdays and until noon on Saturday.

Most museums and galleries are open year-round from 9 or 10 am to 5 or 6 pm, daily except Monday and sometimes the first working day after a holiday. You can visit Prague's bigger churches during similar hours.

Castles, chateaux and other historical monuments outside the city are open in summer every day except Monday and the first working day after a holiday, from 8 or 9 am to 5 or 6 pm, except for a lunch break. Most shut down from November through March, with some limited to weekends in October and April. But Karlštejn and Křivoklát castles and Březnice chateau are open seven days a week year-round except Christmas Eve and New Year's day, from at least 9 am to 4 pm.

PUBLIC HOLIDAYS

Following are the Czech Republic's public holidays, when banks, offices, department stores and some shops close. Restaurants, museums and tourist attractions tend to stay open:

1 January
: *Nový rok* (New Year's Day)

March or April
: *Pondělí velikonoční* (Easter Monday) – The country collapses in a mirthful rite of spring. Czech men of all ages swat their favourite women on the legs with willow switches, and the women respond with gifts of hand-painted eggs, after which everybody parties; the culmination of several days of serious spring-cleaning, cooking and visiting

1 May
: *Svátek práce* (Labour Day) – Once the Communist 'holy' day, now it's just a chance for a picnic or a day in the country, often preceded by an all-night party (see 30 April in the following Festivals & Events section)

8 May
: *Den osvobození* (Liberation Day) – Liberation of Prague by its citizens in 1945. Under Communism this was celebrated on 9 May, when the Red Army marched in

5 July
: *Den Cyrila a Metoděje* (SS Cyril & Methodius Day) – Recalls the Slavs' introduction to literacy and Christianity by the two Greek missionary monks

6 July
: *Den Jana Husa* (Jan Hus Day) – Commemorates the 1415 burning at the stake of the great Bohemian religious reformer; kicked off by low-key celebrations and bell-ringing at Prague's Bethlehem Chapel the evening before

28 October
: *Den vzniku Československa* (Independence Day) – Anniversary of the founding of the Czechoslovak Republic in 1918, now celebrated as the day of independence from the Austro-Hungarian Empire

24 December
: *Štědrý den* ('Generous Day', Christmas Eve) – The big day for evening family meals and gift-giving

25 December
: *Vánoce* (Christmas Day) – The day for visiting friends and relatives, and the turkey lunch

26 December
: *Štěpána* (St Stephen's Day, equivalent to Boxing Day)

FESTIVALS & EVENTS

The following are not public holidays but special days *(významné dny)* for remembrance or celebration:

19 January
: *Anniversary of Jan Palach's Death* – In memory of the Charles University student who, in 1969, burned himself to death in protest against the Soviet occupation

7 March
Birthday of Tomáš Masaryk – Commemorates Czechoslovakia's national father figure and first president

30 April
Pálení Čarodějnic (Burning of the Witches) – Czech version of the German *Walpurgisnacht*, a pre-Christian festival for warding off evil, now an opportunity for all-night, end-of-winter bonfire parties on Kampa island and in suburban backyards

5 May
České povstání (Czech Uprising) – Anniversary of Prague's 1945 anti-Nazi uprising preceding liberation

12 May to 4 June
Pražské Jaro (Prague Spring) International Music Festival – Classical music concerts in theatres, churches and historic buildings; kicked off on the anniversary of Smetana's death (12 May) with a procession from his grave at Vyšehrad to the Obecní dům

Mid-May
Prague International Book Fair

September
Mozart Festival

17 November
Start of the 'Velvet Revolution' – Anniversary of the beating of student demonstrators by security police, triggering the fall of the Communist regime

24 December to 1 January
Christmas/New Year – While many Czechs celebrate an extended holiday, stuffing themselves with carp, Prague is engulfed by revellers from all over Europe and the tourist season is on again, briefly and furiously

6 January
Tři králové (Three Kings' Day) – Formal end of the Christmas season, sometimes celebrated with carol-singing, bell-ringing, and gifts to the poor

Saints' Days

Practically every day of the year is the day of a particular saint, something Catholics will be familiar with. To Czechs, one's 'name day' (the day of the saint whom a person may be named after) is very much like a birthday, and a small gift or gesture on that day never goes amiss.

POST & TELECOMMUNICATIONS

The main post office is at Jindřišská 14, just off Wenceslas Square. It is open 24 hours a day for postage, parcels, telegrams, faxes and unassisted telephone calls.

The main telephone bureau (from 7 am to 11 pm) is to the left inside the front entrance of the main post office, and the fax/telegram/telex bureau (24 hours a day) is to the right. Poste restante (Monday to Friday from 7 am

View from Charles Bridge towards Prague Castle (JK)

to 8 pm, Saturday to 1 pm) is in the main lobby. Most other services, and all services at the city's 115 other post offices, are available Monday to Friday from 8 am to 6 pm and Saturday until noon.

Post

Buy stamps at windows 18 to 22 in the main post office, or from street vendors or PNS newsagents. Letters go in the orange boxes outside post offices and around the city. International parcels can be sent from window 7, and poste restante *(uložené zásilky)* is at window 28. The information window, No 30, sometimes has an English-speaker.

Letters The Czech postal service seems fairly efficient. Mail to Europe (automatically air mail) is 8 Kč for a letter, 5 Kč for a postcard. To anywhere else by air, a letter is 10 Kč and a postcard 6 Kč. Express service is 10 Kč extra, registration 20 Kč. There are no aerogrammes, but stamp counters will sell you an envelope and a few sheets of air-mail paper for 1 Kč.

Parcels A two-kg parcel to Europe (automatically air mail) is about US$10; to anywhere else it's about US$25 by air and about half that by sea. Books and printed matter can go for reduced rates in bundles up to five kg. Larger post offices will allow you to send parcels of books or printed matter of up to 15 kg at even lower rates.

See the earlier Customs section if you want to mail antiques out of the country. In the interests of safety, however, it's best to carry anything of value out of the country yourself, as things sometimes do 'disappear' in the Czech postal system.

In principle, anything else can be posted internationally from any major post office. But in practice, many postal employees retain Communist-era anxieties about 'regulations', and may send you off to customs if you have anything over two kg, no matter what it is.

Parcels containing glass and crystal will not be accepted by the postal systems in the USA, Australia and New Zealand.

Warning Always ask for a receipt *(paragon)* when sending anything larger than a letter by air mail or a more expensive service. Post-office staff are notorious for charging for such services and then sending the item by surface mail.

Poste Restante Mail should be addressed to Poste Restante, Hlavní pošta, Jindřišská 14, 110 00 Praha 1, Czech Republic. You must present your passport to claim mail. Check under your first name, too.

Holders of American Express and Thomas Cook cards and travellers' cheques can have letters sent to the Prague offices (for addresses, see the earlier Money section); the British and Canadian embassies will hold letters for their citizens for a few months. None of them will accept registered letters or parcels.

Telephone

Public coin telephones accepting only one or two-crown coins are just for local calls, which cost 2 Kč in Prague. Those taking larger coins can also be used for long-distance and international calls. Newer telephones, such as in the post office, accept extra coins and return the unused ones. Calls from hotel telephones usually involve substantial extra charges.

A more convenient alternative is a *telekart* (telephone card), good for local, long-distance and international calls. There are now many card telephones in Prague. Cards are sold in post offices, newsagents and the main telephone bureau; each is good for up to 200 Kč worth of calls.

Since summer 1993, the Prague telephone system has been undergoing a complete overhaul including new local numbers across the board, a process that will continue for some time. Although efforts have been made to use new numbers in this guidebook where they were available, you may well find that some numbers don't work. If so, talk to PIS, look at the latest telephone book, or ring directory assistance on ☎ 120 (for numbers in Prague) or ☎ 121 (for numbers elsewhere in the Czech and Slovak republics).

Long-Distance & International Calls You can make long-distance and international calls from public telephones, eg in the 24-hour lobby of the main post office. Or for the same rates you can pay a deposit in the telephone bureau and make your call in a sound-proof booth, where a little meter ticks off your money.

To call another city in the Czech or Slovak Republic, dial 0 plus the telephone code plus the number; no country code is yet needed for calls to the Slovak Republic. The telephone bureau has directories for Prague and major cities.

To call out of the Czech Republic, dial 00 followed by the country code for your target country, the area code for your target city (you'll probably have to drop the first zero) and then the number. Country codes include Australia 61, Canada 1, France 33, Germany 49, Irish Republic 353, Netherlands 31, New Zealand 64, UK 44 and USA 1. To make calls to Prague, dial your country's international access code plus 42 (Czech and Slovak republics) plus 2 (Prague) and then the number.

International direct dialling (IDD) rates from Prague are about US$1 a minute to the UK and US$2 a minute to the USA and Australia; operator assistance adds about 35 US cents a minute. For international directory enquiries, dial ☎ 0 149; for international telephone services, ☎ 0 139.

You can place an international collect (reverse-charges) call from the telephone bureau without putting down any cash, or from a public telephone for the price of a local call. Tell the operator *účet volaného*. Collect calls are not possible to Australia.

Certain countries also have arrangements for direct connection to an operator in that country for collect calls etc. To do this, dial 00 42 00 plus: 0101 (USA/AT&T), 0112 (USA/MCI), 0151 (Canada), 3101 (Netherlands), 3301 (France), 4401 (UK), or 4949 (Germany), among others.

Fax, Telegram & Telex

Faxes, telegrams and telex messages can be sent and received 24 hours a day at the fax bureau of the main post office.

Fax rates are the same as telephone rates, with an A4-sized page taking about 1½ minutes. Many hotels and agencies have fax services too, but rates are around twice the post office rate.

Telegrams are about 65 US cents per word to Europe, North America and Australasia.

TIME

Czechs tend to use the 24-hour clock and there is no equivalent of 'am' and 'pm', though they commonly add *ráno* (morning), *dopoledne* (before noon), *odpoledne* (afternoon) or *večer* (evening).

The Czech Republic is on Central European Time, ie GMT/UTC plus one hour. Clocks are reset to daylight-saving time, ahead one hour on the last weekend in March and back one hour on the last weekend in September. When it's noon in Prague in summer (winter), it's:

3 am (3 am) in San Francisco & Vancouver
6 am (6 am) in New York & Toronto
11 am (11 am) in London & Dublin
noon (noon) in Paris, Berlin, Vienna, Budapest & Warsaw
8 pm (10 pm) in Sydney
10 pm (midnight) in Wellington

ELECTRICITY

Electricity is 220 volts, 50 Hz AC, and quite reliable in Prague. Nearly all outlets have the two small round holes common throughout Continental Europe; some

Malá Strana bridge towers with St Nicholas Church in background (RN)

also have a protruding earth (ground) pin. If you have a different plug or want to use the earth pin, bring an adapter, as they don't seem to be sold in the Czech Republic. North American appliances will also need a transformer if they don't have built-in voltage adjustment.

WEIGHTS & MEASURES

The metric system is in use. A comma is used instead of the decimal point, and full stops are used at thousands, millions etc. A dash is used after prices rounded to the nearest crown. Thus, for example, 3000 crowns would be written 3.000,–.

LAUNDRY

Prague's first self-service laundy *(samoobslužná prádelna)* is the cheerful, expat-run Laundry Kings (☎ 312 37 43). A normal load costs about US$3 to wash and dry, and there's also a drop-off service. It's open weekdays from 6 am to 10 pm, Saturday and Sunday from 8 am. From Metro station Hradčanská, take the 'Praha Dejvice' exit, turn left into Dejvická and it's at No 16.

A sign on a place under renovation at Londynská 71, off náměstí Míru (Prague 2), states that a new self-service laundry will be opening there.

Locally run laundries are hard to find, and a load can take up to a week. There's one in the shopping arcade opposite the Hotel Olšanka in Žižkov, or you can look in the Yellow Pages under *prádelny* (laundries). Hotels sometimes offer pricey services.

If you'd rather do yours in the hotel sink, bring along a universal sink plug and a bit of line. Detergent is easy to find in the shops.

TOILETS

Public toilets are free in state-run museums, galleries and concert halls, and most cafés and restaurants don't seem to mind non-guests using theirs (ask for *záchod, vé cé* (WC) or *toalet)*.

Elsewhere, eg in train, bus and metro stations, they're staffed by attendants who ask for a crown or two for use of the toilet (their only pay) and a further donation to use the washbasin, and may sell a few bits of toilet paper *(toaletní papír)*. Most places are fairly clean. Men's are marked *muži* or *páni*, women's *ženy* or *dámy*.

BOOKS & MAPS

Current Affairs

The Europe-based journalist Timothy Garton Ash's *We the People: the Revolutions of 1989* features gripping I-was-there accounts of the revolutions that swept away the region's old guard in 1989. William Shawcross's *Dubček & Czechoslovakia* is a biography of the late leader of Prague's original Spring, with a hasty post-1989 update. Another biography is Michael Simmons' *The Reluctant President: A Political Life of Václav Havel*.

Essays & Memoirs

Several books contain the essays and memoirs of the dissident-turned-president Václav Havel. *Disturbing the Peace* is a collection of recent historical musings. *Letters to Olga* is a collection of letters to his wife from prison in the 1980s. *Living In Truth* is a series of absorbing political essays.

Patrick Leigh Fermor's *A Time of Gifts* is the luminous first instalment of his trek through Europe, including Czechoslovakia, in the early 1930s.

Fiction

Bruce Chatwin's*Utz* is a quiet, absorbing novella about a porcelain collector in Prague's old Jewish quarter. Jaroslav Hašek's *The Good Soldier Švejk* is good low-brow WW I humour about the trials of Czechoslovakia's literary mascot, written in instalments from Prague's pubs. Alois Jirásek's *Old Czech Legends* is a compendium of Bohemian legends by a leading light of the Czech National Revival. *The Trial* and *The Castle* are Franz Kafka's two complex and claustrophobic masterpieces.

One of the Czech Republic's best known authors-in-exile is Milan Kundera, who wrote about life under the Communist regime. Probably his best novel is *The Joke*. Two other notable works are *The Book of Laughter and Forgetting* and *The Unbearable Lightness of Being*. Other enjoyable novels are *Cowards* by Josef Škvorecký and *The Ship Named Hope* by Ivo Klíma.

Guidebooks

The somewhat disjointed *Prague: Insight City Guide* (ed Joachim Chwaszcza) has few practicalities but good background information. Rob Humphries' *Prague: the Rough Guide* is a detailed and intelligent guide to the city. Sadakat Kadri's *Prague: Cadogan City Guide* is a poetic and easy-to-read guidebook, though its information is becoming a bit dated. The *Blue Guide to Czechoslovakia* by Michael Jacobs focuses on architecture and is aimed at visitors travelling by car.

If you're doing any further travelling in the region, Lonely Planet's *Eastern Europe on a shoestring* by David Stanley is a practical and well-informed guidebook written by a committed backpacker. LP's *Eastern Europe phrasebook* has an extensive section on Czech.

Maps

Numerous maps are available at Prague newsagents, bookshops and travel agencies for around US$1. The most precise and readable map of the city's historical heart is Žaket's 1:6500 *Praha – historické centrum*, though it has no transport information. Kartografie Praha's 1:20,000, city-wide *Praha – plán města* is crammed with data and includes a detailed street index and public transport routes.

A big headache for travellers and Czechs alike has been the rush to erase cartographic reminders of Communism. Scores of Prague's streets, squares, bridges and parks have been re-named since 1989. Not all maps have kept pace, and trying to use an old one will drive you up the wall. The Žaket maps seem to be the most up-to-date. A map's copyright blurb will show its publication date.

For excursions around Prague, Kartografie Praha's excellent 1:100,000 contour map, *Výlety do okolí prahy* (Excursions to the Environs of Prague), has parks, preserves and forests, sites of historical interest, roads, campsites and 56 hikes (from four to 18 km long), colour-coded to their trail markers. Unfortunately the hike descriptions are only in Czech.

Bookshops

Prague is full of interesting bookshops *(knihupectví)*, but those that stock English-language titles tend to favour coffee-table books and paperback English classics. You'll find surprisingly few books on Czech history, culture or translations of Czech writers other than Václav Havel and Franz Kafka. Following are the best of the lot for English-speaking book junkies:

Academia, Wenceslas Square 34, is good for books on art and architecture.

Albatros, Národní 29, has children's books and a big rock-CD and tape department; a branch on the corner of Havelská and Melantrichova has children's books and classical CDs.

Československý spisovatel (Monday to Friday from 10 am to 6 pm, Saturday from 9 am to 2 pm), Národní 9, has a big map department.

Charles University Philosophy Faculty student bookshop (☎ 231 95 16, Monday to Friday from 9 am to 5 pm), náměstí Jana Palacha 2, Staré Město, has some Czech history and Czech writers among the Penguin Classics. A sister shop is at Michalská 18 near Old Town Square.

Cizojazyčná literatura (Monday to Friday from 8.30 am to 8 pm, Saturday to 6 pm), Na příkopě 27, has many books about Prague and the Czech Republic.

Fišer, Kaprova 10, is a small place aimed at Czech readers but with a good map selection.
Globe, Janovského 14 (near Strosmayerovo náměstí) in Holešovice, is a pleasant bookshop-cum-coffee shop.
International Bookstore (☎ 231 28 12, daily from 10 am to 8 pm) claims to have Prague's biggest English-language inventory, heavy on art books, cheap novels, guidebooks and magazines; temporarily housed in the student union, on the corner of Pařížská and 17.listopadu.
Melantrich (☎ 26 71 66, weekdays from 8.30 am to 8 pm, Saturday and Sunday to 6 pm), Na příkopě 3 (plus half a dozen other locations), has a good selection of city and country maps.
Nadas (Monday to Friday from 9 am to 6 pm, Saturday 8.30 am to 1 pm), Hybernská 5, publishes train and bus timetables, and is very good for Prague maps and guidebooks.
Olympia, Opletalova 1, is good for maps and guidebooks.

Second-hand bookshops *(antikvariat)* dotted around the Old Town and Malá Strana have few English titles but make great browsing.

MEDIA

Newspapers & Magazines

Prague has no English-language daily newspaper, but its weekly *Prague Post* and bi-weekly *Prognosis*, at 25 Kč each, are good value for visitors. Along with local news and features, both have 'facts for the visitor' sections, travel tips, concert and restaurant reviews and day-by-day arts and entertainment listings.

The *Central European Business Weekly* is aimed at the growing expatriate business community, with business-oriented regional news plus a few entertainment and restaurant listings.

Major European and American newspapers and a few magazines are on sale at kiosks in tourist zones and at the main train station.

Radio

BBC World Service news and cultural programming is broadcast locally on 101.1 MHz FM, with some Czech and Slovak-language inserts. Club VOA (Voice of America pop music and news) is on 106.2 MHz FM, with Czech-language news at half-past the hour. World Service and VOA are also easy to receive on short-wave. Radio 1 (91.9 MHz FM) has tourist news and information in English on Monday to Friday from 3.30 to 4 pm. The

FM dial is full of Czech DJs playing Western pop and rock.

TV

Of Prague's four state-run TV channels, ČT3 is 'international', which means it broadcasts midday and late-night CNN news – roughly from 11.30 pm (weekends from 1 am) to 10 am and from around noon to 3 or 4 pm. Prague is due to get its first private channel in 1994.

FILM & PHOTOGRAPHY

Forty-five years of secret police lurking behind every shrub may have made some people uneasy about being photographed, so ask first. 'May I take your photograph?' is *Mužu si váš vifotit?*

Airport X-Rays

One dose of x-rays for carry-on bags won't harm slow or medium-speed film, but the effects are cumulative and repeated doses can fog your pictures. Lead-lined, 'film-safe' pouches help, but most officials will hand-inspect your film if you ask.

Film & Processing

The Old Town and Malá Strana have numerous small shops with Western print film and D&P service. Some also stock video cassettes. Reliable-looking shops in the Old Town are at Panská 4, Jungmannova 20, and in the Kotva and Krone department stores. Some Kodak franchises also have overpriced Ektachrome (but not Kodachrome) slide film. The biggest is a lab at Národní 39; another is at Celetná 3.

Avoid Czech colour and slide film, as you may not be able to process it outside the country. You can get prints developed in Prague, but Czech photo shops are *not* good places to get slides processed – two reputable labs scratched many of the slides submitted by one of this book's researchers. Better to get them done at home.

For passport/visa photos, two studios near the embassies in Malá Strana are Foto Expres Minilab, Lázeňská 15, and another on the corner of Valdštejnská and Pod Bruskou. A shop in the Můstek metro station lobby below Wenceslas Square offers four Polaroid passport photos for about US$3.

For camera repairs, try Profoto at Pařížská 12 in Josefov.

HEALTH

No immunisations are required for entry into the Czech Republic.

Precautions

Most Praguers insist that you can drink the tap water, but there have been instances of contamination in outer districts. In any case it's an unpleasant brew of chlorine and other additives. Bottled or fully boiled water is available almost everywhere.

Most restaurant and take-away food is as hygienic as in the West, but you're safest with hot, freshly made items. Bottled milk is pasteurised, and yoghurt is always hygienic; the dates stamped on them are manufacture dates, not use-by dates.

Ticks

Ticks *(klíště)* are a common nuisance in forests and even in suburban gardens. If you see that one has buried itself in your skin, *don't* pick it off, but coax it out by covering it in vaseline or oil. If it has been there some time, a red blotch may appear around it, though long-term ill effects are rare.

But about 5% of ticks carry tick encephalitis, a cerebral inflammation that can cause death. In this case, the blotches can be several cm or more across, sometimes pale in the centre. In some cases, there may be no blotches but only temporary flu-type symptoms or no symptoms at all. Victims may feel extremely tired and weak.

You can get a short-lasting vaccine against tick encephalitis in the Czech Republic, and a vaccine is available in the West that immunises you for years. Avoid ticks by wearing socks and long trousers when walking in woods and tall grass.

Respiratory Problems

For people with respiratory problems, Prague is not a fun place to be in winter, as pollution from cars and the widespread burning of soft coal periodically turns the air dangerously foul.

Medical Services

Emergency treatment and non-hospital first aid are free for all visitors to the Czech Republic. You must pay for any other hospital care unless you're an EU citizen, in which case you may get cheap or free treatment under reciprocal health-care treaties (check before you leave home).

Others must pay for treatment, normally in crowns, and at least some of it must be paid up front. A travel insurance policy that covers medical treatment abroad is a good idea – those offered by various 'student' travel agencies are good value. Everyone must pay for prescribed medications.

Prague's best hospital, equipped and staffed to Western standards, is Na Homolce Hospital at Na Homolce 724 (on older maps this street is called Nad motolskou nemocnice) in Motol, Prague 5; take bus No 167 from Anděl metro station. This used to be just for diplomats and Party bigwigs, and to most Praguers it's still the 'rich people's hospital'. The foreigners' polyclinic and emergency entrance (☎ 529 221 46 from 7.30 am to 4 pm; after hours 529 221 91 or 529 211 11) are on the north side, 2nd level. There's a separate children's clinic (☎ 529 220 25).

For anything other than a life-threatening injury or illness, the drop-in Fakultní poliklinika (☎ 29 06 51, ext (*linka*) 316, or 29 83 41 or 29 93 81) is geared for foreigners and has English-speaking staff. It's at Karlovo náměstí 32, in southern Nové Město, and is open Monday to Friday from 7.30 am to 3.30 pm. Payment is in crowns.

District clinics have after-hours emergency services (from 7 pm to 7 am and all weekend). The city's biggest polyclinic is at Antala Staška 80 in Prague 4, south-west of metro station Budějovická. The Prague 1 clinic (☎ 236 14 08) is at Palackého 5 off Jungmannova in southern Nové Město. For Prague 2 it's on U nemocnice, south-east of Karlovo náměstí in southern Nové Město.

Dental Services

There are dental clinics at Na Homolce Hospital (☎ 529 221 55 from 7.30 am to 4 pm, after hours 529 221 91 or 529 211 11), the Fakultní Poliklinika, and the big Prague 4 polyclinic (see the previous Medical Services section). District clinics for after-hours emergencies include those at Vladislavova 22 opposite Národní Třída metro station (☎ 26 13 74), and at Ječná 1 on Karlovo náměstí.

Medicines & Pharmacies

Pharmacies (*lekárna*) are plentiful, and each city district has one that stays open 24 hours a day. For Prague 1 it's at Na příkopě 5 (☎ 22 00 81). Prague 2's is at Ječná 1 on

Photos : Top left JK, others RN

Karlovo náměstí (☎ 20 19 15), Prague 3's at Koněvova 150 (☎ 89 42 03). But over-the-counter and prescription medicines are not always available, so it's wise to bring what you need.

Spas

The Czech Republic has hundreds of mineral springs whose waters are said to be good for various ailments, and Czechs and foreigners take the cure at dozens of spas around the country. A spa visit – typically about three weeks – must be booked in advance through Balnea (☎ 232 37 67), Pařížská 11, 110 01 Prague 1, or a Čedok office abroad. Room, board and treatment start at about US$60 per person a day in summer, less in winter. But you can bring your own glass to the public springs and drink the local water at no cost.

The closest spa town to Prague is Poděbrady, convenient but not very exciting. The most famous, attractive and touristed ones are Karlovy Vary (Karlsbad) and Mariánské Lázně (Marienbad) in West Bohemia, within reach of Prague as excursions.

WOMEN TRAVELLERS

Women (especially solo) may find the atmosphere in most non-touristy pubs a bit raw, as they tend to be male territory. *Kavárnas* (coffee shops) often dispense beer and wine too, and are more congenial. *Vinárnas* (wine bars) are another good place for drinks and a meal.

To many Westerners the Czech Republic seems to be picking up, sexually speaking, where it left off in 1948. Newsstands groan under porno rubbish; the expatriate press bubbles with arguments about whether this is sexism or freedom of expression, while on the whole Czechs seem to be less fussed about the matter than foreigners are.

The darker side is that sexual violence is on the rise since 1989. Most Czech women we asked said they experience routine whistling and catcalls. Attacks on Czech women now happen throughout the city, and it's not a good idea to wander anywhere alone at night, even in Old Town Square and Wenceslas Square.

DANGERS & ANNOYANCES

Emergency telephone numbers in Prague include:

Police: ☎ 158
Fire: ☎ 150

Ambulance: ☎ 155
Road accidents: ☎ 236 64 64 or 2121 37 47

Theft & Other Rip-Offs

Tourism and heady commercialism have spawned an epidemic of petty (and not-so-petty) crime. Where tourists are concerned, this mainly means pickpockets. Naturally enough, the prime trouble spots are where tourists gather in crowds. These include Prague Castle, Charles Bridge, Old Town Square (especially by the Astronomical Clock), the entrance to the Old Jewish Cemetery, Wenceslas Square, and in the metro and on trams.

There's no point in being paranoid, but it makes obvious sense to keep valuables well out of reach, such as inside your clothing. Be alert in crowds.

Lost or Stolen Belongings

It's usually helpful to go to your embassy first. The staff ought to give you a letter to take to the police, preferably in Czech, asking for a police report, without which you cannot collect on insurance. Try to get the embassy to provide its own report in English too.

The British Embassy has this down to a fine art, and will also help you get in touch with mum and dad or your bank to get more money. For British, Irish and unrepresented Commonwealth citizens, it may even arrange an emergency passport to get you home.

For a police report, go to the Prague 1 police station at Konviktská 14. If your passport has been stolen, apply for a replacement visa at the Foreigners' Police & Passport Office at Olšanská 2 in Žižkov (see Visa Extensions under Visas & Embassies earlier in this chapter). On the subject of lost or stolen travellers' cheques and credit cards, see Money in this chapter.

For anything except travel documents, you might get lucky at the city's lost & found office (*ztráty a nálezy*, ☎ 236 88 87) at Bolzanova 5, north-east of the main train station. There's also one (☎ 334 442 85) at the airport.

Racism

You may be surprised at the level of casual prejudice directed at Romanies (Gypsies), whom people are quick to blame for the city's problems. A beauty-pageant contestant in northern Bohemia made headlines in 1993 by revealing her aspiration to be a public prosecutor so she could rid her town of Romanies. If you are dark-skinned you may encounter low-level discrimination yourself, though overt hostility towards visitors is unlikely.

WORK

There are numerous schools where you can find short or long-term work teaching English (or other languages). Some trustworthy ones are:

Angličtina Expres (☎ 29 06 19), Pasáž Světozor, Vodičkova 39, Prague 1
Aspekt – Americká Jazyková Škola (☎ 74 85 27, fax 692 18 43), Ohradní 24, Prague 4
Berlitz (☎ 287 20 52), Na poříčí 12, Prague 1
Canadian Club (☎ 22 77 95), Národní 37, Prague 1
Jazyková Škola (☎ 20 38 14; for other languages, 20 62 41), Národní 20, Prague 1
London School of Modern Languages (☎ 25 68 51), Belgická 25, Prague 2
SPUSA (an agency for English teachers, ☎ 20 45 63), Navrátilova 2, Prague 1

If you can prove your qualifications to them, they'll take care of the paperwork for a work permit.

If you want to stay to do business, talk to the Commercial Section of your embassy in Prague, or the American Chamber of Commerce (☎ 29 98 87, 26 67 78), Karlovo náměstí 24, about work permits and other matters. The Business Club (☎ 26 57 01) at Karlova 21 is a meeting place for Czech and foreign entrepreneurs. Another place for tips is the American Hospitality Center (☎ 26 15 74), Na můstku 7.

If you're staying in the Czech Republic for more than six months, you must register as a permanent resident and get a Czech green card (which also entitles you to lower fees and hotel rates). Go to the Foreigners' Police & Passport Office (☎ 27 95 43) at Olšanská 2, Žižkov. You must submit information on your work and your accommodation, and a medical report. The process takes several months.

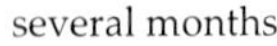

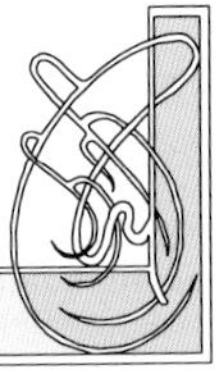

Getting There & Away

Students and people aged under 26 or over 59 can get some big travel discounts. See Money in the Facts for the Visitor chapter for information about student, youth and senior ID cards.

AIR

Prague Ruzyně on the western outskirts of the city, the Czech Republic's only international airport, is served by about two dozen international carriers, including ČSA (Československé aerolinie), the state airline. The high season for travel to Prague is roughly June or July through September, plus Christmas/New Year.

Buying a Ticket from Home

You won't save much money buying tickets in Prague, so if you're going only to the Czech Republic, take advantage of the lower cost of a return (round-trip) ticket bought at home.

Airlines themselves don't usually offer the cheapest tickets. For these you must shop around the travel agencies; several of them specialise in finding low air fares. Look for adverts in major newspapers' travel sections, and watch for special offers. You're safest if an agency belongs to the International Air Transport Association (IATA) or a national body like the American Society of Travel Agents (ASTA), the Association of British Travel Agents (ABTA) or the Australian Federation of Travel Agents (AFTA).

Fares quoted here are approximate, and based on advertised rates at the time of writing. None of them constitutes a recommendation for any airline.

Reconfirmation

To minimise your chances of being 'bumped' from an onward or return flight because of overbooking, reconfirm directly with the airline at least 72 hours before departure.

To/From Europe

Discount air travel is big business in London. In addition to the travel sections of the major dailies, check the Travel classifieds in London's weekly *Time Out* entertainment magazine. A good bargain-ticket agency, especially for those aged under 26, is Campus Travel (☎ 071-730 3402), 52 Grosvenor Gardens, London SW1W 0AG. Trailfinders (☎ 071-937 5400), 42-50 Earl's Court Rd, Kensington, London W8 6EJ, and STA Travel (☎ 071-937 9921), 74 Old Brompton Rd, London SW7, and 117 Euston Rd, London NW1, are also good. All three have branches all over the UK. Another agency aimed at independent travellers to the old Eastern bloc is Regent Holidays (☎ 0272- 211711), 15 John St, Bristol BS1 2HR.

Flying London-Prague (about two hours) can be cheaper than the train. Campus Travel has charter flights for £159 to £189 return (less for under-26s, ISIC cardholders and their dependants), and occasional last-minute specials for £99 return. British Airways and ČSA have daily direct flights; these and KLM also fly from other UK cities. The best ordinary discounted summer fare is about £240, with low-season fares about £20 less.

A reliable source of bargain tickets on the continent is NBBS Travels (☎ 020-638 17 38), Leidsestraat 53, 1017 NV Amsterdam. A discounted return ticket to Prague from Amsterdam is about £180, and from Berlin, Vienna, Warsaw or Budapest, about £100.

To/From North America

ČSA flies directly to Prague from New York four times a week, and jointly with Air Canada from Montreal two or three times weekly. But the cheapest way is probably to fly to London and buy an onward ticket there.

Council Travel and STA sell discounted tickets in the USA from offices all around the country. Council's national toll-free number is ☎ 1-800-223 7402, STA's is ☎ 1-800-777 0112. Another agency recommended by individual travellers is Travel Avenue (☎ 312-876-1254), 641 West Lake St, Chicago, IL 60661. For an ISIC cardholder, a return fare to Prague in July would be about US$880 from Los Angeles, US$750 from New York; earlier or later, subtract at least 10%.

Canada's best bargain-ticket agency is Travel Cuts, with some 50 offices in major cities. The parent office (☎ 416-979-2406) is at 187 College St, Toronto M5T 1P7.

To/From Australasia

Flight Centres International and STA Travel are major dealers in cheap air fares, each with offices throughout Australia and New Zealand. Flight Centres' main offices are at 19 Bourke St (☎ 03-650 2899) and 317 Swanston St, Melbourne 3000; and 82 Elizabeth St, Sydney 2000 (☎ 02-235 3522). STA's are at 224 Faraday St, Carlton, Vic 3053 (☎ 03-347 6911), and 732 Harris St, Ultimo, NSW 2007 (☎ 02-281 9866); in New Zealand, 10 High St, PO Box 4156, Auckland (☎ 09-309 9995).

The best available high-season return fare from east-coast Australia is about A$2200 with Qantas/ČSA, or about A$400 less in the low season, and ČSA throws in a free domestic flight.

Arriving in Prague by Air

The arrivals hall in Ruzyně Airport has several currency exchange offices; AVE, a reliable accommodation agency (though it does charge high commissions); and half a dozen pricey car-rental agencies. A Čedok desk (☎ 334 45 12, open from 8 am to 6 pm daily, to 8 pm April to October) has maps and information, and can book cars and mid-range hotels. See the Getting Around chapter for transport to/from the city.

Leaving Prague by Air

ČSA's ticketing office (☎ 2146, 235 27 85 or 231 25 95) at Revoluční 1, náměstí Republiky, is open Monday to Friday from 7 am to 6 pm, Saturday from 8 am to 4 pm. Other airline offices include:

Aeroflot, Pařížská 5 (☎ 232 80 47)
Air France, Wenceslas Square 10 (☎ 26 01 55)
Air India, Wenceslas Square 15 (☎ 22 38 54)
Alitalia, Revoluční 5 (☎ 231 05 35)
Austrian Airlines, Revoluční 15 (☎ 232 27 95)
British Airways, Old Town Square 10 (☎ 232 90 20)
Delta, Pařížská 11 (☎ 232 47 72)
Finnair, Španělská 2 (☎ 22 64 89)
KLM, Wenceslas Square 37 (☎ 26 43 62/9)
LOT, Pařížská 18 (☎ 231 75 24)
Lufthansa, Pařížská 28 (☎ 231 75 51)
Malév Hungarian, Pařížská 5 (☎ 232 79 95)
SAS, Štěpánská 61 (☎ 22 81 41)
Sabena, Ruzyně Airport (☎ 36 78 13)
Swissair, Pařížská 11 (☎ 232 47 07)

A departure tax of around US$7 is normally included in the ticket price.

TRAIN

Trains go daily to Prague from most major European cities. Fares quoted here are based on advertised rates at the time of writing. In summer you should book at least a few weeks ahead.

In the UK, it's cheapest to buy tickets through British Rail International (☎ 071-834 2345), Victoria Station, London SW1V 1JY; or Eurotrain (071-730 3402), 52 Grosvenor Gardens, London SW1W 0AG. A 2nd-class return ticket from London via Cologne – the cheapest and most direct of half a dozen routes – is £235 (£150 for under-26s), plus about £10 for a couchette or £25 for a sleeper. Tickets are good for two months and you can break your journey anywhere en route. London-Prague takes 25 to 30 hours.

There's no need to book domestic rail travel before you get there.

Rail Passes

If you plan to travel widely in Europe, or in the Czech and Slovak republics, the following special tickets and rail passes may be better value for you. Some of these may have different names in different countries.

Inter-Rail Pass This £249 pass gives people aged under 26 unlimited 2nd-class travel for one month on most of the state railways of western and central Europe (except their own country). There's also an Inter-Rail pass for people aged 26 and over, at £209 for 15 days or £269 for one month. Both can be used in the Czech and Slovak republics. There are also plans to issue cheaper passes good only for certain zones in Europe.

Circuit Tour Ticket This fixed-route return ticket (Eurotrain's version for those aged under 26 is called an Explorer ticket) links six or eight major European cities, going out one way and returning another. Two Eurotrain routes that include Prague are £240 and £265; British Rail International has a non-youth version for £337, plus 1st-class options.

Czech Explorer Pass This Eurotrain pass is £24 for a week's unlimited 2nd-class travel within the Czech and Slovak republics (£35 for 1st class). It's available to people aged under 26, ISIC card-holders, teachers and their spouses and children. Explorer passes are also available for Hungary, Poland and a few other countries. You must buy it *outside* the country where it is to be used.

Euro-Domino Freedom Pass If you don't plan to be on the move all that much, this pass allows a few days per month of unrestricted train travel within a particular country. In the Czech and Slovak republics, for example, any three/five/10 days in a designated month is £40/56/96 respectively, travelling in 2nd class (for under-26-year-olds it's £31/42/72). This pass cannot be bought in the intended country of travel.

Eurail Pass This pass for 1st-class travel in a limited number of European countries is normally sold only outside Europe and is meant for non-Europeans. It's not yet valid in the Czech and Slovak republics, though this may change.

Arriving in Prague by Train

Most international trains arrive at Prague's main station, Praha hlavní nádraží. A few go to Praha-Holešovice or Praha-Smíchov. All these stations have metro stops. Masarykovo nádraží, two blocks north of the main station, is the primary domestic station.

Praha Hlavní Nádraží (Main Train Station) You disembark at level 3 into a swarm of currency-exchange desks, accommodation offices and people offering places to stay. Get your bearings and a map at the very helpful PIS booth on level 2 (weekdays from 9 am to 7 pm, weekends to 6 pm).

Up on level 4 is the original Art-Nouveau station; levels 3, 2 and 1 are the modern extension beneath Wilsonova třída. Buses are outside the north (right) end of level 3 and out the front on Opletalova. Taxis are outside the south end, and there's a metro station entrance on level 2. Public-transport information is available at the ČAD booth beside the metro entrance. Level 1 has a left-luggage office (*úschovna*), open 24 hours, and day-use lockers (set your own combination inside the door, insert two 2-Kč coins, close it and turn the handle). There are showers beneath level 2.

If you arrive in the middle of the night without a hotel booking, store your bags and take a long walk until the sun rises. This station is a magnet for pickpockets, crazies and urine-soaked drunks, and at night it's a bad place to hang out. Money exchange and accommodation offices here all close from 11 pm to at least 6 am.

The closest hostel with a night desk is the Kolej Jednota at Opletalova 38, just north of the station. The closest 24-hour currency exchange is at the Hotel Jalta on Wenceslas Square. At the time of writing, the FX Café and Club Radost, both a 15-minute walk south to Bělehradská 120 in Vinohrady, were open until 6 am. The Repre Klub in Obecní dům stays open until 5 am.

Leaving Prague by Train

The state railway company is ČD (České dráhy). With some exceptions, domestic train travel is more leisurely than bus travel, sometimes to extremes. Foreigners and Czechs pay the same fares.

You can buy a ticket *(jízdenka)*, or a ticket with a reservation *(místenka)* for a seat *(místo)*, couchette *(lehátkový vůz)* or sleeper *(spací vůz)*. You cannot get a reservation without a ticket. Certain services are reservation-only – marked with the letter R in a box on timetables.

Doing It Yourself In Prague, information about connections is available on ☎ 235 38 36 or 26 49 30. Station lobbies have timetables on rotating drums. The main station has an information office at the north end of level 3, and several ČD travel agency offices. You can buy your own regional or national timetables from the ČD agency outside level 3, or from the publisher at Nadas bookshop, Hybernská 5, northern Nové Město.

Domestic tickets are sold at the odd-numbered windows on level 2 of the main station; go to the even-numbered windows for ticket-plus-reservation. It's easiest to write down your intended destination, time and date (month in Roman numerals); if you don't specify anything else, you'll probably get a 2nd-class, one-way ticket. 'Return ticket' is *zpáteční lístek*.

International tickets are sold at the *mezinárodní jízdenky* window on level 3. For a reservation, you must *then* take your ticket to the right-hand ČD agency office on level 2 – up to six hours before departure for a seat or couchette, between eight and 30 days beforehand for a sleeper. You can save a bit by buying a ticket only to the border, and getting your onward ticket in the 'onward' country.

Travel Agencies It's easy to see why most people let an agency do the work, especially with international bookings. Booking a few days ahead is usually enough, even in summer.

Čedok (☎ 212 73 50 or 212 76 42), Na příkopě 18, isn't the cheapest but it's efficient with both domestic and international bookings. Also good for domestic train trips is the ČD agency (☎ 236 53 32 or 26 64 69) in the Sevastopol Cinema passage between Na příkopě 31 and Celetná, open weekdays from 8 am to 5 pm, weekends from 9 am to 3 pm.

For international train bookings, go to the ČD agency (☎ 236 41 40 or 22 84 36) at the main station, outside level 3, open Monday to Friday from 9 am to 1 pm and 2 to 5 pm, Saturday from 8.30 am to noon; or to the youth-travel agency CKM (☎ 20 33 80), Žitná 9, open Monday to Friday from 9 am to noon and 1 to 5 pm (also for Inter-Rail passes and Eurotrain packages).

Train Rip-Offs Overnight Prague-Berlin and Prague-Budapest trains have experienced some bold thefts from sleeping passengers, so keep a grip on your bags.

BUS

This is the cheapest way to travel across Europe. It's easiest to book with Eurolines, a consortium of coach lines with offices all over Europe. Coaches are comfortable, air-conditioned and as fast as the train, and stop frequently for food and bodily functions. You can usually get away with booking a few days ahead of departure, even in summer.

Eurolines goes to Prague from London's Victoria Coach Station daily in summer for £95 return (£85 for people aged under 26 and over 59); book through any National Express office. Smaller lines that go from London for a few pounds less are Kingscourt Express (☎ 081-769 9229) and Adco Travel (☎ 071-372 0323). The trip takes about 23 hours.

Eurolines also has flexible two-month 'Euro Explorer' itineraries with unlimited stopovers en route – eg London-Budapest-Prague-London for £105.

For details on domestic connections to/from Prague, see the following Leaving Prague by Bus section.

Arriving in Prague by Bus

Most international buses arrive at Florenc, the city's main bus station, although it wouldn't hurt to ask when you book; some London connections go to/from metro station Roztyly in the southern outskirts.

Florenc Station By the platforms is an information window where some English is allegedly spoken. There are day-use lockers of dubious security by the platforms and inside, and an expensive currency-exchange office. Metro station Florenc is beside the bus station.

Leaving Prague by Bus

Domestic The state bus company is ČAD (Česká autobusová doprava). Its long-distance coaches tend to be faster, more frequent and marginally cheaper than trains. For the time being, 'domestic' includes the Slovak Republic, though this is certain to change. Foreigners and Czechs pay the same fares.

Long-distance coaches depart from Florenc, as do buses to most regional destinations – eg excursions around Prague. Some regional buses start from stands near metro stations Anděl, Hradčanská, Nádraží Holešovice, Palmovka, Radlická, Roztyly, Smíchovské nádraží and Želivského; the stand at Želivského has moved eastward on Vinohradská to Počernická – a five-minute walk or one stop on any tram.

Agencies do not book domestic buses, but Čedok and others can tell you which stand is best for a particular trip – or indeed whether you're better off taking the

Butchers at work, Golden Gate, St Vitus Cathedral (RN)

train. You might get some help from ČAD's information line (☎ 221 44 59 or 22 14 45, 6 am to 8 pm).

Florenc offers a maze of charts, though they're not impossible to sort out. One gives the route numbers and departure platforms for each major destination. Others give all departure times for each route number. Then there are timetables for every route. To figure out when the next bus leaves, you'll probably have to look at timetables for more than one route number. You can buy your own regional timetables from the Nadas bookshop, Hybernská 5, northern Nové Město.

Short-haul tickets are sold on the bus. Long-distance domestic tickets are sold in Florenc, weekdays from 6 am to 6.30 pm, Saturday to 1 pm, Sunday from 8.30 am to noon and 12.30 to 3.30 pm.

There are at least two private coach lines that cost a shade less than ČAD. Čebus (☎ 24 81 16 76) goes to Brno, Karlovy Vary, Liberec, Pardubice and Teplice; its booking office on Za Poříčskou bránou near Florenc is open weekdays from 9 am to 5 pm, weekends from 10 am to 6 pm. Ceres (also called Český národní expres) goes to Brno and Hradec Králové; its office near the City Museum is open weekdays from 6 am to 8 pm, Saturday from 7 am to 3 pm, Sunday from noon to 8 pm. By the time you read this, both will probably be offering additional destinations.

International Nearly all international buses leave from Florenc (although a few UK-bound buses leave from Roztyly metro station). Window No 5 sells international tickets and is open weekdays from 6 am to noon and 12.40 to 6 pm, Saturday to 12.30 pm only, Sunday from 8.30 am to noon and 12.30 to 3 pm.

But it is much simpler to book through a good agency. The price is the same, and you're more likely to get discounts. Following are some reliable ones (they don't all book the same destinations):

Adco Travel, Bulovka 19/368, Libeň (☎ 683 04 29)
American Hospitality Center, Na Můstku 7, Staré Město (☎ 26 15 74)
Bohemiatour, Zlatnická 7, northern Nové Město (☎ 232 38 77, 232 39 89)
CKM, Žitná 9, southern Nové Město (☎ 20 33 80)
ČAD-Kličov (the main Prague agent for Eurolines), Štěpánská 63 (three flights up), southern Nové Město
ČD, Sevastopol Cinema passage between Na příkopě 31 and Celetná (☎ 236 53 32, 26 64 69); and outside level 3 of the main train station, does a few coach routes (☎ 236 41 40 or 22 84 36)
Čedok, Na příkopě 18 (☎ 212 73 50, 212 76 42)

Kingscourt Express, Antala Staška 60, near metro station Budějovická (☎ 49 92 56; info 75 24 22)

CAR & MOTORBIKE

See Car & Motorbike in the Getting Around chapter for details about car rental, breakdown support and driving in Prague itself.

Czech Border Crossings

Following are border posts which can process Western foreigners. At the time of writing, only those marked with * were able to issue tourist visas on the spot; at the others you could only get a 48-hour, non-extendable transit visa (though it's likely some of them may soon be able to issue tourist visas as well). Fees for on-the-spot visas are around US$35, approval is at the officials' discretion, and visas are normally issued only during daytime business hours. All of these border posts are open 24 hours, except as noted:

With Austria:
- Studánky, South Bohemia (Weigetschlag)
- * Dolní Dvořiště, South Bohemia (Wullowitz)
- České Velenice, South Bohemia (Gmünd)
- Halámky, South Bohemia (Neu Nagelberg)
- Nová Bystřice, South Bohemia (Grametten)
- * Hatě (Znojmo), South Moravia (Kleinhaugsdorf)
- Hevlín, South Moravia (Laa an der Thaya)
- Mikulov, South Moravia (Drasenhofen)

With Germany:
- Varnsdorf, North Bohemia (Seifhennersdorf)
- Hřensko (Děčín), North Bohemia (Schmilka)
- Petrovice, North Bohemia (Bahratal)
- Cínovec, North Bohemia (Zinnwald)
- Hora sv Šebestiána, North Bohemia (Reitzenhain)
- Boží Dar, West Bohemia (Oberwiesenthal)
- Vojtanov, West Bohemia (Schönberg)
- Aš, West Bohemia (Selb); limited hours
- Pomezí nad Ohří (Cheb), West Bohemia (Schirnding)
- Svatý Kříž (Cheb), West Bohemia (Waldsassen); limited hours
- Broumov (Planá), West Bohemia (Mähring)
- * Rozvadov, West Bohemia (Waidhaus)
- Lísková (Domažlice), West Bohemia (Waldmünchen)
- Česká Kubice (Domažlice), West Bohemia (Furth im Wald)
- Všeruby (Domažlice), West Bohemia (Eschlkam)
- Železná Ruda, West Bohemia (Bayerisch Eisenstein)
- Strážný, South Bohemia (Phillippsreuth)

With Poland:

- Český Těšín, North Moravia (Cieszyn)
- Bohumín, North Moravia (Chalupki)
- Mikulovice, North Moravia (Glucholazy); limited hours
- Dolní Lipka (Králíky), East Bohemia (Boboszów)
- Náchod, East Bohemia (Kudowa Slone)
- Harrachov, East Bohemia (Jakuszyce)

You can often save hours by detouring away from popular crossings to smaller ones nearby. Rozvadov is a notorious bottleneck on weekends; other busy ones are Cínovec, Strážný and Dolní Dvořiště.

Czech-Slovak Border Points New border facilities between the Czech and Slovak republics are still being sorted out. You cannot count on getting an on-the-spot visa at any of them, but you should still insist on stopping for an entry stamp in your passport, to avoid any later headaches over the question of how long you were actually in the Czech Republic.

Documents

Officially you should carry an International Driving Permit, though all the Czech officials (and car-rental agencies) we dealt with were satisfied with just our home driving licences. Drivers must also have passport, vehicle registration papers and the 'green card' that shows they carry full liability insurance (see your domestic insurer about this). Without proof of insurance, you'll be forced to take out insurance at the border, for around 250 Kč a month for a car, 50 Kč a month for a motorbike. If the car isn't yours, avoid potential headaches by carrying a notarised letter from the owner saying you're allowed to drive it.

Road Rules

As in the rest of continental Europe, you drive on the right here. The legal driving age is 18. *Don't* drink *any* alcohol if you'll be driving – regulations permit *no* blood-alcohol level, and penalties are severe.

Speed limits vary in built-up areas from 40 to 60 km/h between 5 am and 11 pm, and 90 km/h outside these hours. On major roads the maximum speed is 90 km/h, and on motorways (freeways) 110 km/h. Although the official speed limit at the country's many rail crossings is 30 km/h, you're better off to stop and look, as many well-used crossings have no barriers and some don't even have flashing lights.

If the car has seat belts, they must be worn by all passengers. Children under 12 years old aren't allowed in the front seat. Each vehicle must be equipped with a first-aid kit and a red-and-white warning triangle (to be set up behind your car if you break down), and must display a sticker on the rear indicating the country of registration.

Riders of motorbikes greater than 50 cc must wear helmets and goggles, and their passengers must wear helmets. Headlights must be switched on day and night. The maximum speed for motorcycles is 90 km/h, and the police make a point of booking foreign motorcyclists who keep up with cars on the freeways.

You may not overtake a tram, trolleybus or bus if it is stationary and there is no passenger island. In Prague you may only overtake trams on the right; anywhere else you can do so on the left if it is not possible on the right.

Road Signs Standard European signs are in common use. Intersections are frequently marked with only a small black-and-white sign showing which direction has the right of way. In cities and towns, watch out for *Pěší zona* signs, which indicate pedestrian-only zones; there may be few other clues that you're not meant to be driving there. Some signs that don't conform with international conventions include:

Průjezd zakázán – closed to all vehicles
Objížďka – detour
Jednosměrný provoz – one way
H or *Nemocnice* – hospital

Driving Offences

Fines for driving offences seem to be around 200 to 300 Kč. Fines for foreigners are commonly inflated, and if no docket/receipt *(paragon)* is given, you may be getting overcharged and may wish to bargain it down.

Fuel

Petrol or gasoline *(benzín)* is widely available, but not all stations are open on Sundays and after 6 pm on weeknights. Leaded petrol (*special* at 91 octane and *super* at 96 octane) is widely available. Unleaded petrol (*natural*, 95 octane) is available at an increasing number of stations. Diesel *(nafta)* is readily available. At the time of writing, petrol was about 20 Kč per litre, diesel about 17 Kč. See the Getting Around chapter for details about fuel in Prague.

TOURS

After decades of being the only game in town, Čedok, the state travel bureau, still has the widest range of short trips and package tours to the Czech Republic – generally at the highest prices.

Depending on choice of accommodation, its land-only cost (exclusive of air fare) for a two-night city excursion with breakfast and a city tour is US$100 to US$300 per person sharing a double room, with cheaper winter trips available. Three-night 'summer breaks' with an out-of-town trip are US$300 to US$500, and a five-night package is about US$600. Čedok also offers driving tours and escorted coach tours around the Czech Republic.

Čedok offices abroad, listed under Tourist Offices in the Facts for the Visitor chapter, can make the arrangements or identify local agents who sell the packages.

From the UK

New Millennium (☎ 021-711 2232), 20 High St, Solihull, W Midlands B91 3TB, runs nine-night coach holidays to Prague for £145 to £225 per person. Travellers Czech (☎ 081-907 7049), 56 Oakfield Ave, Kenton, Harrow, Middlesex HA3 8TJ, offers similar trips, and two to seven-night holidays by air. A 'city break' (including air fare) with Travelscene (☎ 081-427 8800), 11-15 St Ann's Rd, Harrow, Middlesex HA1 1AS, starts at £395 for three nights, £565 for seven nights.

VegiVentures (☎ 0760-755888) does the improbable with a seven-night vegetarian tour of Prague and eastern Bohemia, for about £500 including air fare. Martin Randall Travel (☎ 081-742 3355), 10 Barley Mow Passage, Chiswick, London W4 4PH, offers guided art and music tours to Bohemia and Moravia.

Accommodation-Only The travel classifieds of UK papers list a growing number of low-overhead outfits who can arrange private, pension or cheap hotel accommodation in and around Prague. Some better-looking ones are:

Auto Plan, Energy House, Lombard St, Lichfield, Staffordshire WS13 6DP (☎ 0543-257777)

Bridgewater Travel, 217 Monton Rd, Monton, Manchester M30 9PN (☎ 061-707 8547)

Czech Travel, 21 Leighlands Rd, South Woodham Ferrers, Essex CM3 5XN (☎ 0245-328647)

Czechbook, 52 St John's Park, Blackheath, London SE3 7JP (☎ 081-853 1168)
Czechscene, 63 Falkland Rd, Evesham, Worcestershire WR11 6XS (☎ 0386-442782)
Mary & Francis Villas, Chester Close, Belgravia, London SW1X 7BQ (☎ 071-235 8825, fax 259 6093)
TK Travel, 154 Camberwell Grove, London SE5 8HR (☎ 071-737 4952)

From the USA

American-International Homestays (☎ 303-938 8257; toll-free in the USA, 800-876 2048), 2823 Jay Rd, Boulder, CO 80301, organises multi-city homestays in which host families act as de facto guides to their city. The 17-day programmes (Prague plus Budapest-Kraków, Budapest, or St Petersburg) are US$2200 to US$2500 from New York. It also arranges ordinary bed-&-breakfast accommodation.

Goulash Tours (☎ 616-349 8817), 1707 Olmstead Rd, PO Box 2972, Kalamazoo, MI 49003, organises two-week to 12-week bicycle tours around the old Eastern bloc.

From Australasia

One agency organising tours to Prague is Eastern Europe Travel Bureau at 272 Clovelly Rd, Clovelly (Sydney) 2031 (☎ 02-262 1144); and 343 Little Collins St, Melbourne 3000 (☎ 03-600 0299). Its packages include three to seven days in Prague for A$172 to A$1495, plus tours around the Christmas period.

Getting Around

Prague's compact historical centre (Hradčany, Malá Strana, Staré Město and Nové Město) is best appreciated on foot, with the help of cheap and good public transport. Pollution, traffic congestion and traffic vibration damage to old buildings have resulted in pedestrian-only zones and restrictions on vehicle traffic. Since parking in the historical centre is permit-only, there's little point in trying to see it in your car.

TO/FROM THE AIRPORT

City bus No 119 plies between Ruzyně Airport, on the western outskirts of the city, and metro station Dejvická every half an hour or less from 4.30 am to 11.30 pm (buy a 6-Kč bus ticket from the lobby newsstand or the yellow machine near Čedok); the trip takes about 40 minutes including the metro trip to/from the city centre. ČSL, the Czech airport authority, runs comfortable shuttle buses between the airport and metro station Dejvická for 15 Kč, or ČSA's city terminal at Revoluční 25 for 20 Kč (tickets on board); from the airport, take the bus marked 'Centrum'. They run at least every half an hour, daily from 6 am to 6.30 pm. The city terminal is linked by tram No 14 to náměstí Republiky and Wenceslas Square. Čedok runs a daily shuttle every two hours from 9 am to 5 pm to/from the Atrium and Panorama hotels, for a cheeky 150 Kč. They prefer that you book ahead (☎ 284 20 42). All buses leave the airport from in front of the terminal.

Prague's unprincipled taxi drivers, especially those stalking the airport, should be avoided. From the city, avoid hailing a taxi off the street; taxi drivers often jack up the fare for tourists. It's marginally better to telephone for one (see the Taxis section later in this chapter).

PUBLIC TRANSPORT

It costs just 6 Kč to use the metro, tram or bus, and half that for 10 to 16-year-olds and for parents accompanying children aged under three; kids aged under 10 and adults over 69 ride free.

The same ticket *(jízdenka)* is used on all parts of the system. They're sold from the yellow machines in metro stations, and individually or in discounted books of 25 at newsstands, Trafiky snack shops, PNS and other tobacco kiosks. Except on the metro, each ride costs a separate fare (ie there are no transfers). Validate your ticket by punching it in a little machine in the metro station lobby or on the bus or tram.

Cheaper and more convenient is a travel pass from the city transport department (Dopravní podnik or DP), good for unlimited travel on trams, city buses and the metro. A tourist day-pass *(denní jízdenka)*, good for one, two, three, four or five days, is 30, 50, 65, 80 or 100 Kč from ticket outlets and PIS offices.

A tourist pass called the Prague Card is good for unlimited public transport plus free admission to state-run museums, galleries and other attractions, plus some shopping discounts. It's available from Čedok (Na příkopě 18), Pragotur (U Obecního domu 2), American Express (Wenceslas Square 56) and other agencies.

Longer-term visitors can get a one, three or 12 calendar-month pass *(měsíční jízdenka)* for 200, 500 or 1700 Kč. These are sold in the DP office at Na bojišti 5, near metro station I P Pavlova, and between the 25th and 8th of the month at about half the city's metro stations. Bring your passport and one passport-size photo. The passes remain valid three days before or after the validity dates mentioned on the back, allowing time to 'switch' to a new pass.

Inspectors do pounce now and then, and they can fine you 200 Kč on the spot if you don't have a pass or validated ticket.

Metro

Like other Soviet-designed underground systems, Prague's 38-station network is safe, reliable and clean. A 6-Kč ticket lets you ride anywhere with unlimited transfers, for an hour or until you emerge from a station. Trains run from 5 am to midnight daily.

A polite recorded voice announces each station. At the station, it warns, *Ukončete výstup a nástup, dveře se zavírají* ('Finish getting on and off, the doors are closing'). As the train pulls away, it says, *Příští stanice...* ('The next station is...'), perhaps noting that it's a *přestupní stanice* (transfer station). When you disembark, signs point you towards the *výstup* (exit) or to a *přestup* (connecting line).

Trams & Buses

The metro is quickest as far as it goes, but trams are much more relaxed. Buses cover all the areas that trams miss,

LE GRAND MAGASIN KOTVA EST LA POUR VOUS
KOTVA

ČERNÍ
ČERNÍ

22
7133

CAMEL
CAMEL

Trams (RN)

but are dismally slow. Most trams and buses operate from 4.30 am to 11.30 pm daily, and a few only at peak hours. Routes and schedules are posted at each stop. Tram-line numbers have one or two digits, buses three.

There is limited night service on certain lines from midnight to 5 am, at roughly 40-minute intervals: tram Nos 51 through 58 all pass the corner of Lazarská and Spálená (north of Karlovo náměstí) so you can transfer, and bus Nos 501-505, 508-510 and 512 connect with the trams. These are indicated by reverse-colour signs at stops. You might be able to bag a copy of DP's map, *Noční provoz* (Night Service).

In summer and on weekends, vintage tram cars are used on special sightseeing routes. No 91 runs from Masarykovo train station via Wenceslas Square and the National Theatre to Malá Strana, for 10 Kč (kids 5 Kč). No 92 runs from Malostranské náměstí to Hradčany and back for 5 Kč. Ordinary tickets and passes cannot be used on these lines.

TAXI

Prague is plagued with unscrupulous cabbies. Theoretically, anything labelled 'taxi' must display and charge official rates; at the time of writing, the maximum price a registered taxi could charge was 6 Kč flagfall plus 12 Kč per km. Anything else (including look-alike taxis with the word 'taxi' spelt incorrectly) can legally charge whatever they wish. Some tourists have been asked for as much as US$7 per km!

Hailing a taxi on the street is inviting trouble, and even a Czech-speaking interlocutor may not be able to help much. If you do take one, find out the approximate fare in advance and ask the driver to use the meter *(zapněte taximetr, prosím)*. If it's 'broken', find someone else. Before paying, ask for a receipt *(paragon)*, with the distance and fare shown. If you get the rare driver who willingly turns on the meter, he probably deserves a tip. The taxi stands at Wenceslas Square and Old Town Square are notorious for rip-offs.

It's somewhat safer to telephone for a taxi. The cheapest is said to be Interkontact (☎ 22 12 55). Some others – all with 24-hour service – are AAA (☎ 32 24 44), Nonstop Radio Taxi (☎ 35 13 36), Franco-Taxi (☎ 858 74 41) and Reax-Taxi (☎ 472 14 53). To book one more than 24 hours in advance, call ☎ 235 28 11 or 236 58 75, Monday to Friday between 6 am and 5.30 pm.

CAR & MOTORBIKE

For information about driving in the Czech Republic in general, including border crossings, documents and road rules, see the Getting There & Away chapter.

Driving in Prague is no fun. Trying to find your way around – or a legal parking space – while coping with trams, belching buses, other drivers, cyclists and pedestrians, and police on the lookout for a little *baksheesh*, can make you wish you'd left the car at home.

You can ease the trauma by avoiding weekday peak-traffic hours – in central Prague from 4 pm onward (on Fridays as early as 2 pm). Try not to arrive or leave on a Friday or Sunday afternoon or evening, when half the population seems to head to/from their *chaty* (weekend houses).

Most Old Town streets are narrow, and many are cobbled. Central Prague has many pedestrian-only streets, including Wenceslas Square, parts of 28.října and Na příkopě, most of Old Town Square and some streets leading into it. Most are marked with *Pěší zona* (Pedestrian Zone) signs, and only service vehicles and taxis have special permits in these areas.

Parking

Street parking in most of Prague 1 is permit-only. Traffic inspectors need little encouragement to hand out fines, clamp your wheels or tow away vehicles. Parking in one-way streets is normally only allowed on the right-hand side.

There are several parking lots at the edges of the Old Town and around the outer city. Most are marked on the 1:20,000 Kartografie Praha and Žaket city maps. Most charge about 21 Kč per hour or 265 Kč per day. Public transport from these lots into the centre is very good. Parking lots include:

- Hlavní nádraží (main train station)
- Hlavní nádraží, Bolzanova street entrance
- Konstruktiva, under náměstí Jana Palacha
- Hotel Opera Těšnov, Těšnov
- Masarykovo train station
- Tržnice Smíchov, náměstí 14.října

More central (and expensive) parking lots include:

- Kotva department store, náměstí Republiky
- Hotel Inter-Continental, Pařížská
- Hotel Slovan, Wilsonova

- Smetana Theatre (Opera House), Wilsonova
- Národní divadlo (National Theatre), Divadelní

Car Theft

A Western car with foreign plates is a prime target for thieves, especialy in central Prague. Several gangs are said to operate in the republic, stealing cars for the Polish and Russian markets, and a stolen car can be across the border in a matter of hours. Also popular are smaller items like windscreen wipers, antennas and car emblems. Of course, don't leave your possessions visible in the vehicle. Prague's worst street for car thefts is the

Thunovská ulice, Malá Strana (JK)

quiet Mánesova in Vinohrady, Prague 2, nicknamed *Bermudovský trojúhelník* (the Bermuda Triangle).

Tram Rules

In Prague you may overtake a tram only on the right, and only if it is in motion. You must stop for any tram taking on or letting off passengers where there is no passenger island. A tram has the right of way when making any signalled turn across your path. For more road rules, see the Getting There & Away chapter.

Fuel

At the time of writing, you could get leaded and unleaded fuel at the following places in Prague (those marked * are open 24 hours, or nearly so):

- Svatoplukova, Prague 2
- Olšanská, Prague 3 *
- Újezd u Průhonic LS, Prague 4 *
- Vrbova, Prague 4
- K Barrandovu, Prague 5 *
- Strakonická, Malá Chuchle, Prague 5 *
- Plzeňská, Motol, Prague 5 *
- Bělohorská, Prague 6
- Mackova, Prague 6
- Evropská (Ruzyně Airport), Prague 5
- Argentinská, Prague 7 *
- Karlínské náměstí, Prague 8
- Českobrodská, Prague 9 *
- Horní Počernice (along the freeway), Prague 9 *
- Horní Počernice, Náchodská ulice, Prague 9
- Poděbradská, Prague 9
- Na hroudě, Prague 10

Emergencies

In case of an accident the police should be contacted immediately if damage exceeds 1000 Kč (about US$40). For emergency service, the ÚAMK (also called Automotoklub), the Czech automobile and motorcycle club, provides emergency service nationwide. Its 24-hour service numbers are Prague ☎ 123 and 0123. Prague offices are at Mánesova 20, Vinohrady, open from 8 am to 3.30 pm (☎ 236 00 22; info 74 74 00 or 26 52 64); and at Černomořská 9, Prague 10 (☎ 74 60 00).

The ÚAMK has agreements with the Alliance Internationale de Tourisme, Fédération Internationale de l'Automobile and numerous national auto and tourist clubs. If you're a member of one of these, the ÚAMK will help you on roughly the same terms as your own club would. If not, you must pay for all services.

Other places offering round-the-clock repair services throughout the republic are Autoturist (☎ 154 or 77 34 55), Limužská 12, Prague 10, and ADOS (☎ 73 33 51).

Spare parts (other than for Škodas) are hard to find, but most well-known models can be repaired at a basic level by at least one garage in Prague. Don't expect any help with high-grade electronic components. Repair shops for major foreign brands include:

Fiat
: Na strži 35, Prague 4 (☎ 692 24 34)

Ford
: K učilišti 5, Prague 10 (☎ 70 31 30)

Chrysler
: Novostrašnická 46, Prague 10 (☎ 782 15 01)

Nissan
: Severní XI, Prague 4 (☎ 76 67 52 – 4)

Renault
: Ďáblická 2, Prague 8 (☎ 88 82 57)

Toyota
: Padbabská 2a, Prague 6 (☎ 311 92 79)

Volkswagen
: Auto Adámek, K Vltavě 1114, Prague 4 (☎ 76 67 52 – 3)

Most models
: Uni Car Service, Dudkova 187, Prague 9 (☎ 855 25 68)

Car Rental

Esucar (☎ 691 22 44), Husitská 58, Prague 3, claims to be Prague's cheapest car-hire company, charging about US$10/day and 10 cents/km, plus 5% tax. Other cheap (and small) places include:

Josef Stašek – Půjčovna osobních automobilů (☎ 39 85 78), 194 Horoměřice; about US$24/day plus six cents/km beyond 200 km/day for a Škoda or Lada

Discar Marcel Vlasák (☎ 687 05 23), Hovorčovice 192; same price and choice as Stašek

Secco Car (☎ 80 06 47, 684 34 03), Přístavní 39, Prague 7; Škodas for about US$40/day (discounts after three days) or US$700/month.

Mainstream agencies tend to charge US$80 or more per day for a basic model. They have desks at the airport, as well as the following offices in Prague 1:

Pragocar/Avis (☎ 24 22 98 48), Opletalova 33
Budget (☎ 231 95 95), Hotel Inter-Continental, Pařížská
Hertz (☎ 236 16 37), Palace Hotel, Panská 1
Europcar (☎ 24 81 05 15), Pařížská 28.

BOAT

In summer, cruise boats of Prague Passenger Shipping (Pražská paroplavební společnost, ☎ 29 83 09) chug up and down from the central quay *(centrální přístaviště)* on the east bank north of Palackého most. The closest metro station is Karlovo náměstí (exit to Palackého náměstí).

Most photogenic is a two-hour jaunt north to Hradčany and south to Vyšehrad, daily at 11 am, 2.30 and 6 pm, for 70 Kč. At 10.30 am, 1.30 and 5.30 pm a 1½-hour tootle goes north around Střelecký ostrov and south to the outskirts of Prague at Barrandov cliffs, for 60 Kč. If there are enough passengers, a one-hour trip goes to Barrandov and back hourly from 10 am to 4 pm, daily except Monday. Other sailings go up and down while you lunch, snack or dine expensively on board.

Every day except Monday, boats go north to the zoo and chateau at Troja, departing at 9.30 am and 1.30 pm and stopping at Kampa, Čechův most and Nádraží Holešovice for 20 Kč return. On weekends (plus Thursdays and Fridays from late June to early September), at 9 am, a boat goes 40 km south (upstream) through a wild, green landscape to Štěchovice, almost to the big dam across the Vltava at Slapy, arriving back at 6.30 pm. This fine escape is 70 Kč return.

All river transport shuts down in winter.

Boat Rental

If you just want a quiet float on the river to watch the sunset, consider renting a rowing boat or pedal-boat on Slovanský ostrov (see the Islands of Prague section in the Things to See & Do chapter); but you can't take these beyond the upstream and downstream weirs. Another place that rents out rowing boats by the hour is just north of the Charles Bridge on the Old Town side, at the end of Platnéřská, off Křižovnická.

BICYCLE

Prague is not a brilliant place to ride a bike. Traffic is heavy, the pollution can be choking, and there are no bicycle lanes. The cobblestones in older streets will loosen your teeth, and tram tracks are treacherous, especially when wet. Have a good lock and chain for both wheels and frame – Western bikes are a popular target. Spare parts are available in the city's numerous bike shops, but scarcer outside Prague.

If you're at least 12 years old you can take your bicycle on the metro for an extra 6 Kč. You must keep it near the last door of the carriage and only two bikes per carriage are allowed. You may not take a bike on board from 5.30 to 8.30 am and 2.30 to 5.30 pm on working days, nor at any time when the carriage is full, nor if there's already a pram in the carriage.

Bicycle Rental

Rent a Bike (☎ 22 10 63), Školská 12 (off Vodičkova), rents bicycles for 280 Kč a day or 700 Kč for three days, with a 3500-Kč deposit.

You can rent a mountain bike from Cyklocentrum (☎ 20 54 51), Karlovo náměstí 27-29. But you must book

Organ grinder on Hradčanské naměstí (RN)

in advance (with cash or credit card) at Resources (☎ 20 54 51, ext 216 or 217, fax 20 18 12), Lazarská 3, Staré Město. It's 300 Kč for a day, 750 Kč for a weekend, 1500 Kč for a week or 2500 Kč for two weeks, with a 10,000-Kč deposit. Cyklocentrum is open weekdays from 9 am to noon and 1 to 6 pm, Saturday to 12.30 pm.

We've also heard that 'student' operations rent bikes at Old Town Square in the summer.

TOURS

Čedok has the widest selection of English-language city tours and out-of-city excursions, which can be arranged at its offices at Na příkopě 18 (☎ 212 73 50), Bílková 6 (☎ 231 82 55) or Rytířská 16 (☎ 26 36 97). Following are some worthwhile possibilities; only the 'Historical Prague' tour is offered year-round:

Old Prague on Foot (Monday and Thursday): a four-hour walking tour of Staré Město and Josefov; 300 Kč
Historical Prague (daily): a three-hour dash around the city by coach, with a walk through Hradčany and Prague Castle; 450 Kč
Panoramic Tour of Prague (daily except Sunday): two hours by coach around the edges of the historical centre, recommended only for those unable/unwilling to walk; 300 Kč

Čedok also offers river cruises, but you can do these more cheaply on your own (see the earlier Boat section).

If you're short on time, some of Čedok's all-day, out-of-city excursions (high season only) are worth considering; lunch is included in the price:

Karlštejn & Konopiště (Tuesday, Thursday, Saturday, Sunday), 1350 Kč
Karlšejn, Křivoklát & Lány (Wednesday), 1150 Kč
Kutná Hora & Český Šternberk (Thursday, Sunday), 1150 Kč

Others go farther afield, eg day trips to the West Bohemian spa towns of Karlovy Vary or Mariánské Lázně, or around České Budějovice in South Bohemia, for 1350 Kč.

PIS will arrange a group tour or a private guide, at Panská 4 (☎ 22 43 11). Upper-end hotels and agencies offer city tours, but most are just Čedok's with extra fees added on.

Some smaller, independent agencies are Martin-Tour (☎ 52 74 56) and Prague Sightseeing (☎ 232 36 93); both also go to Karlštejn and Konopiště. A problem with smaller outfits is that they may lump customers speaking various languages into one group and split the talking time between them, leaving no room for questions.

An off-the-wall agency called Provocatours claims to offer a look at 'the things others ignore' on a two-hour walking tour of the city centre, with plenty of beer stops. Look for its sign near the Jan Hus statue.

Things to See & Do

Prague's prime attraction is its physical face. The city centre is a haphazard museum of 900 years' worth of architecture – stodgy Romanesque, sublime Gothic, handsome Renaissance, dazzling Baroque, 19th century revivals of all of them, and mouthwatering Art Nouveau – amazingly undisturbed by the 20th century and folded into a compact network of lanes, passages and culs-de-sac.

Also on offer is a heady menu of entertainment: classical music, from world-class festivals to tourist concerts in every other church; opera and ballet; avant-garde drama; jazz and rock; a few excellent museums; and dozens of art galleries. There are some good restaurants, and plenty of ordinary ones full of good cheer and world-famous Czech beer. Within reach as day trips are a dozen medieval chateaux and castles.

Prague's greatest *dis*traction is that it is now one of Europe's most popular tourist destinations, and choked with summer crowds.

HIGHLIGHTS

The historical core of the city – Hradčany (the Castle District) and Malá Strana (the Small Quarter) west of the river, Staré Město (the Old Town) and Václavské náměstí (Wenceslas Square) to the east, and Charles Bridge between – covers only about three sq km and is pedestrian-friendly, so you can see a lot even on a short visit.

If you're on a weekend break, a walk down the Royal Way *(Královská cesta)* – the route of ancient coronation processions – takes in the best of the city's architectural treasures, beginning with Prague Castle and St Vitus Cathedral. From the castle, descend to St Nicholas Church, the centrepiece of Malá Strana. After lunch, make your way across Charles Bridge and through the backstreets of Staré Město to Old Town Square.

Next day, see the Old Jewish Cemetery and return via Pařížská třída to Old Town Square, where the view from the Old Town Hall tower and a look inside Týn Church are recommended. Don't miss the striking of the town hall's Astronomical Clock. Complete the Royal Way down Celetná to the Powder Tower, stopping to look

Top : Vltava & Prague bridges from Letná (RN)
Bottom : Convent & Church of St George (RN)

inside St James Church and the beautiful Obecní dům (Municipal House). Return along Na příkopě to historic Wenceslas Square.

On a longer stay, linger in Hradčany to see the Strahov Monastery, the Loreta and the Summer Palace, and climb Petřín Hill for a splendid view over the city. In Josefov, go inside the Old-New Synagogue; in Nové Město, stroll down Národní třída to the National Theatre; and take a few hours to lose yourself in Staré Město's backstreets. It's also worth riding a tram or the metro south to the ancient stronghold of Vyšehrad.

The finest places to see a classical music concert are the Smetana Hall in Obecní dům, and the Rudolfinum. In summer, chamber concerts are held in many halls and churches; equally impressive are organ recitals, for which St James Church is said to have the best acoustics.

If you like museums, don't miss the amazing model of 19th century Prague at the Museum of the City of Prague in northern Nové Město. Best of the permanent collections of the National Gallery are those of 19th and 20th century European art at Šternberk Palace in Hradčany, and of 19th century Czech painting and sculpture at the Convent of St Agnes in Staré Město.

Don't forget that most (but not all) state-run museums and galleries are closed on Monday, and that the Old Jewish Cemetery and synagogues of Josefov are closed to the public on Saturday. Most museums and galleries and some sights charge a nominal admission fee of 15 to 20 Kč (at the time of writing), except where noted in the following text. Very often youth, student and senior discounts are available if you ask.

Architectural Highlights

The city's best standing Romanesque structure is the Basilica of St George at Prague Castle. St Vitus Cathedral, one of Europe's finest churches, is the clear winner in the Gothic category. The Summer (or Belvedere) Palace at Hradčany is probably the finest Renaissance building.

Of Prague's many Baroque masterpieces, one of the most elegant exteriors is the almost Rococo façade of the Kinský Palace on Old Town Square, while St Nicholas Church in Malá Strana draws fans of Baroque from all over Europe. The city has a high concentration of fine Art-Nouveau buildings; top of the line, inside and out, is the Obecní dům (Municipal House).

Cubism found its architectural voice in Prague, and there are more Cubist buildings here than in any other city in the world. Some striking façades are at Celetná 34 in Staré Město, and at Neklanova 30 near Vyšehrad.

PRAGUE CASTLE

Prague Castle (Pražský hrad, simply called *hrad* by the Czechs) is the most popular and visited sight in Prague; if you don't like crowds, try to get there early or late. According to the *Guinness Book of Records*, it's the largest ancient castle in the world – 570 metres long, an average of 128 metres wide and occupying 7.28 hectares.

Its history goes back to the 9th century when Prince Bořivoj established a fortified settlement here. It grew as rulers made their own additions, which explains its mixture of styles. It has always been the seat of Czech rulers, although the current president, Václav Havel, has chosen to live in his own house on the outskirts of the city.

The castle has had four major reconstructions, from that of Prince Soběslav in the 12th century to a Classical facelift under Empress Maria Theresa. In the 1920s, President Masaryk contracted a Slovene, Josef Plečnik, to renovate the castle.

First Courtyard

On either side of the main gate are the *Battling Titans* by Ignác Platzer (1767-70). Below them stand the **castle guards**, who are known to crack smiles now and then. President Havel hired the costume designer for the film *Amadeus* to replace their Communist-era khaki uniforms with the present ones, reminiscent of the First Republic. The guard is changed every hour from 5 am to 11 pm, but the most spectacular display is at noon, with an exchange of banners to a 15-minute fanfare by a six-piece brass band. The pointy flagpoles in the first courtyard are among Plečnik's controversial 1920s additions.

Second Courtyard

The second courtyard is entered through the Baroque **Matthias Gate** (1614). The Spanish Hall (Španělský sál) and Rudolf Gallery (Rudolfova galerie) here are the most beautiful in the castle, but like all other western parts of the castle they're only for state use.

The **Chapel of the Holy Cross** (Kaple sv Kříže, 1763) on the right was once the treasury of St Vitus Cathedral. In the middle of the courtyard is a Baroque fountain and a 17th century well with Renaissance lattice work.

At the northern end, the **Prague Castle Gallery**, open Tuesday to Sunday from 10 am to 6 pm, features 16th and 17th century European and Czech paintings and sculptures.

Powder Bridge Street (U Prašného Mostu) A detour past the gallery crosses the **Powder Bridge** (Prašný most), built in 1540. The **Stag Moat** (Jelení příkop) below it was later used for raising game animals, hence the name. Today it's closed to the public. To the left is a gate into a bomb shelter started by the Communists in the 1950s but never completed. Its tunnels run under most parts of the castle.

Royal Garden (Královská Zahrada) This garden on the far side of the Stag Moat is open Tuesday to Sunday from 10 am to 5.45 pm. Ferdinand I built a

Castle Services & Approach Routes

In some ways Prague Castle is a mini town, with many services within its walls. The castle itself is open daily from 5 am to midnight from April to September, and to 11 pm the rest of the year. Most sights are open from 9 am to 5 pm except Mondays, although the hours vary.

Information An information centre (☎ 21 01) at Vikářská 37 is open from 9 am to 5 pm (in winter until 4 pm). There are maps posted around the castle.

Post Office The post office is in the third courtyard, opposite the main entrance to St Vitus Cathedral.

Money There is an exchange office by the post office, open during regular castle hours.

Emergency The castle police station is opposite the post office, but its main function is to look after the president and the castle. It has limited jurisdiction in other matters; for these you must visit the main city police at Konviktská 14 in Staré Město.

Approach Routes Most approaches to the castle require some walking. The usual ones are from the trams in Malostranské náměstí, up Nerudova and Ke Hradu to the main gate; and from Malostranská metro station, up the Old Castle Steps (Staré zámecké schody). You can also enter along Powder Bridge Street (U Prašného mostu) from the Pražský hrad stop on tram No 22 – this requires the least walking. ■

▼ PLACES TO EAT

1 Café Poet
13 Vikárka
15 Reataurace U Kanovníků
21 Bonal Café

OTHER

2 Spanish Hall (Španělský sál)
3 Prague Castle Gallery (Obrazárna pražského hradu)
4 Plečník Hall (Plečníkova síň)
5 Matthias Gate (Matyášova brána)
6 Chapel of the Holy Cross (Kaple sv Kříže)
7 Post Office
8 Čekobanka Exchange Office
9 Castle Police Station
10 Plečník's Monolith
11 Statue of St George
12 President's Office
14 Information Centre
16 Vladislav Hall
17 All Saints' Chapel (Kaple Všech svatých)
18 Basilica of St George (Bazilika sv Jiří)
19 Convent of St George (Klášter sv Jiří) & National Gallery
20 Institute of Noblewomen (Ústav šlechtičen)

Singing Fountain, Royal Garden (RN)

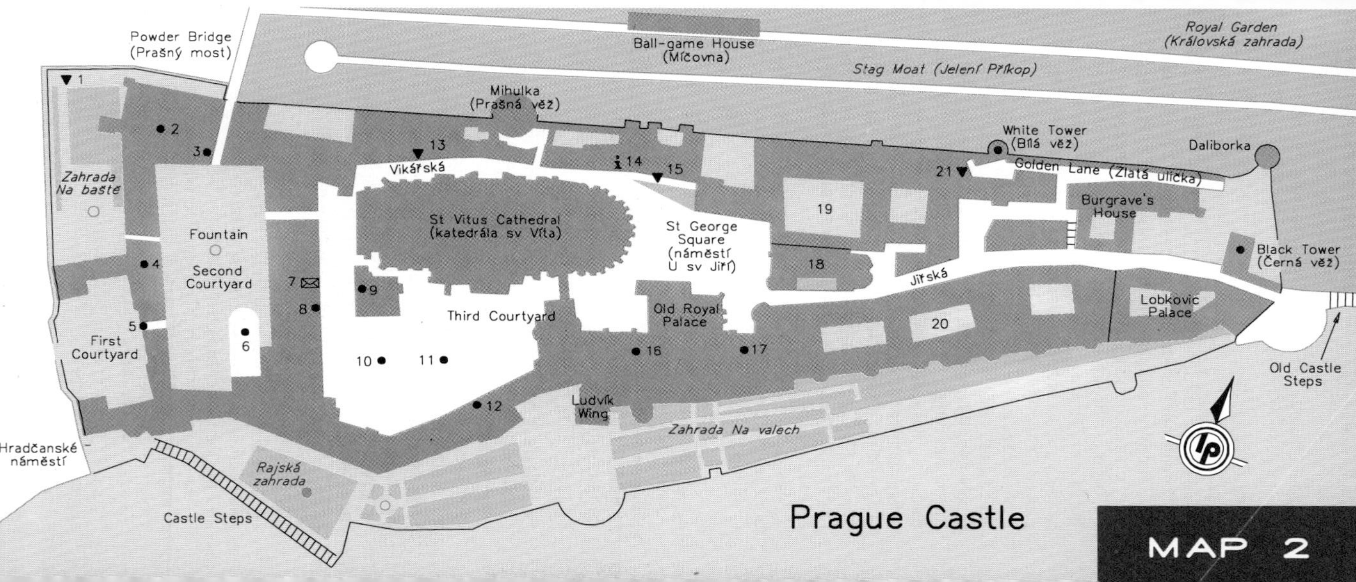
MAP 2
Prague Castle
Powder Bridge
(Prašný most)
Ball-game House
(Míčovna)
Royal Garden
(Královská zahrada)
Stag Moat (Jelení Příkop)
Mihulka
(Prašná věž)
White Tower
(Bílá věž)
Daliborka
Golden Lane (Zlatá ulička)
Burgrave's
House
Black Tower
(Černá věž)
Lobkovic
Palace
Old Castle
Steps
Jiřská
Vikářská
St Vitus Cathedral
(katedrála sv Víta)
St George
Square
(náměstí
U sv Jiří)
Old Royal
Palace
Third Courtyard
Ludvík
Wing
Zahrada Na valech
Zahrada
Na baště
Fountain
Second
Courtyard
First
Courtyard
Hradčanské
náměstí
Rajská
zahrada
Castle Steps
1
2
3
4
5
6
7
8
9
10
11
12
13
14
15
16
17
18
19
20
21

Renaissance garden here in 1534. To the left of the entrance from Powder Bridge Street is the **Lion's Court** (Lví dvorek), named for the lions and other animals that were once kept here in Prague's first private zoo.

The most beautiful of the garden's buildings is the **Ball-Game House** (Míčovna) built by Bonifác Wohlmut in 1569, but it's only open for exhibitions. The Habsburgs played an early version of badminton here.

Walking east through a well-kept park popular for its tulips and azaleas – Europe's first tulip garden, from where they later went to the Netherlands – you come to the bronze Singing Fountain (Zpívající fontána) and the **Summer Palace** (Letohrádek), also (and incorrectly) called the Belvedere Palace. The palace, built in 1538-64, is the most authentic Italian Renaissance building outside Italy, with arcades and a copper roof that looks like an inverted ship's hull. It houses temporary modern art exhibitions.

West of the Royal Garden is the former **Riding School** built in 1695, now a venue for temporary modern art exhibitions.

Third Courtyard

Entering from the second courtyard brings you straight to the main entrance of St Vitus Cathedral, the largest in the country, with a main steeple 97 metres high.

St Vitus Cathedral (Katedrála Sv Víta) This Gothic cathedral, blackened by age and pollution, was built on the site of a Romanesque rotunda by Duke Wenceslas in 929 and enlarged in the 11th century.

The cathedral's foundation stone was laid in 1344 by Emperor Charles IV. His architect, Matthias of Arras, began work in the French Gothic style but died eight years later. The German Peter Parler completed much of the structure in a freer, late-Gothic style before he died in 1399. Details were added in Renaissance and Baroque styles over the following centuries, but it was only in 1861, during the Czech National Revival, that a concerted effort was made to finish Parler's work. Many architects were involved, most notably Josef Mocker, and the job was completed in 1929.

The doorways are richly decorated with carvings of historical and biblical scenes, the most beautiful of which is the *Last Judgment* (1370-71) on the southern doorway, the **Golden Gate** (Zlatá brána). Its wrought-iron gate has scenes of people at work – blacksmith, shoemaker, butcher.

The interior is enhanced by traditional and modern **stained-glass windows**. Of its numerous side chapels, the most beautiful is the **Chapel of St Wenceslas** (Kaple sv Václava), built in the 14th century by Peter Parler and full of frescoes and 1345 semiprecious stones. On the south side of this chapel, a small door – locked with seven locks – hides a staircase leading to the Coronation Chamber above the Golden Gate, where the Czech **crown jewels** are held. They're rarely exhibited to the public (you can see replicas at the museum in the Lobkovic Palace) and include the gold crown of St Wenceslas, which Charles IV had remade from the original Přemysl crown in 1346.

A **wooden relief** by Caspar Bechterle (1623) beside the Chapel of St Anne shows the escape from Prague of Frederick of the Palatinate after the Battle of the White Mountain. One of the best modern sculptures is the wooden ***Crucifixion*** by František Bílek, in the cathedral since 1927.

There is no charge to enter the cathedral but three places inside charge admission, payable to the left of the western entrance. The Royal Crypt and the choir are open daily from 9 am to 5 pm. The **choir** includes the ornate Royal Mausoleum with images of Ferdinand I, his wife Anna Jagellonská and son Maxmilián II. In the **Royal Crypt** are the remains of Charles IV, Wenceslas IV, George of Poděbrady and Rudolf II.

The **Great Tower** is open Tuesday to Sunday from 10 am to 4 pm, and on a clear day the views are great. You can also study part of the 1597 clockworks. One of the bells, the Sigismund Bell, is the largest in Bohemia, made by Tomáš Jaroš in 1549.

In the courtyard is Plečník's 16-metre granite **monolith** (1928) dedicated to the victims of WW I. At the south-east end of the courtyard, a gate leads to the **Garden on the Ramparts** (Zahrada Na valech), an elegant manicured space with fine views over the city.

Old Royal Palace (Starý Královský Palác) This is one of the oldest parts of the castle. Dating from 1135, it was originally a castle for Czech princesses; from the 13th to the 16th century it was the king's palace. It is open daily from 9 am to 5 pm (to 4 pm in winter).

At the heart of the palace is the **Vladislav Hall** (Vladislavský sál), one of the best examples of late Gothic architecture in Prague. It was used for banquets, councils and coronations – and in case of bad weather, jousting! Hence the **Riders' Staircase** (Jezdecké schody) leading in from one side. The presidents of the republic have also been sworn in here.

Top : Battling Titans guarding Prague Castle (RN)
Bottom : Changing of the guards at the main gate (JK)

St Vitus Cathedral (RN)

MAP 3

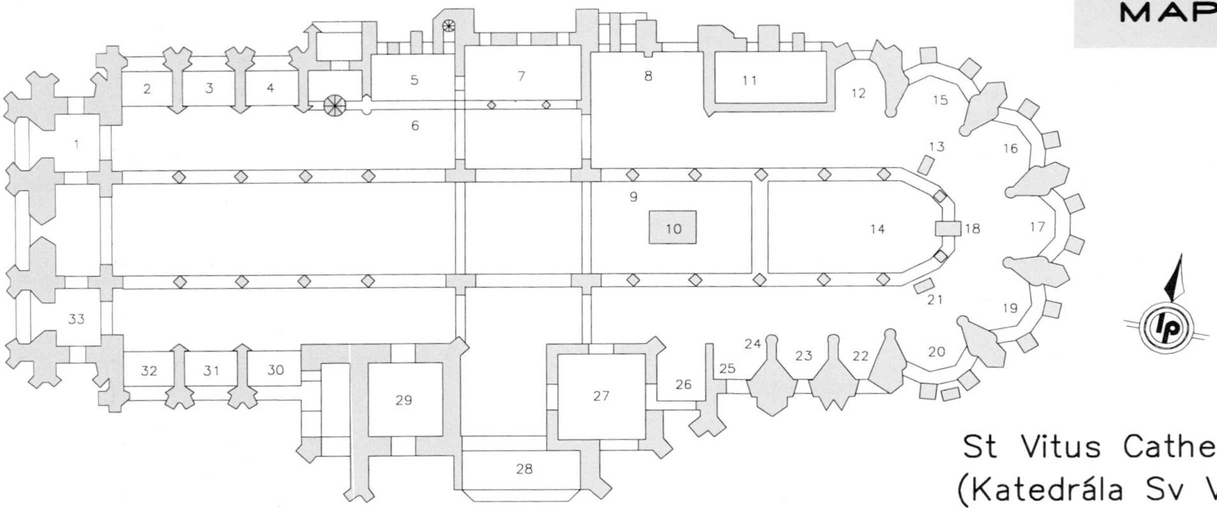

St Vitus Cathedral
(Katedrála Sv Víta)

1 Northern Tower (Severní věž)
2 Chapel of Bartoňů z Dobenína
3 Schwarzenberg Chapel
4 New Archbishops' Chapel
5 New Sacristy
6 Bílek's Crucifixion Statue
7 Kůrova Chapel
8 St Sigismund Chapel
9 Pulpit
10 Royal Mausoleum
11 Old Sacristy
12 Chapel of St Anne
13 Cardinal Schwarzenberg Monument
14 Choir with the Main Altar
15 Old Archbishop's Chapel
16 Chapel of St John the Baptist
17 Chapel of Our Lady
18 St Vitus Altar
19 Saxon Chapel
20 Chapel of St John of Nepomuk
21 Tombstone of St John of Nepomuk
22 Wallenstein Chapel
23 Royal Oratory
24 Chapel of the Holy Cross
25 Entrance to the Royal Crypt
26 Chapel of Martin
27 Chapel of St Wenceslas
28 Golden Gate (Zlatá brána)
29 Házmburská Chapel & Great Tower
30 Thun Chapel
31 Chapel of the Tomb of God
32 Chapel of St Ludmilla
33 Southern Tower (Jižní věž)

In one corner of the hall is the entrance to the **Ludvík Wing**. On 23 May 1618, nobles rebelling against Emperor Rudolf II threw two of his councillors out of the window of the chancellery here. They survived, their fall broken by the moat that was there in those days, but the event triggered off the Thirty Years' War.

Across the hall from the Ludvík Wing is the **New Land Rolls Room**, the old map repository for land titles, where the walls are covered with the coats of arms of the clerks who kept them. At the eastern end of the Vladislav Hall is the **All Saints' Chapel** (Kaple Všech svatých), and to its right a terrace with great views of Prague.

St George Square (Náměstí U Sv Jiří)

This is the plaza behind the cathedral, and the heart of Prague Castle.

Convent of St George (Klášter Sv Jiří) This very ordinary-looking building was Bohemia's first convent, established in 973 by Boleslav II, and closed and converted to an army barracks in 1782. It's now a branch of the National Gallery, open Tuesday to Sunday from 10 am to 6 pm, for Kč 40 (free on the first Sunday of each month). Here you'll find an excellent collection of Czech Gothic, Renaissance and Baroque art, including the jewel of 14th century Czech Gothic art, a trio of panels by the Master of the Třeboň Altar.

Basilica of St George (Bazilika Sv Jiří) The striking church adjoining the convent was established in the 10th century by Vratislav I (the father of St Wenceslas), and is the best preserved Romanesque structure in the Czech Republic. What you see is mostly the result of attempts in 1887-1908 to give it back a pure Romanesque look. The Přemysl princes are buried here. It's open Tuesday to Sunday from 9 am to 5 pm (to 4 pm in winter).

Inside are some fine, partially preserved frescoes. Beside the altar is an unusual statue of St Ludmilla lying down with hands at prayer. On the left wall is a hole through which nuns from the convent next door communicated with the rest of the world. The basilica's acoustics make it a good venue for classical concerts.

Mihulka Powder Tower (Prašná Věž)

This tower on the north side of St Vitus was built at the end of the 15th century as part of the castle's defences. Later it was the workshop of the cannon and bell-maker Tomáš Jaroš, who cast the bells of St Vitus. Alchemists employed by Rudolf II worked here. It got its name in the 19th century from the *mihule* (lamprey eels) bred in the area. Today it's a museum of alchemy and bell and cannon-forging, and of Renaissance life in Prague Castle, open from 9 am to 4 pm Tuesday to Sunday.

On the wall opposite the entrance is a peculiar clock: a globe with the days of the week written in Czech, around which a little plane is meant to fly every hour, though it hasn't worked for years.

Jiřská Ulice

Off Jiřská, along the northern wall of the castle, is the **Golden Lane** (Zlatá ulička), also known as Goldsmiths' Lane (Zlatnická ulička). Its tiny colourful cottages were built in the 16th century for the sharpshooters of the castle guard, and later used by goldsmiths. In the 18th and 19th centuries they were occupied by squatters, and

Basilica of St George (RN)

later by artists like the writer Franz Kafka (who stayed at No 22 in 1916-17) and the Nobel-laureate poet Jaroslav Seifert. Today, most are souvenir shops.

At the west end of the lane is the **White Tower** (Bílá věž), where the hapless Irish alchemist Edward Kelley was imprisoned by Rudolf II. At the east end is the **Daliborka** tower, which got its name from the knight Dalibor of Kozojed, imprisoned here in 1498 for supporting a peasant rebellion, and later executed. According to an old tale, he played a violin during his imprisonment, which could be heard throughout the castle. Smetana based his opera *Dalibor* (1868) on the tale.

Just inside the eastern gate, with its **Black Tower** (Černá věž), is the **Lobkovic Palace** (Lobkovický palác), built in the 1570s. On the 1st and 2nd floors is a good museum of Czech history from the arrival of the Slavs until 1848. Exhibits include copies of the Czech crown jewels (the originals are locked up in St Vitus Cathedral), the sword of Prague's executioner Jan Mydlář (who lopped off the heads of 27 rebellious Protestant nobles in Old Town Square in 1621) and some of the oldest marionettes in the Czech Republic. It's open Tuesday to Sunday from 9 am to 4.30 pm.

HRADČANY

Hradčany is the residential area around the west gate of Prague Castle. In 1320 it was made a town in its own right. Before it became a borough of Prague in 1598, it twice suffered heavy damage: in the Hussite wars and in the Great Fire of 1541. After this, palaces were built in place of the older town houses, some by Habsburg nobility in hopes of cementing their power at Prague Castle.

Today Hradčany district reaches as far as Pohořelec and the Strahov Monastery. There are a few government offices around Hradčanské náměstí and along Loretánská, but the rest is still basically residential.

Hradčanské Náměstí

Hradčanské náměstí has kept its shape since the Middle Ages. At its centre is a plague column by Ferdinand Brokoff (1726). Several former canons' residences (Nos 6 to 12) have richly decorated façades.

The **Schwarzenberg Palace** (Schwarzenberský palác) sports a sgraffito façade that stands out from the others. The Schwarzenbergs acquired the palace in 1719, and it's now a Museum of Military History, open daily from 9.30 am to 4.30 pm. Don't miss the special exhibit of tin soldiers.

Opposite is the Rococo **Archbishop's Palace** (Arcibiskupský palác), bought and remodelled by Archbishop Antonín Bruse of Mohelnic in 1562, and the seat of archbishops ever since. Its wonderful interior, including a chapel with frescoes by Daniel Alexius (1600), is only open to the public on the last Thursday before Easter.

Diagonally behind is the Baroque **Sternberg Palace** (Šternberský palác, 1707), home to the National Gallery's splendid collection of 19th and 20th century European art, open Tuesday to Sunday from 10 am to 6 pm (free admission on the first Sunday of each month). The ground floor has a very good French art collection, and on the 1st floor are 14th to 16th century European paintings.

Loretánské Náměstí

From Hradčanské náměstí it's a short walk to Loretánské náměstí, created early in the 18th century when the **Černín Palace** (Černínský palác) was built. This palace today houses the foreign ministry. In 1948, Jan Masaryk, son of the founding president of Czechoslovakia, allegedly committed suicide by jumping from his bathroom window. The new Communist government would have had good reasons to get rid of this democrat and staunch anti-Communist, but the true facts may never be known.

At the north end of the square is a **Capuchin Monastery** (1600-02), the oldest operating monastery in Bohemia.

The Loreta Without a doubt, however, the square's main attraction is the Loreta, an extraordinary Baroque place of pilgrimage founded by Benigna Kateřina Lobkovic in 1626 to resemble the house of the Virgin Mary (the Santa Casa), which legend says was carried by angels to the Italian town of Loreto as the Turks were advancing on Nazareth. The duplicate **Santa Casa** (Svatá chýše) is in the centre of the courtyard.

Across from it is the **Church of the Nativity of Our Lord** (Kostel Narození Páně), built in 1737 by Kristof Dientzenhofer, with a bizarre interior. Two skeletons, of the Spanish saints Felicissima and Marcia, are dressed in nobles' clothing with wax masks over their skulls.

Finally there is the **Chapel of Our Lady of Sorrows** (Kaple Panny Marie Bolestné), featuring a crucified bearded lady – St Starosta (St Liberatou to the Spanish), daughter of a Portuguese king who promised her to the king of Sicily against her wishes. After a night of tearful prayers she awoke with a beard, the wedding was called off, and her father had her crucified. She was later made patron saint of the needy and godforsaken.

The most eye-popping sight is the **treasury** on the 1st floor. Though its treasures have been ransacked at least four times over the centuries, there are still some amazing items. Most valuable and decorative (or over the top, depending on your perspective) is an 89.5-cm-tall monstrance called the *Prague Sun* (Pražské slunce), of solid silver with plenty of gold and 6222 diamonds.

Above the Loreta's entrance are 27 **bells** made in Amsterdam in the 17th century that play *We Greet Thee*

The Loreta (RN)

a Thousand Times every hour to a gob-smacked audience of tourists and locals.

The Loreta is open Tuesday to Sunday from 9 am to 12.15 pm and 1 to 4.30 pm.

Strahov Monastery (Strahovský Klášter)

This former monastery complex was founded in 1140 by Vladislav II for the Premonstratensians. Today's structure, completed in the 17th and 18th centuries, functioned until the Communist government closed it and imprisoned most of the monks, who have recently returned.

Inside is the 1612 **Church of St Roch** (Kostel sv Rocha), now an exhibition hall. The **Church of the Assumption of Our Lady** (Kostel Nanebevzetí Panny Marie) was built in 1143. Mozart allegedly played the organ here.

The monastery's biggest attraction is the **Strahov Library** (Strahovská knihovna), the largest monastic library in the Czech Republic. You can look but you can't go into the two-storey Philosophy Hall (Filozofický sál), with its carved floor-to-ceiling shelves lined with beautiful old tomes and, covering the ceiling, the *Struggle of Mankind to Gain Real Wisdom,* a fresco by Franz Maulbertsch. Down the hallway is the Theology Hall, with a ceiling fresco by Siard Nosecký. The library is open from 9 am to 12 pm and 1 to 5 pm.

In the second courtyard is the **National Literature Museum**, open from 9 am to 12.30 pm and 1 to 5 pm.

MALÁ STRANA

Malá Strana (the Small Quarter) clusters at the foot of Prague Castle. Most tourists climb to the castle on the Royal Way, along Mostecká and Nerudova, but the narrow side streets of this Baroque quarter have plenty to offer. Almost too picturesque for its own good, it's now a favourite movie and commercial set.

Malá Strana started in the 8th or 9th century as a market settlement. In 1257 Přemysl Otakar II granted it town status. Fortifications were built by Charles IV – the so-called 'Hunger Wall' (Hladová zeď).

Malá Strana was twice almost destroyed – during battles between the Hussites and the Prague Castle gar-

Malá Strana from Prague Castle (RN)

rison in 1419, and in the Great Fire of 1541. Renaissance buildings and palaces replaced destroyed houses. In the 17th and 18th centuries the Baroque churches and palaces that give Malá Strana its present charm were built. The largely residential quarter is a historical reserve.

Nerudova Ulice

Nerudova, part of the Royal Way, is architecturally the quarter's most important street. Most of its old Renaissance façades were later 'Baroquefied'. Many still have their original shutter-like doors.

At No 47 is the **House of Two Suns** (Dům U dvou slunců), an early Baroque building where the Czech poet Jan Neruda lived from 1845 to 1891. At No 34 is the **House at the Golden Horseshoe** (Dům U zlaté podkovy), so called for the statue of St Wenceslas, whose horse was said to be shod with gold. In 1749, the first pharmacy in Hradčany opened here and is still functioning next door.

On the corner with Janský vršek is the **Bretfeld Palace,** which from 1765 Josef of Bretfeld made a centre for social gatherings; among his guests were Mozart and Casanova.

At No 24 is the Baroque **Church of Our Lady of Unceasing Succour** (Kostel Paní Marie ustavičné pomoci). From 1834 to 1837 it was the Divadlo U Kajetánů, a theatre that featured Czech plays during the Czech National Revival.

Most houses have emblems of some kind on them. At No 18 is one named after **St John of Nepomuk**, patron saint of the Czechs; it was built in 1566 and the saint's relief was added about 1730. The **House at the Three Fiddles** (Dům U tří housliček) was originally a Gothic building, rebuilt in Renaissance style in the 17th century, and belonged to a family of violin makers.

Úvoz, Nerudova's uphill extension, takes you to the Strahov Monastery, with fine views over the city.

Malostranské Náměstí

This is really two squares, with the Church of St Nicholas (Kostel sv Mikuláše) – Malá Strana's primary landmark – between them. It has been the hub of Malá Strana from the 10th century, though it lost some of its character at the turn of this century when Karmelitská was widened. Today it's a mixture of official buildings and touristy restaurants, with a tram line through the middle.

What is today a restaurant called Malostranská beseda, at No 21, was the **old town hall**, where in 1575 the non-Catholic nobles wrote the so-called *Czech Confession* (České konfese), a pioneering demand for religious tolerance addressed to the Habsburg emperor and eventually passed into Czech law by Rudolf II in 1609. On 22 May 1618, Czech nobles gathered at the Smiřický Palace at No 18; the next day they flung two Habsburg councillors out a window in Prague Castle, setting off the Thirty Years' War.

St Nicholas Church (Kostel Sv Mikuláše) This beautiful, heavily decorated church with the huge green cupola that dominates Malá Strana is one of central Europe's finest Baroque buildings. (Don't confuse this church with the other St Nicholas Church on Old Town Square.) It was begun by Kristof Dientzenhofer; his son Kilian Ignatz continued the work and Anselmo Lurago finished the job in 1755.

The **ceiling fresco** by Johann Kracker (1770) portraying the life of St Nicholas is the largest fresco in Europe. In the first chapel on the left is a mural by Karel Škreta, into which he has painted the church official who kept track of him as he worked; he is looking out through a window in the upper corner. The most unusual of the church's paintings is the *Death of St Francis Xavier* by F X Balko, in the third chapel.

The church is open from 9 am to 5.30 pm (to 4 pm on concert days) May to September, and in winter to 3.30 or 4.30 pm.

Below the Castle to Klárov

The **Castle Steps** (Zámecké schody) were originally the main route to the castle; the houses around them were built later. The steps merge into Thunovská street. Around the corner at Sněmovní is the **former Parliament House** (Sněmovna) in the Thun Palace, seat of the national assembly which on 14 November 1918 deposed the Habsburgs from the Czech throne.

At Tomášská 4 is the **House at the Golden Stag** (Dům U zlatého jelena), with a statue by Ferdinand Brokoff (1726) of St Hubert and a stag with a cross between its antlers.

Wallenstein Palace (Valdštejnský Palác) On Valdštejnské náměstí is the first of the monumental Baroque structures built by Albrecht of Wallenstein, generalissmo of the Habsburg armies, in 1630. The vast palace, which displaced 23 houses, a brickworks and

House at the Three Fiddles (RN)

three gardens, was financed by Wallenstein's confiscation of properties from Protestant nobles who lost the Battle of the White Mountain.

It's now occupied by the Ministry of Culture and the **Komenský Pedagogical Museum** (Pedagogické muzeum J A Komenského), named after the 17th century Protestant teacher and theologian Jan Ámos Komenský, known in the West as Comenius. The museum, with a small exhibition of his works and those of two other well-known Czech philosophers, Tomáš Masaryk and Jan Patočka, is open from 10 am to noon and 1 to 5 pm Tuesday to Sunday, with free admission.

Top : Čertovka channel (RN)
Bottom : John Lennon Wall (RN)

Beside the palace is the huge **Wallenstein Garden** (Valdštejnská zahrada), open from 10 am to 6 pm. At the east end of the garden is the Wallenstein Riding School (Valdštejnská jízdárna), home to changing exhibitions of modern art, Tuesday to Sunday from 10 am to 6 pm.

Other Parks & Gardens The quiet **Vojan Park** (Vojanovy sady), entered from U lužického semináře, is all that remains of Prague's oldest park, established in 1248. Up the hill towards Dejvice is **Chotek Park** (Chotkovy sady), Prague's first public park, established in 1833.

South of Nerudova to Kampa

The buildings in Vlašská and Tržiště suffered serious neglect under the Communists, and lower Tržiště is getting a total facelift. Vlašská has another Lobkovic Palace, this one home to the **German Embassy**. In summer 1989 it was besieged by thousands of East Germans trying to get into West Germany. After their departure, Vlašská was littered with abandoned Trabant cars.

The fine Baroque **Vrtbov Garden** (Vrtbovská zahrada), entered through house No 25 on the corner of Karmelitská and Tržiště, has statues and vases by Matthias Braun and a terrace with good views of Prague Castle and Malá Strana.

In Karmelitská is the unimposing 1613 **Church of Our Lady Victorious** (Kostel Paní Marie Vítězné). On its central altar is a waxwork figure of the baby Jesus brought from Spain in 1628, the so-called ***Infant of Prague*** (*Pražské jezulátko*, also known by its Italian name of *Bambino di Praga*). It is alleged to have worked numerous miracles, including saving Prague from the plague and the destruction of the Thirty Years' War, and is visited by a steady stream of Roman Catholic pilgrims, especially from Italy, Spain and Latin America. The 18th century German prior E S Stephano wrote of the Infant's miracles, starting a European cult of worship that spread to all the world's corners. The Infant's wardrobe consists of 60 costumes donated from all over the world, changed in accordance with a religious calendar.

Maltézské Náměstí This quiet square gets its name from the Maltese Knights, Czech crusaders who established a monastery beside the **Church of Our Lady Below the Chain** (Kostel Paní Marie pod řetězem) in 1169. All that remains today are sections of the church. Beyond the statue of St John the Baptist is a music school from whose windows classical melodies drift, and nearby at Lázeňská 2 is a small Museum of Musical Instruments (Hudební muzeum).

A short way east is Velkopřevorské náměstí, and opposite the French Embassy is the **John Lennon Wall** (Lennonova zeď), a kind of political focus for Prague's pre-1989 youth. After his death, Lennon became a pacifist hero in the Czech subculture, and the wall served as a monument to him and his ideas. Most Western pop music was banned by the Communists, and some Czech musicians who played it went to jail. Beatles lyrics began appearing on the wall in the 1980s under the constant eye of the secret police, but they never managed to keep the wall clean. Nowadays, lightweight graffiti has buried the potent political messages.

Kampa Lying off the Malá Strana bank, with Charles Bridge passing over one end, this is the most picturesque of Prague's islands. It was once used as farmland and was home to a popular pottery market. In the 13th century the town's first mill, the Sovovský mlýn, was built on Čertovka (Devil's Stream) separating Kampa from the mainland, and other mills followed.

The area along the stream and under Charles Bridge is sometimes called 'Prague's Venice' because the buildings rise straight out of the water. **Na Kampě** square below the bridge, with its sunny cafés, makes a pleasant diversion.

The southern part of Kampa is a park. Near the tip of the island is another wall venue for graffiti artists. The views of the Old Town from here are excellent. For more on Kampa, see the Islands of Prague later in this chapter.

Around Újezd

On Říční is one of the oldest Gothic buildings in Malá Strana, the **Church of St John at the Laundry** (Kostel sv Jana Na prádle), built in 1142 as a local parish church. Inside are the remains of 14th century frescoes. In 1784 it was converted to a laundry, hence the name. In 1935 it was reconsecrated by the Czechoslovak Hussite Church.

At Újezd 40 is the **Museum of Physical Education & Sport** (Muzeum tělovýchovy a sportu), on the history of Czech sport, including the Sokol movement which mobilised the masses in the name of sport early this century. It's all in Czech but some staff speak English, or for 1 Kč you can listen to a multilingual tape. It's open Tuesday to Sunday from 9 am to 5 pm, for 7 Kč.

Petřín Hill (Petřínské Sady)

This 318-metre hill, simply called Petřín by Czechs, is actually a network of eight parks (Strahovská, Lobkovická, Schönbornská, Vrtbovská, Seminářská, Kinského, Růžový and Petřínský), together comprising the largest green space in Prague. It's great for cool, quiet walks and fine views of the 'city of 100 spires', a phrase that becomes quite clear from here. Once upon a time there were also vineyards, and a quarry from which most of Prague's Romanesque and Gothic buildings were assembled.

Petřín is easily accessible from Hradčany and Strahov, or you can ride the **cable car** *(lanová dráha)* from Újezd (at U lanové dráhy) up to Růžový sad. It runs from 9.15 am to 8.45 pm, for the same price as a bus ride (you can use ordinary city transit tickets). You can also get off halfway up and dine with a great view at the Nebozízek Restaurant.

Just south of the cable-car terminus is the **Štefánik Observatory & Planetarium** (Štefánikova hvězdárna), a 'people's observatory' open April to August on Tuesday to Friday from 2 to 7 pm and 9 to 11 pm, Saturday and Sunday from 10 am to noon, 2 to 7 pm and 9 to 11 pm; during the rest of the year, hours vary. For 6 Kč you can view the stars if it's clear, and look at the exhibition.

North of the terminus on the summit is the **Petřín Tower** (Petřínská rozhledna), a 62-metre Eiffel Tower lookalike built in 1891 for the Prague Exposition. You can climb its 299 steps for 20 Kč, daily from 9.30 am to 10 pm. Some of the best views of Prague are from here, and on clear days you can see the forests of central Bohemia.

Church of St Lawrence (RN)

On the way to the tower you cross the **'Hunger Wall'** (Hladová zeď), running from Újezd to Strahov, the fortifications completed in 1362 under Charles IV. The name comes from the fact that it was to be built by the poor of the city in return for food.

Below the tower is **The Maze** (Bludiště), also built for the 1891 Exposition and later moved here. Inside is a mirror maze good for a laugh, and a diorama of the 1648 battle between Praguers and Swedes on Charles Bridge.

Opposite is the **Church of St Lawrence** (Kostel sv Vavřince), with a ceiling fresco depicting the founding of the church in 991 at a pagan site with a sacred flame. In the Middle Ages executions took place in the area. Close by is the Chapel of the Tomb of Christ (Kaple Božího hrobu) from where the Stations of the Cross (Křížová cesta) commence along the 'Hunger Wall', part of the way down to Malá Strana. Each station is a little chapel with a painting of Jesus struggling through Jerusalem to his crucifixion.

STARÉ MĚSTO & JOSEFOV

A settlement and marketplace existed on the east bank of the Vltava by the 10th century. In the 12th century this was linked to the castle district by the forerunner of the Charles Bridge, and in 1231 Wenceslas I honoured it with a town charter and the beginnings of a fortification. This 'Old Town' – Staré Město – has been Prague's working heart ever since. The town walls are long gone, though still traced by Národní třída, Na příkopě and Revoluční streets.

Staré Město shared in the boom when Charles IV gave Prague a Gothic face befitting its new status as capital of the Holy Roman Empire. Charles founded the Karolinum (Charles University) in Staré Město in 1348, and began the Charles Bridge in 1357. When Empress Maria Theresa amalgamated Prague's towns into a single city in 1748, the Old Town Hall became its seat of government.

Many of Staré Město's buildings have Gothic insides and Romanesque basements. To ease the devastation of frequent flooding by the Vltava, the level of the town was gradually raised, beginning in the 13th century, with new construction simply rising on top of older foundations. A huge fire in 1689 contributed to an orgy of rebuilding in the re-Catholicised 17th and 18th centuries, giving the formerly Gothic district a heavily Baroque face.

The only intrusions into Staré Město's medieval layout have been appropriation for the Jesuits' massive college, the Klementinum, in the 16th and 17th centuries, and the 'clearance' of Josefov, the Jewish quarter, at the end of the 19th century.

At the centre of everything is Old Town Square. If the maze of alleys around it can be said to have an 'artery', it is the so-called Royal Way, the ancient coronation route to Prague Castle; in this part of the city, it runs from the Powder Tower, down Celetná to Old Town Square, along Karlova and over the Charles Bridge.

Josefov (The Old Jewish Quarter)

The slice of Staré Město within Kaprova, Dlouhá and Kozí streets contains the remains of the once thriving mini town of Josefov, Prague's former Jewish ghetto.

The Jews of Prague Prague's Jewish community was first moved into a walled ghetto in about the 13th century, in response to directives from Rome that Jews and Christians should live separately. Subsequent centuries of pogroms and official repression culminated in Ferdinand I's threat, only grudgingly withdrawn, to throw all Jews out of Bohemia.

The reign of Rudolf II saw honour bestowed on Prague's Jews, a flowering of Jewish intellectual life, and prosperity in the ghetto. Mordechai Maisel (or Maisl), mayor of the ghetto, Rudolf's finance minister and Prague's wealthiest citizen, bankrolled some lavish redevelopment. Another major figure was Judah Löw ben Bezalel, or Rabbi Löw, prominent theologian, chief rabbi, student of the mystical teachings of the cabbala, and nowadays best known as the creator of the mythical golem – a kind of proto-robot made from the mud of the Vltava.

When they helped repel the Swedes on the Charles Bridge in 1648, Prague's Jews won the favour of Ferdinand III – to the extent that he had the ghetto enlarged. But a century later they were driven out of the city for over three years, to be welcomed back only because Praguers had begun to miss their business. In the 1780s Emperor Joseph II outlawed many forms of discrimination, and in 1848 the ghetto walls were torn down and the Jewish quarter was made a borough of Prague, named Josefov in honour of Joseph II.

The demise of the Jewish quarter (which had slid into squalor as its Jewish population fell) came in 1893-1910 when it was cleared, ostensibly for public health reasons, slashed through the middle by Pařížská třída and lined with new Art-Nouveau housing.

The community itself was all but wiped out by the Nazis, with almost three-quarters of the city's Jews – and some 90% of all the Jews in Bohemia and Moravia – dying of starvation or exterminated in camps from 1941. The Communist regime slowly strangled what was left of Jewish cultural life, and thousands emigrated. Today a few thousand Jews live in Prague, compared with some 50,000 in the 1930s.

The 'State Jewish Museum' (Státní Židovské Muzeum) is an umbrella-word for what's left of the Jewish Quarter – half a dozen synagogues, the town hall, a ceremonial hall and the powerfully melancholy Old Cemetery. In a grotesquely ironic act, the Nazis spared these to be a 'museum of an extinct race' – thanks to which they have instead survived as a memorial to seven centuries of oppression. The Old-New Synagogue is still used for religious services; the others have been converted to exhibition halls for what is probably the world's biggest collection of sacred Jewish artefacts, many of them saved from demolished Bohemian synagogues.

All are open from 9.30 am to 6 pm but closed to the public on Saturday. A 30-Kč ticket at the High Synagogue admits you to that and the Old-New Synagogue, and an 80-Kč ticket from the Klaus Synagogue is good there, for the cemetery and the Maisel and Pinkas synagogues.

Old-New Synagogue (Staronová Synagóga)

Completed about 1270, this is Europe's oldest 'working' synagogue and one of Prague's earliest Gothic buildings. You step *down* into it because it predates the raising of Staré Město's streets against floods.

Men must cover their heads (a hat or bandanna serves better than the complimentary paper *yarmulkas* outside). Around the central chamber are an entry hall, a winter prayer hall and the room from which women watch the men-only services. The interior, with a pulpit surrounded by a 15th century wrought-iron grille, looks much as it would have 500 years ago. The 17th century scriptures on the walls were recovered from beneath a later 'restoration'. On the east wall is the Holy Ark that holds the Torah scrolls. In a glass case at the rear, little light bulbs beside the names of prominent deceased are lit on their death days.

With its steep roof and 'crowstep' gables, this looks like a place with secrets, and at least one version of the golem legend ends here: the creature, left alone on the sabbath, runs amok; Rabbi Löw rushes out in the midst of a service, removes its magic talisman and carries the

Top : Široká ulice, Josefov (JK)
Bottom : Old Jewish Cemetery, Josefov (JK)

lifeless body into the synagogue's attic, where some insist it still lies.

High Synagogue (Vysoká Synagóga) Opposite the Old-New Synagogue is the elegant 16th century High Synagogue, so called because its prayer hall is upstairs. It now houses an exhibit of sacramental textiles and silver implements.

Jewish Town Hall (Židovská Radnice) Built by Maisel in 1586 and given its Rococo façade in the 18th century, the Jewish Town Hall is closed to the public except for the Shalom Kosher Restaurant on the ground floor. It has a clock tower with one Hebrew face whose hands, like the Hebrew script, run 'backwards'.

Klaus Synagogue (Klauzová Synagóga) In this 1694 Baroque building by the cemetery entrance is a well-done exhibit on Jewish artefacts and ceremonies of birth, death, worship and special holy days.

Ceremonial Hall (Obřadní Síň) This was built around 1906 by the cemetery entrance. Its collection of paintings and drawings by children held in the Terezín (Theresienstadt) concentration camp during WW II was closed to the public at the time of writing.

Pinkas Synagogue (Pinkasova Synagóga) This handsome synagogue on Široká was built in 1535 and used for worship until 1941. After WW II it was converted into a powerful memorial, with the names, birth dates and dates of disappearance of the 77,297 Bohemian and Moravian victims of the Nazis, inscribed across wall after wall. 'Renovated' away during the Communist era, it's now being painstakingly reconstructed.

Maisel Synagogue (Maiselova Synagóga) This neo-Gothic synagogue at Maiselova 10 replaced a Renaissance original built by Maisel and destroyed by fire. It houses another exhibit of synagogue silver.

Spanish Synagogue (Španělská Synagóga) Named for its striking Moorish interior, this neglected 1868 building is used as a museum depository and is closed to the public.

Old Jewish Cemetery (Starý Židovský Hřbitov) Founded in the early 15th century, this is

Europe's oldest surviving Jewish cemetery, truly a monument to dignity in the face of humiliation. It has a palpable atmosphere of mourning even after two centuries of disuse (it was closed in 1787).

Some 12,000 crumbling stones (some brought from other, long-gone cemeteries) are heaped together, but beneath them are perhaps 100,000 graves, piled in layers because of space limitations. Most contain the name of the deceased and his/her father, the date of death (and sometimes of burial), and poetic texts. Elaborate markers from the 17th and 18th centuries have bas-relief and sculpture, some of it indicating the deceased's occupation and lineage. The oldest standing stone (now replaced by a replica), from 1439, is that of Avigdor Karo, a chief rabbi and court poet to Wenceslas IV.

The most prominent graves, marked by pairs of marble tablets with a 'roof' between them, are near the main gate. They include those of Mordechai Maisel and Rabbi Löw.

You enter the cemetery beside the Ceremonial Hall on U starého hřbitova. This is one of Prague's most popular sights, and the queue of chattering tour groups tends to break its spell.

Since this cemetery was closed, burials have been at the New Jewish Cemetery in Žižkov. Remnants of another old Jewish burial ground are at the foot of the TV tower in Žižkov.

Pařížská Třída Despite their association with the demise of the Jewish quarter, Pařížská třída ('Parisian Avenue') and adjacent streets are themselves a kind of museum. The ghetto was cleared at a time of general infatuation with the French Art-Nouveau style, and its old lanes were lined with courtly four- and five-storey residential buildings – their stained glass and sculptural flourishes now slipping into disrepair.

Museum of Decorative Arts (Uměleckoprůmyslové Muzeum) This wonderful museum of European and Czech 'applied art' arose as part of a European movement to encourage a return to aesthetic values sacrificed to the Industrial Revolution. Its four halls full of 16th to 19th century furniture, tapestries, porcelain and a fabulous trove of glasswork are a feast for the eyes. Don't miss the Rococo grandfather of all grandfather clocks in room No 3.

Labels are in Czech but detailed English texts are available in each room. What you see is only a fraction of the collection; other bits appear now and then for single-theme exhibitions. The museum's French neo-Renaissance quarters, built in 1890, are at 17.listopadu 2, opposite the Rudolfinum. It's open from 10 am to 6 pm except Monday and holidays.

Rudolfinum & Jan Palach Square Jan Palach Square (náměstí Jana Palacha or Palachovo náměstí) is a memorial to the Charles University student who in January 1969 set himself alight in Wenceslas Square in protest of the Soviet invasion. Across the road on the philosophy faculty building, where Palach was a student, is a plaque with a spooky death mask.

Presiding over the square is the Rudolfinum, home of the Czech Philharmonic. This and the National Theatre, both designed by the architects Josef Schulz and Josef Zítek, are considered Prague's finest neo-Renaissance buildings. Completed in 1884, it served between the wars as the seat of the Czechoslovak Parliament. In the basement is a good classical CD shop.

The street into the square from the north is called 17.listopadu (17 November), which now has a dual meaning. It originally honoured students killed in an anti-Nazi demonstration in 1939. Exactly 50 years later, students marching in memory of that day were clubbed by police, triggering the national outrage that brought the Communist government down.

Charles Bridge (Karlův Most)

Charles Bridge was begun by Charles IV on the foundations of the earlier Judith (Juditin) Bridge (named after Vladislav I's queen), washed away by floods. Designed by Peter Parler, it was completed about 1400, though it only got Charles' name in the 19th century. Despite occasional flood damage, it withstood wheeled traffic for 600 years without a shudder – thanks, legend says, to eggs mixed into the mortar – until it was made pedestrian-only after WW II.

Crossing it is everybody's favourite Prague activity. By 9 am it's a 500-metre-long fairground, with an army of tourists squeezing through a gauntlet of hawkers and buskers, beneath an outer rank of imposing Baroque statuary.

In the crush, don't forget to look at the bridge itself and the grand views up and down the river. In summer you can climb up into the towers at either end – built originally for its defense – for a few crowns; they're normally open from 10 am to 6 pm. To have the bridge more or less to yourself in the high season you'd have to get here by about 8 am.

Top : Charles Bridge (JK)
Bottom : Old Town & Charles Bridge (RN)

Top : Old Town Square (JK)
Bottom : Malá Strana bridge towers (RN)

Towers & Statues of Charles Bridge

Of the two Malá Strana bridge towers (Malostranské mostecké věžé), the lower one was originally part of the long-gone 12th century Judith Bridge. The taller tower was built in the mid-15th century in imitation of the one at the Staré Město end.

The bridge's first monument was the crucifix near the east end, erected in 1657. The first and still most popular statue – the Jesuits' 1683 monument to St John of Nepomuk – inspired other Catholic orders, and a score more went up, like ecclesiastical billboards, over the next 30 years. New ones were added in the late 1800s, and one (plus replacements for some lost to floods) in this century.

Most statues were of soft sandstone, and several weathered originals have been replaced with copies. Some of the originals are in an exhibit in the casemates under the walls at Vyšehrad, others are in the Lapidárium at the Fairgrounds in Holešovice. There are apparently plans to replace all of them with copies eventually.

From the west (Malá Strana) end, the monuments are:

Left, SS Cosmas and Damian, charitable 3rd century physician brothers (1709); right, St Wenceslas (1858)

Left, St Vitus (1714); right, SS John of Matha and Félix de Valois, 12th century French founders of the Trinitarian order, for the ransom of enslaved Christians (represented by a Tatar standing guard over a group of them), with St Ivo (1714)

Left, St Philip Benizi (1714); right, St Adalbert, Prague's first Czech bishop, canonised in the 10th century (1709, replica)

Left, St Cajetan, Italian founder of Theatine order in the 15th century (1709); right, *The Vision of St Luitgard*, agreed by most to be the finest piece on the bridge, in which Christ appears to the blind saint and allows her to kiss his wounds (1710)

Left, St Augustine (1708, replica); right, St Nicholas of Tolentino (1706, replica)

Left, St Jude Thaddaeus, Apostle and patron saint of hopeless causes (1708); right, St Vincent Ferrer, a 14th century Spanish priest, and St Procopius, Hussite warrior-priest (1712)

Right, beyond the railing is a column with a statue of the eponymous hero of the 11th century epic poem, the *Song of Roland* (Czech: *Bruncvík)*

Left, St Anthony of Padua, 13th century Portuguese disciple of St Francis of Assisi (1707); right, St Francis (1855)

Left, St John of Nepomuk, patron saint of Czechs: according to the legend illustrated on the base of the statue, Wenceslas IV had him trussed up and thrown off the bridge in 1393 for refusing to divulge confessions by the queen, though the real reason had to do with the bitter conflict between church and state; the stars in his halo allegedly followed his corpse down the river (bronze, 1683); right, St Wenceslas as a boy, with his grandmother and guardian St Ludmilla, patroness of Bohemia (about 1730)

Left, St Wenceslas with St Sigismund, son of Charles IV and Holy Roman Emperor, and St Norbert, 12th century German founder of the Premonstratensian order (1853); right, St Francis Borgia, 16th century Spanish priest (1710)

Left, a bronze cross on the railing marks the place where St John of Nepomuk was thrown off (see above)

Left, St John the Baptist (1857); right, St Christopher, patron saint of travellers (1857)

Left, SS Cyril and Methodius, who brought Christianity and a written language to the Slavs in the 9th century (the newest statue, 1938); right, St Francis Xavier, 16th century Spanish missionary celebrated for his work in the Orient (1711, replica)

Left, St Anne, Madonna and Child (1707); right, St Joseph (1854)

Left, Crucifix (gilded bronze, 1657), with an invocation in Hebrew, saying 'holy, holy, holy Lord', funded by the fine of a Jew who had mocked it (1696), and stone figures (1861); right, Pietà (1859)

Left, Madonna with St Dominic, Spanish founder of the Dominicans in the 12th century, and St Thomas Aquinas (1709, replica); right, St Barbara, 2nd century patron saint of miners, St Margaret, 3rd or 4th century patron saint of expectant mothers, and St Elizabeth, a 13th century Slovak princess who renounced the good life to serve the poor (1707)

Left, Madonna with St Bernard, founder of the Cistercian order in the 12th century (1709, replica); right, St Ivo, 11th century bishop of Chartres (1711, replica)

The elegant Old Town Bridge Tower (Staroměstská mostecká věž) was, like the bridge, designed by Peter Parler. Here the Swedish army was finally turned back at the end of the Thirty Years' War by a band of students and ghetto residents. Looking out from the east face are SS Adalbert and Procopius, and below them Charles IV, St Vitus and Wenceslas IV. The tower also features a bit of 'Gothic porno': below these worthies on the left side of the arch is a stone relief of a man with his hand up the skirt of what appears to be a nun. ■

Gangs of pickpockets work the bridge during the day, so keep track of your purse or wallet.

Old Town Square (Staroměstské Náměstí)

The huge (about 1.7 hectares) Old Town Square has been Prague's heart since the 10th century, and was its main marketplace until the beginning of this century.

Despite over-the-top commercialism and swarming tourists, it's impossible not to enjoy the place – the cafés spilling onto the pavement, the buskers and performing dogs, the silly horse-drawn beer wagons, the crowds at Jan Hus' feet. Its pastel gingerbread Baroque and neo-Renaissance façades reveal nothing about their crumbling interiors, and there's hardly a hint of the square's harrowed history.

Czech History in the Old Town Square

The Old Town Square has been the scene of some momentous events in Czech history:

1338: John of Luxembourg grants Staré Město the right to a town hall, and a private house is purchased for the purpose
1422: Execution of Jan Želivský, the Hussite preacher who led Prague's first defenestration, touching off the Hussite Wars
1437: Execution of 57 more Hussites
1458: Election of the Hussite George of Poděbrady as King of Bohemia, in the Town Hall
21 June 1621: Beheading of 27 Protestants after the Battle of the White Mountain
1784: The Town Hall becomes the governmental seat of a newly unified Prague city
6 July 1915: Unveiling of the statue of Jan Hus on the 500th anniversary of his martyrdom
2 November 1918: The 270-year-old column commemorating the end of the Thirty Years' War is toppled
8 May 1945: Nazi SS units try to demolish the Old Town Hall as German troops begin pulling out after three days of fighting against Prague residents; the following day, the Red Army marches in
21 February 1948: Klement Gottwald proclaims a Communist government from the balcony of the Kinský Palace
21 August 1968: Warsaw Pact tanks roll across the square as the 'Prague Spring' comes to an end; the Jan Hus statue is draped in black. ■

Top : Old Town Hall tower (RN)
Bottom : Czech coats of arms, Old Town Hall (RN)

Jan Hus Statue Ladislav Šaloun's brooding Art-Nouveau sculpture of Jan Hus dominates the square as Hus' mythic memory dominates Czech history. It was unveiled on 6 July 1915, the 500th anniversary of Hus's death at the stake, to patriotic noises but less than total artistic approval. The steps at its base – being just about the only place in the square where you can sit down without having to pay for something – are a magnet for footsore Praguers and visitors.

A brass strip on the pavement nearby is the so-called **'Prague Meridian'**. Until 1915 the square's main ornament was a 17th century column commemorating Habsburg victory in the Thirty Years' War, whose shadow used to cross the meridian at high noon. Three years after the Hus statue went up, and five days after Czechoslovakia's declaration of independence, the column was toppled by jubilant Praguers.

Old Town Hall (Staroměstská Radnice) Staré Město's ancient town hall, founded in 1338, looks like a row of private buildings with a tower at the end – the result of its having been gradually assembled from existing buildings by a medieval town council short on funds.

The arcaded building at the corner, covered with Renaissance sgraffito, is called **Dům U minuty**. Franz Kafka lived in it as a child just before it was bought for the town hall.

A Gothic chapel and a neo-Gothic northern wing were destroyed by Nazi shells in 1945, on the day before the Soviet Army marched into Prague. The chapel has been laboriously reconstructed.

A plaque on the tower's east face contains a roll-call of the 27 Czech Protestant nobles beheaded in 1621 after the Battle of the White Mountain; crosses on the ground mark the spot where the deed was done. Another plaque commemorates a critical WW II victory by Red Army and Czechoslovak units at Dukla Pass in Slovakia.

It is de rigueur to wait for the hourly show by the hall's splendid **Astronomical Clock** or *orloj*. There's an on-the-hour tour of selected rooms of the town hall, but aside from the clock the hall's best feature is the **view** from the 60-metre tower, open from 9 am to 5 pm except Monday and certainly worth the 20-Kč price.

St Nicholas Church (Kostel Sv Mikuláše) The Baroque wedding cake in the north-west corner of the square is St Nicholas Church, built in the 1730s by Kilian Dientzenhofer. (It's not to be confused with at least two other St Nicholas churches in Prague, including Kilian's and his father's masterwork in Malá Strana.) He managed to work considerable grandeur into a very tight space, wedged at the time behind the north wing of the Old Town Hall which was destroyed in 1945.

Kafka's World

Literary Prague at the turn of the century was a unique melting pot of Czechs, Germans and Jews. Though he wrote in German, Franz Kafka is a son of Prague; he lived here all his life, haunting the city and haunted by it, needing it and hating it. One could look at *The Trial* as a metaphysical geography of Staré Město, whose Byzantine alleys and passages break down the usual boundaries between outer streets and inner courtyards, between public and private, new and old, real and imaginary.

Most of Kafka's life was lived around Josefov and Old Town Square. He was born on 3 July 1883 in an apartment beside St Nicholas Church ; only the stone portal remains from the original building. As a boy, he lived at: Celetná 2 (1888-89); 'U minuty', the Renaissance corner building that's now part of the Old Town Hall (1889-96); and Celetná 3 (1896-1907), where his bedroom window looked into Týn Church. He took classes in 1893-1901 at the Old Town State Gymnasium in the Kinský Palace on the square, and for a time his father Hermann ran his clothing shop on the ground floor there.

On the south side of the square, at No 17, Berta Fanta ran an intellectual salon in the early 1900s to which she invited fashionable European thinkers of the time, including Kafka and fellow writers Max Brod (Kafka's friend and biographer), Franz Werfel and Egon Erwin Kisch.

After earning a law degree from the Karolinum in 1906, Kafka took his first job in 1907-08, an unhappy one as an insurance clerk with the Italian firm Assicurazioni Generali, at Wenceslas Square 19 (on the corner of Jindřišská). At Na poříčí 7 in northern Nové Město is the former headquarters of the Workers' Accident Insurance Co, where he toiled on the 5th floor from 1908 until his retirement in 1922.

The last place where he lived with his parents (1913-14) – and the setting for his horrific parable, *Metamorphosis* – was a top-floor flat across Pařížská from St Nicholas Church, facing Old Town Square. At the age of 33 he finally moved into a place of his own at Dlouhá 16 (at the narrow corner with Masná) where he lived from 1915 to 1917, during which time he also spent a productive winter (1916-17) at a cottage rented by his sister at Zlatá ulička (Golden Lane) 22, inside the Prague Castle grounds. By now ill with tuberculosis, he took a flat for a few months in 1917 at the Schönborn Palace at Tržiště 15 in Malá Strana (now the US Embassy).

Kafka died in Vienna on 3 June 1924 and is buried in the New Jewish Cemetery in Žižkov. ■

Top : Rooftops, Old Town Square (RN)
Bottom : St Nicholas Church, Old Town Square (RN)

Top : Kinský Palace, Old Town Square (RN)
Bottom : Týn Church façade, Old Town Square (RN)

Frequent chamber concerts are held beneath its stucco decorations, a visually splendid (though acoustically mediocre) setting.

Next door to the west, at the corner of Maiselova, is a privately operated **Franz Kafka Exhibition** (Expozice Franze Kafky) at the site of the author's birthplace. It's open Tuesday to Friday from 10 am to 6 pm, Saturday to 5 pm, closed Sunday and Monday.

Kinský Palace (Palác Kinských) Fronting the late-Baroque Kinský or Goltz-Kinský Palace at No 12 is

The Astronomical Clock

The Old Town Hall tower was given a clock in 1410 by the master clockmaker Mikuláš of Kadaně; this was improved in 1490 by one Master Hanuš, producing the mechanical marvel you see today. Legend has it that Master Hanuš was afterwards blinded so he could not duplicate the work elsewhere, and in revenge crawled up into the clock and disabled it. (Documents from the time suggest that he carried on as clock master for years, unblinded, although the clock apparently didn't work properly until it was repaired in about 1570.)

Four figures beside the clock represent 15th century Praguers' deepest civic anxieties: Vanity, Greed (originally a Jewish money-lender, cosmetically altered after WW II), Death and Pagan Invasion (represented by a Turk). The four figures below these are the Chronicler, Angel, Astronomer and Philosopher.

On the hour, Death rings a bell and inverts his hourglass, and a parade of Apostles passes two windows, nodding to the crowd: on the left side, Paul (with a sword and a book), Thomas (lance), Jude (book), Simon (saw), Bartholomew (book) and Barnabas (parchment); on the right side, Peter (with a key), Matthew (axe), John (snake), Andrew (cross), Philip (cross) and James (mallet). At the end a cock crows and the hour is rung.

On the upper face, the disk (A) in the middle of the fixed part depicts the world known at the time – with Prague (B) at the centre, of course. The gold sun (C) traces a circle through the blue zone of day, the brown zone of dusk *(CREPUSCULUM* in Latin) in the west *(OCCASUS*, D on the diagram), the black disk (E) of night, and dawn *(AURORA)* in the east *(ORTUS*, F on the diagram). From this the hours of sunrise and sunset can be read. The curved lines (G) with black Arabic numerals are part of an astrological 'star clock'.

The sun-arm (H) points to the hour (adjusted for daylight-saving time) on the Roman-numeral ring (I); the top XII is noon and the bottom XII is midnight. The outer ring probably the city's finest Rococo façade, completed in 1765 by the redoubtable Kilian Dientzenhofer.

Alfred Nobel, the Swedish inventor of dynamite, once stayed here; his crush on pacifist Bertha Kinský may have influenced him to establish the Nobel Peace Prize. Many living Praguers have a darker memory of the place, for it was from its balcony in February 1948 that Klement Gottwald proclaimed Communist rule in Czechoslovakia.

Here the National Gallery stages changing exhibitions drawn from its collection of prints and 19th and 20th century graphics; there's also a good music shop.

(J), with Gothic numerals, reads traditional 24-hour Bohemian time, counted from sunset; the number 24 (K) is always opposite the sunset hour on the fixed (inner) face.

The moon (L), with its phases shown, also traces a path through the zones of day and night, riding on the offset moving ring (M). On the ring you can also read which houses of the zodiac the sun and moon are in. The hand with a little star at the end of it (N) indicates stellar time.

The calendar-wheel beneath all this astronomical wizardry, with 12 seasonal scenes in praise of rural Bohemian life, is a duplicate of one painted in 1866 by the Czech Revivalist Josef Mánes. You can have a close look at the beautiful original in the Museum of the City of Prague (see the Nové Město section). Most dates are marked with the name of the relevant saint; 6 July is in honour of Jan Hus. ■

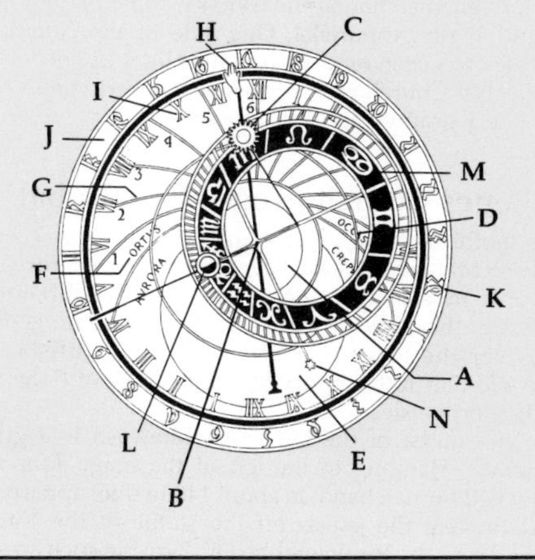

House at the Stone Bell (Dům U Kamenného Zvonu) Next door at No 13, its 14th century Romanesque dignity rescued in the 1960s from a second-rate Baroque renovation, is the House at the Stone Bell, named for the house sign at the corner of the building. Inside, two restored Gothic chapels now serve as a private gallery of modern art and a chamber-concert venue.

Church of Our Lady Before Týn (Kostel Panny Marie Před Týnem) Gloomy inside but oddly appealing outside, the spiky-topped 'Týn Church' is early Gothic, though it takes some imagination to visualise the original. It's strangely hidden behind the four-storey **Týn School** (not a Habsburg plot to obscure this 15th century Hussite stronghold, but almost contemporaneous with it). Inside it's smothered in heavy Baroque.

The entrance is up a passage beside the Caffè Italia. Two of the church's most striking features are a huge Rococo altar on the north wall, and the beautiful north-east entrance. On the lower south wall are two tiny windows that once looked in from the house at Celetná 3 – one from the bedroom of the teenage Franz Kafka in 1896-1907. The Danish astronomer Tycho Brahe, one of Rudolf II's most illustrious 'consultants' (who died in 1601 of a burst bladder during a royal piss-up) is buried near the chancel.

The church's name comes from a medieval courtyard for foreign merchants, the **Týnský dvůr** or just Týn, behind it on Štupartská. One side of the courtyard complex has been renovated as the Hotel Ungelt.

The Týn Church is an occasional concert venue, and has a very grand-sounding pipe organ.

St James Church (Kostel Sv Jakuba)

This Gothically long, tall church, behind the Týnský dvůr on Malá Štupartská, began in the 14th century as a Minorite monastery church. It got a beautiful Baroque facelift in the early 18th century. Pride of place goes to the over-the-top tomb of Count Jan Vratislav of Mitrovice, an 18th century lord chancellor of Bohemia, on the north aisle.

In the midst of the gilt and whitewash is a grisly memento. Hanging to the left of the main door is a shrivelled human hand. In about 1400 a thief apparently tried to steal the jewels off the statue of the Virgin. Legend says the Virgin grabbed his wrist in such an iron

Týn Church (RN)

grip that his hand had to be lopped off. The truth may not be far behind: the church was a favourite of the guild of butchers, who may have administered their own justice.

It's well worth a visit to enjoy St James' splendid pipe organ and famous acoustics. Recitals – eg free ones after the 9.15 am Sunday Mass – and concerts are not always noticed by ticket agencies, so check the notice-board outside.

Along the Royal Way

The lanes from the Powder Tower to Charles Bridge are part of the original route of coronation processions held right into the 19th century. Nearly all of this Royal Way in Staré Město is pedestrianised. We follow the coronation route in reverse direction from Charles Bridge.

The Klementinum To boost the power of Rome in Bohemia, Ferdinand I invited the Jesuits to Prague. Selecting one of the city's choicest bits of real estate, they set to work in 1578 on Prague's flagship of the Counter-Reformation, the Church of the Holy Saviour (Kostel sv Salvátora).

After gradually buying up most of the adjacent neighbourhood, the Jesuits broke ground in 1653 for their college, the Klementinum, which by the time of its completion a century later was second in size only to Prague Castle. When the Jesuits fell out with the pope in 1773, all of it became part of Charles University.

The western façade of the **Church of the Holy Saviour** faces Charles Bridge, its sooty stone saints glaring down at merrymakers and the traffic ripping through Křižovnická náměstí. Alongside the church, Karlova ulice does a jog at the little round **Assumption Chapel** (Vlašská kaple Nanebevzetí Panny Marie), completed in 1600 for the Italian artisans who worked on the Klementinum (it is still technically the property of the Italian government).

Eastward on Karlova you can look inside **St Clement Church** (Kostel sv Klimenta), lavishly rehabilitated in Baroque style in 1711-15, to plans by Kilian Dientzenhofer. It's now Greek Orthodox, with services in Old Church Slavonic daily at 5 pm and on Sunday at 8.30 and 10 am, to which conservatively dressed visitors are welcome.

The three churches form most of the southern wall of the Klementinum, a vast complex of beautiful Rococo halls now occupied by the Czech National Library. Tragically, it's closed to the public. From gates on

Křižovnická, Karlova and Seminářská you can detour through several courtyards, and inside the library entrance in the south-east courtyard is a tiny exhibit about the Klementinum. In a courtyard at the centre of the complex is an 18th century observatory tower.

A room you might be able to see is the **Chapel of Mirrors** (Zrcadlová kaple), a frequent concert venue (see the notices posted outside). One architectural handbook suggests that this over-the-top room with mirrors on the ceiling looks more like a boudoir than a chapel!

Near the Klementinum Beside the Staré Město tower of Charles Bridge is the 17th century **Church of St Francis Seraphinus** (Kostel sv Františka Serafinského), its dome inside decorated with a fresco of the Last Judgment. The church belongs to the Order of Knights of the Cross, the only Bohemian order of Crusaders.

Just south of the bridge, at the site of the former Old Town mill, is Novotného lávka, a pedestrian lane full of sunny, overpriced vinárnas, and a smashing view of the bridge and castle. At No 1, the private **Opera Mozart Theatre** is a venue for chamber concerts, opera and Sunday jazz (see the Entertainment chapter). An uninspiring museum devoted to Bedřich **Smetana**, Bohemia's sentimental favourite composer, is upstairs.

At Karlova 18, on the corner of Liliová, the building called **The Golden Snake** (U zlatého hada) was Prague's first coffee house, opened in 1708 by an Armenian named Deomatus Damajan; it's now a T-shirt shop with an espresso machine in the corner, serving coffee in paper cups – tasteless in every sense.

At Husova 19-21, on the corner of Karlova, are two good modern-art galleries, the **Central Bohemian Gallery** (Středočeská galerie) and the **Central European Gallery** (Středoevropská galerie, both ☎ 236 07 00). Down at Husova 10, the associated Centrum České Grafiky (☎ 232 79 40) often has more than just graphics.

At Žatecká 1 is an old theatre called **Marionette Kingdom** (Říše loutek), which got a new lease on life when the respected Kladno puppet troupe moved in with a puppet show for adults – Mozart's opera *Don Giovanni* at US$15 a throw – and a sell-out for several years now. The name 'National Marionette Theatre' was a joke that has stuck.

Malé Náměstí In the 'Little Square', the south-western extension of the Old Town Square, is a Renaissance **fountain** and 16th century wrought-iron grille. Several fine Baroque and neo-Renaissance ex-

Hradčany (RN)

teriors decorate some of Staré Město's oldest and most dilapidated structures.

Celetná Ulice This pedestrianised lane from Old Town Square to the Powder Tower is an open-air museum of well-groomed, pastel-painted Baroque façades over Gothic frames (and Romanesque foundations, deliberately buried to raise Staré Město above the Vltava's floods).

But the most interesting façade only dates from 1912: Josef Gočár's delightful Cubist front on the so-called **House at the Black Madonna** (Dům U černé Matky Boží). It's at No 34, at the corner of the Old Fruit Market (Ovocný trh), with its Baroque predecessor's Madonna house-marker. It was Prague's first Cubist building, and there has been talk of opening a museum of Cubism here.

Powder Tower (Prašná Brána) The 65-metre-tall Powder Tower was begun in 1475 for King Vladislav II Jagiello at the site of one of Staré Město's original 13 gates. After the defenestration of the mayor in 1483, the king moved to Prague Castle and the tower was left unfinished. The name comes from its use as a gunpowder magazine in the 18th century. Josef Mocker rebuilt, decorated and steepled it in 1875-86. It's been closed for several years, its neo-Gothic icing hidden behind scaffolding.

Municipal House (Obecní Dům) Don't miss the 'Dům', Prague's most sensually beautiful building, with an unrivalled Art-Nouveau interior and a façade that looks like a Victorian Easter egg.

The site is that of the royal court, seat of Bohemia's kings from 1383 to 1483 (when Vladislav II moved to Prague Castle) and only demolished at the turn of this century. In 1906-12 the Obecní dům was built in its place – a lavish joint effort by some 30 of the leading artists of the day, a cultural centre that was to be the architectural climax of the Czech National Revival.

The exterior mosaic, *Homage to Prague*, is set between sculptures representing the oppression and rebirth of the Czech people. You enter beneath a wrought-iron and glass canopy into an interior that is Art Nouveau down to the doorknobs.

The restaurant and the kavárna flanking the entrance are like museums of design, and the basement club is like a gallery. Upstairs are half a dozen over-the-top salons – including the Lord Mayor's Hall, done up entirely by Alfons Mucha, whose paintings and posters have made him an international symbol of Art Nouveau, and Smetana Hall, Prague's biggest concert hall.

Among symbolic moments here have been the proclamation of an independent Czechoslovak Republic on 28 October 1918, and meetings between Civic Forum and the Jakeš regime in November 1989. The Prague Spring Music Festival always opens on 12 May, the anniversary of Smetana's death, with a procession from Vyšehrad to the Obecní dům, and a gala performance of his symphonic cycle *Má vlast* (My Country) in Smetana Hall.

Smetana Hall, Obecní dům (JK)

Around Obecní Dům Across náměstí Republiky looms **Hibernian House** (Dům U hybernů). In 1810 this monstrous Empire façade was affixed to a 17th century monastery church by the Viennese architect Georg Fischer, and it became the Prague Customs House. It's now an exhibition hall.

At U Obecního domu 1 is another Art-Nouveau gem, the **Hotel Paříž**, built in 1907 and recently restored.

Na Příkopě

The name means 'on the moat', and with Národní třída and Revoluční this street marks the moat (filled in at the end of the 18th century) by the old Staré Město walls

This was the haunt of Prague's German café society in the 1800s. Today it is, along with Národní, the main shopping precinct, lined with banks, bookshops, tourist cafés and a few interesting buildings. Most of the following buildings can be found on the Southern Nové Město map:

No 20, Živnostenská banka headquarters, with a very grand Art-Nouveau interior completed in 1896 by Osvald Polívka, co-architect of the Obecní dům

No 18, now Čedok headquarters, also designed by Polívka (1912) and linked with No 20 by a bridge over Nekázanka ulice

No 16, the Church of the Holy Cross (Kostel sv Kříže), a leaden Empire-style block by Georg Fischer

No 12, House at the Black Rose (U černé růže); upstairs is an ornate and charming neo-Renaissance interior by Josef Fanta (1880)

No 10, the Sylva-Taroucca Palace, a Rococo masterpiece by Kilian Dientzenhofer (1751), and the oldest building on the street

Na příkopě runs westward from Wenceslas Square as 28.října ('28 October', Czechoslovak Independence Day), and Wenceslas Square runs northward as Na můstku ('On the little bridge', where a footbridge once crossed the moat). Although developers have wet dreams about this junction – nicknamed the **'Golden Cross'** – it's a charmless spot with postcard vendors and loitering heavies.

St Gall's Market Area

About 1230 a new market quarter, Havelské Město or St Gall's Town (named for the 7th century Irish monk who helped introduce Europe to Christianity), was laid out for the pleasure of the German merchants invited into Prague by Wenceslas I.

Modern-day Rytířská and Havelská streets were at that time a single plaza, surrounded by arcaded merchants' houses. Specialist markets *(trh)* included those for coal (Uhelný trh) at the west end and for fruit (Ovocný trh) at the east end. In the 15th century an island of stalls was built down the middle.

Havelská Market All that remains of St Gall's market today is the flower and vegetable market on Havelská ulice, and the clothes hawkers in adjacent V kotcích. No match for the original, it's still Prague's most central open-air market.

Looking down Havelská, and as old as St Gall's Town itself, is the **Church of St Gall** (Kostel sv Havla). Jan Hus and his predecessors preached church reform here. The Carmelites got it in 1627, and in 1723 added its present shapely Baroque face. But the narrow square in front, full of rubbish and parked cars, makes a poor setting. The Czech Baroque painter Karel Škréta (1610-74) is buried in the church.

At the west end of Havelská is Uhelný trh, and nearby the plain 12th century **Church of St Martin in the Wall** (Kostel sv Martina ve zdi), a parish church enlarged and Gothicised in the 14th century. The name comes from its having had the Old Town wall built right round it. Here in 1414 was held the first-ever Hussite communion service *sub utraque specie* ('with both bread and wine', from which the name 'Utraquist' derives).

The Karolinum Charles University – central Europe's oldest university, founded by Charles IV in 1348 – took as its original home the so-called Röthlow House at Železná 9. With Protestantism and Czech nationalism on the rise, the reform preacher Jan Hus became rector in 1402 and soon persuaded Wenceslas IV to slash the voting rights of the university's German students, at which thousands of them left Bohemia.

After the Battle of the White Mountain, the building, called the Karolinum, was handed over to the Jesuits, who gave it a Baroque working-over. When they were booted out in 1773 the university took it back. WW II damage led to remodelling and expansion.

Charles University now has faculties all over Prague, and the Karolinum serves mainly for academic ceremonies. Its finest room is the high-ceilinged assembly hall upstairs. Among pre-university Gothic traces is the Chapel of SS Cosmas & Damian, built around 1370 and

Havelská Market with (top) Church of St Gall (JK)

renovated by Josef Mocker in 1881, whose extraordinary oriel sticks out of the building's south wall. A good private gallery of modern Czech artists now occupies the ground floor.

Tyl Theatre Beside the Karolinum at Železná 11 is Prague's oldest theatre and its finest neo-Classical building. Opened in 1783 as the Nostitz Theatre (after its founder, Count Anton von Nostitz-Rieneck), it was patronised by upper-class German Praguers. It came to be called the Estates Theatre (Stavovské divadlo) – the Estates being the traditional nobility – by which name it's still commonly known.

True Mozart fans know it as the venue for the premières of his operas *Don Giovanni* in 1787 and *La Clemenza di Tito* in 1791. It's the only European opera house that remains, unaltered, from Mozart's day.

After WW II it was renamed the Tyl Theatre (Tylovo divadlo) in honour of the 19th century Czech playwright Josef Kajetán Tyl, from one of whose plays came the Czech national anthem, *Kde domov můj?* (Where is My Home?). Its Czech-language plays occasionally include simultaneous English translation. The theatre is equipped for disabled and hearing-impaired visitors (see the Entertainment chapter).

Around the corner at Ovocný trh 6 is the 17th century Kolowrat Theatre, now also a National Theatre venue.

Convent of St Agnes (Klášter Sv Anežký)

In the north-east corner of Staré Město are the surviving buildings of the former Convent of St Agnes, Prague's oldest standing Gothic structures, now finely restored and used by the National Gallery.

In 1234 the Franciscan Order of the Poor Clares was founded by the Přemyslid King Wenceslas I, who made his sister Anežka (Agnes) its first abbess. Agnes was beatified in the 19th century, and with timing that could hardly be accidental, Pope John Paul II canonised her as St Agnes of Bohemia just weeks before the revolutionary events of November 1989.

In the 16th century the buildings were handed over to the Dominicans, and after Joseph II dissolved the monasteries, they became a squatter's paradise. They've only been restored in the last few decades, and work is ongoing.

The complex consists mainly of the cloister and two churches in French Gothic style. In the **Church of the**

MAP 4

Convent of St Agnes (Anežský klášter)

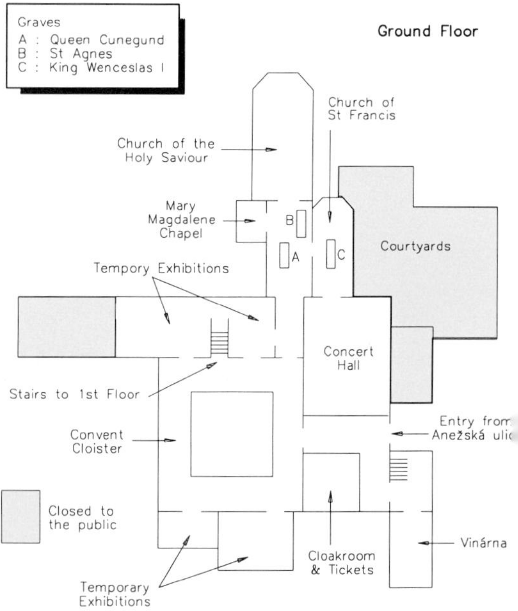

Graves
A : Queen Cunegund
B : St Agnes
C : King Wenceslas I
Ground Floor
Church of St Francis
Church of the Holy Saviour
Mary Magdalene Chapel
B
A
C
Courtyards
Tempory Exhibitions
Concert Hall
Stairs to 1st Floor
Entry from Anežská ulic
Convent Cloister
Closed to the public
Vinárna
Cloakroom & Tickets
Temporary Exhibitions

1st Floor
1
2
3
4
5
6
7
Rooms 1-6 : 19th Century Czech painting & sculpture
Room 7 : European influences
Bookshop

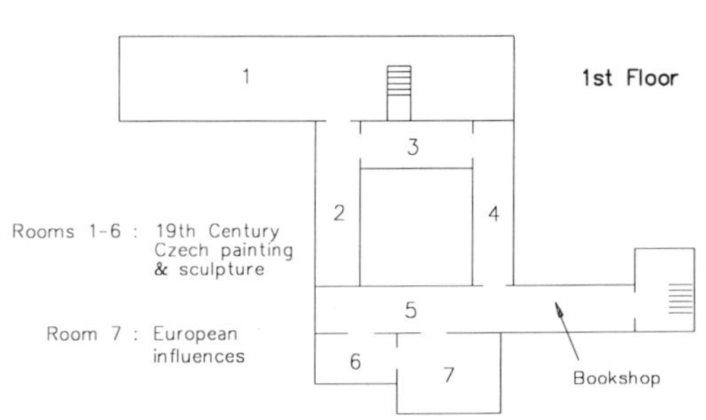

Holy Saviour (Kostel sv Salvatora) are the graves of St Agnes and Wenceslas' queen Cunegund, and the Chapel of Mary Magdalene (Kaple Mařia Magdalena). To the south is the smaller **Church of St Francis** (Kostel sv Františka), in whose chancel Wenceslas I is buried. Part of its ruined nave and other rooms have been rebuilt as a chilly concert and lecture hall.

The 1st floor of the **cloister** now holds the National Gallery's good permanent collection of 19th century Czech painters and sculptors, and in the last room a shifting show of other European artists who influenced them. Included is an eclectic selection from Josef Mánes, the foremost painter of the Czech National Revival. Don't miss the luminous little landscapes of Josef Navrátil.

Everything is open from 10 am to 6 pm daily except Monday. Normal admission is 40 Kč, but 10 Kč for students and free for the disabled – and free for all on the first Sunday of each month. It's at U milosrdných 17, on the corner of Anežská (take any tram along Revoluční, or bus No 207 from Jan Palach Square).

The winding lanes around St Agnes and Háštalské náměstí retain a feeling of earlier times. Only furious lobbying by residents and Prague intellectuals saved it from the same clearance that ravaged Josefov at the turn of the century.

South-West Staré Město

The meandering lanes and passageways in the quarter from Karlova ulice south to Národní třída are Prague's best territory for aimless wandering. When the crowds thin out early or late in the day, this area can cast such a spell that it's a surprise to return to the 20th century outside its borders.

Bethlehem Chapel (Betlémská Kaple) On Betlémské náměstí is one of Prague's most important churches, the real birthplace of Hussitism.

Reformist Praguers won permission for a chapel where services could be held in Czech instead of Latin, and in 1391 proceeded to build the biggest chapel Bohemia had ever seen, for 3000 worshippers. Architecturally it was a radical departure, with a simple square hall focussed on the pulpit rather than the altar. Jan Hus preached here from 1402 to 1412, marking the emergence of the church-reform movement from the safety of Charles University (where he was rector).

In the 18th century the chapel was torn down. Remnants were rediscovered around 1920 and – because

Hussitism had official blessing as an antecedent of Communism – the whole thing was painstakingly reconstructed from 1948 to 1954 in its original form, based on old drawings, descriptions, and traces of the original work in outer walls that were still standing. It's now a National Cultural Monument.

Only the street-facing wall is brand new. You can still see some original bits in the east wall: the pulpit door, several windows and the door to the preacher's quarters. These quarters, including rooms used by Hus and others, are apparently original too; they're now used for exhibits. The wall paintings are modern, based on old Hussite tracts. The indoor well predates the chapel. Additional buildings are now being reconstructed.

It's open weekdays from 9 am to 6 pm, with an English text available at the door. Every year on the night of 5 July, the eve of Hus' burning at the stake in 1415, a commemorative celebration is held here, with speeches and bell-ringing.

Náprstek Museum (Náprstkovo Muzeum) At the west end of Betlémské náměstí is a small museum founded by Vojta Náprstek, a 19th century industrialist with a passion for both anthropology and modern technology. His ethnographical collection, also known as the Museum of Asian, African & American Cultures, is open daily except Monday from 9 am to noon and 12.45 to 5.30 pm (his technology exhibits are now in the National Technology Museum in Holešovice).

St Giles Church (Kostel Sv Jiljí) With stocky Romanesque columns and tall Gothic windows, and oozing Baroque inside, this is a good place to appreciate Prague's passing religio-architectural fortunes. The church, on the corner of Zlatá and Husova, was founded in 1371. The proto-Hussite reformer Jan Milíč of Kroměříž preached here before the Bethlehem Chapel was built. The Dominicans got it during the Counter-Reformation, built a cloister next door and 'Baroquefied' it in the 1730s. Václav Reiner, the Czech painter who did the ceiling frescoes a few years before his death, is buried here.

Chapel of the Holy Cross (Kaple Sv Kříže) A tiny Romanesque rotunda at the west end of Konviktská is one of the oldest buildings in Prague. It started out as a parish church in about 1100. Saved from demolition and restored in the 1860s by a collective of Czech artists, it still has the remnants of some 600-year-old wall frescoes, though you may have to attend Mass to see them (Sunday 9.30 am and 5 pm, Tuesday and Friday 5 pm).

Police & Secret Police Staré Město's charm goes a bit cold along Konviktská and Bartolomějská, and not just because the block between them is full of police offices. Before November 1989, the block was occupied by the StB (Státní bezpečnost, or State Security), the hated secret police. Czechs are still understandably twitchy about police of any shade, and it's a common supposition that a few former StB officers are still there, in new uniforms.

Backing onto Bartolomějská is an old convent and the once lovely 18th century **St Bartholomew Church** (Kostel sv Bartoloměje), for a time part of the StB complex and recently returned to the Franciscans. The church is closed to the public, but the enterprising Unitas Penzion has rented space from the nuns, and guests can now spend the night in refurbished StB prison cells, including one where Václav Havel spent a night (see the Places to Stay chapter).

NOVÉ MĚSTO

Nové Město means 'New Town', although the crescent of land east and south of Staré Město was only 'new' when it was founded by Charles IV in 1348. Its outer fortifications were knocked down in 1875. The layout has been essentially preserved, although most surviving buildings are from the 19th and early 20th centuries. Many blocks are honeycombed with dark, pedestrian-only passages, some lined with shops, cafés and theatres.

Nové Město extends from Revoluční and Na příkopě out to Wilsonova and the main railway line, and south of Národní almost to Vyšehrad. Its focus is Wenceslas Square, a broad, 0.75-km-long boulevard lined with turn-of-the-century buildings, sloping down from the National Museum towards Staré Město. Náměstí Republiky is described in the earlier Staré Město section.

(The following sights are to be found on the Northern Nové Město map.)

Postage Stamp Museum (Muzeum Poštovní Známky)

Philatelists will love this little museum at Nové mlýny 2 near the north end of Revoluční, with its drawers of old postage stamps. It's open from 9 am to 5 pm, except Monday.

Across the street is the **Petrská vodárenská věž** or waterworks tower, built about 1660 on the site of earlier wooden ones. From here, wooden pipes once carried river water to buildings in Nové Město.

Museum of the City of Prague (Muzeum Hlavníhu Města Prahy)

At Na poříčí 52 near the Florenc metro station is an excellent museum of the city's history, built in 1896-98. The ground floor is devoted to the period up to the Battle of the White Mountain in 1620. Upstairs are knick-knacks including the Old Town Hall clock's 1866 calendar-wheel with Josef Mánes' beautiful panels.

But what everybody comes to see is Antonín Langweil's astonishing 1:480 scale model of Prague as it looked in 1826-34. It's most rewarding *after* you've got to know Prague a bit, so you can spot the changes. Other drawings, paintings and woodcuts offer earlier 'snapshots' of the city.

The museum is open from 10 am to 6 pm except Mondays. It's a bargain at 10 Kč (students 5 Kč), and there's a good English text for the asking.

Jindřišská Tower (Jindřišská Věž)

This former watchtower or bell tower, squarely at the end of Jindřišská, was built in the 15th century (a more run-down one is **Petrská věž**, in Petrské náměstí at the north end of Nové Město). Around the corner, at Jeruzalémská 7, is the Moorish-looking **Jubilee Synagogue** (Jubilejní synagoga), also called the Velká (Great) Synagogue, dating from 1906.

(The following sights are to be found on the Southern Nové Město map.)

Main Train Station (Hlavní Nádraží)

Have a look at the fading Art-Nouveau elegance of the original section of the station, designed by Josef Fanta and built in 1901-09. The exterior and vaulted interior are full of bas-relief women's faces from around the world. Under the central dome a plaque says *Praga: mater urbium* (Prague, Mother of Cities). Have a snack at the cavernous restaurant at the end of level 4 and admire its bright tile-work. See the Getting There & Away chapter for a practical tour of the station.

A statue at the north end of the park in front of the station was meant to celebrate the Soviet liberation of Prague after WW II but has always been vaguely insulting, with its submissive Czech soldier embracing his bigger Soviet comrade. Now stripped of its plaque, it looks more like a celebration of gay love in the military.

National Museum (Narodní Muzeum)

Looming above Wenceslas Square is the neo-Renaissance bulk of the National Museum, designed in the 1880s by Josef Schulz as an architectural symbol of the Czech National Revival.

The museum was founded in 1818 primarily as a museum of science, but its rocks, fossils and coins are pretty routine, and devoid of English labels. The truly 'Czech' displays – on the 19th century National Revival and 20th century history – we found closed to accommodate a temporary exhibition; you may have better luck.

Perhaps most appealing is the building itself, especially the grand stairwell, and the upper gallery of the 'pantheon' with (strangely womanless) murals of Czech legend and history by František Ženíšek and Václav Brožík, and pink-bottomed cherubs by Vojtěch Hynais.

Light-coloured patches on the façade of the museum are patched-up bullet holes. In 1968, Warsaw Pact troops apparently took the museum for the seat of government or the radio and TV station, and raked it with gunfire.

The museum is open from 9 am to 5 pm, except Tuesdays. The 20-Kč admission (students 10 Kč) is waived on the first Monday of each month. Across the road to the east is the **National Assembly** (1973), which retains within its walls the former Stock Exchange (1936-38). Next beyond it is the Smetana Theatre or **State Opera** (Statní Opera).

Wenceslas Square (Václavské Náměstí)

A horse market in medieval times, Wenceslas Square got its present name during the nationalist upheavals of the mid-19th century, since when it has been the scene of a great deal of Czech history. A giant Mass was celebrated in the square in 1848. Here in 1918 the new Czechoslovak Republic was celebrated.

In January 1969, in protest against the Warsaw Pact invasion, university student Jan Palach set himself on fire on the steps of the National Museum, staggered into the square and collapsed. The next day some 200,000

Top : Art-Nouveau décor, main train station (JK)
Bottom : Memorial to Soviet liberation of Prague (JK)

Top : Memorial to the victims of Communism (JK)
Bottom : Façade of the State Opera (RN)

people showed up to honour him. It was four agonising days before he died.

Following the 17 November 1989 beating of students on Národní třída, thousands gathered here in anger, night after night. A week later, in a stunning mirror-image of Klement Gottwald's 1948 proclamation of Communist rule, Alexander Dubček and Václav Havel stepped onto the balcony of the **Melantrich Building** to a thunderous, tearful ovation, and proclaimed its end.

At the top of the square is Josef Myslbek's muscular equestrian **statue of St Wenceslas** (sv Václav), the 10th century pacifist Duke of Bohemia, 'Good King Wenceslas' of the Christmas carol – never a king but decidedly good. Flanked by other patron saints of Bohemia – Prokop, Adalbert, Agnes and Wenceslas' grandmother Ludmilla – he has been plastered with posters and bunting at every one of the square's historical moments. Near the statue, where Jan Palach fell, a small **memorial to the victims of Communism** bears photographs and hand-written epitaphs for him and other stubborn rebels.

In contrast to the solemnity of this shrine, the square beyond it has become a monument to the capitalist urge, a gaudy gallery of cafés, shops, greedy cabbies and pricey hotels. Noteworthy buildings (from the top of the square, even numbers on the west side) include:

- The 1906 Grand Hotel Evropa at No 25, the most beautiful building on the square, Art Nouveau inside and out; have a peep at the French restaurant at the rear of the ground floor, and the 2nd-floor atrium
- The Melantrich Building at No 36, from whose balcony Havel and Dubček spoke in November 1989
- The 1896 Wiehl House (named for its designer, Antonín Wiehl) at No 34, its façade decorated with neo-Renaissance murals by Mikulaš Aleš and others
- Peterkův dům (Peterka House) at No 12, Jan Kotěra's 1901 Art-Nouveau building
- The Baťa Shoe Store at No 6, designed by Ludvík Kysela in 1929 for Tomáš Baťa, the art patron, progressive industrialist and founder of the worldwide shoe empire; next door at No 4 is Kysela's Lindt Building, finished the year before and one of the republic's first Constructivist buildings
- The north-east corner building with a tower, at No 1, Antonín Pfeiffer's 1914 Art-Nouveau Koruna Palác; also note its charming tiny façade around the corner on Na příkopě

At the bottom, Wenceslas Square intersects the up-market shopping street of Na příkopě (described under Staré Město) at the so-called 'Golden Cross'.

West of Wenceslas Square

Lucerna Passage The most elegant of Nové Město's many passages runs beneath the Lucerna Palace at Štěpanská 61, bounded by Štěpánská, Vodičkova and V jámé. It was designed by Václav Havel, the president's grandfather (and still owned by the president and his sister-in-law). The Art-Nouveau Lucerna complex includes theatres, a cinema, a night club-cum-restaurant and cafés.

Of numerous entrances to the complex, the most handsome is beneath the 1902 **U Nováků** building at Vodičkova 30, itself with one of Prague's finest Art-Nouveau façades, complete with mosaics of country life.

Church of Our Lady of the Snows (Kostel Panny Marie Sněžné) The most sublime attraction in the neighbourhood is this Gothic church at the bottom end of Wenceslas Square. It was begun in the 14th century by Charles IV but only the chancel was ever completed, which accounts for its proportions, seemingly taller than it is long. Charles had intended it to be the grandest church in Prague; the nave is higher than that of St Vitus, and the altar is the city's tallest. It was a Hussite stronghold, ringing to the sermons of Jan Želivský, who led the 1419 defenestration that touched off the Hussite Wars.

While you're here, go round and look at the church's fine Gothic entryway (and the bizarre Cubist street-lamp nearby). Rest your feet in the **Františkanská zahrada**, the former monastery gardens built beside the church by the Franciscans, now a peaceful park in the middle of the block.

Along Národní Třída Národní třída is central Prague's 'high street', a stately gauntlet of mid-range shops and grand government buildings – above all the National Theatre at the Vltava end. Following are some attractions on a stroll west from Jungmannovo náměstí.

Fronting Jungmannovo náměstí at Národní 40 is an age-blackened, imitation Venetian palace known as the Dům Látek (Cloth House) or **Adria Palace**. Beneath it is the Adria Theatre, original home of Laterna Magika and meeting place of Civic Forum in the heady days of the 'Velvet Revolution'. From here, Dubček and Havel walked through the Lucerna Passage to their 24 November 1989 appearance on the balcony of the Melantrich Building.

The **plaque** reading *17.11.89*, on the wall near No 16, is in memory of the students clubbed here on that date, an event that pushed the Communist government toward its final collapse a few days later.

West of Voršilská the lemon-yellow walls of the **Convent of St Ursula** (Klášter sv Voršila) frame a pink church whose lush Baroque interior includes a battalion of apostle statues. Out front is St John of Nepomuk, and on the building's lower right niche is a gruesome statue of St Agatha holding her severed breasts.

Across the road at No 7 is the fine Art-Nouveau façade (by Osvald Polívka) of the **Viola Building** (see the Staré Město map), former home of the Prague Insurance Co, with huge letters *PRAHA* around five circular windows, and mosaics spelling out *život, kapitál, důchod, věno* and *pojišťuje* (life, capital, income, dowry, insurance). Down the passage is the Viola Jazz Club. The building next door, a former publishing house, is also a Polívka design.

On the south side at No 4, looking like it has been bubble-wrapped by Christo, is Nová Scéna, the 1983 'New National Theatre' building, home of **Laterna Magika**. This pioneering multi-media theatre combining projected images, professional music and live actors, was humbly born at the other end of the street in the Adria Theatre, but has here become a permanent and overpriced tourist attraction.

Finally, facing the Vltava across Smetanovo nábřeží, is the **National Theatre** (Národní divadlo), neo-Renaissance flagship of the Czech National Revival, funded entirely by private donations, decorated inside and out by a roll-call of prominent Czech artists. Architect Josef

Wenceslas Square (JK)

Zítek's masterpiece burned down within weeks of its 1881 opening but, incredibly, was re-funded and restored under Josef Schulz in less than two years. It's now mainly used for ballet and opera performances.

Across Národní from the theatre is the **Slavia Café** (see the Staré Město map), known for its river views and comically awful service, once *the* place to be seen or to grab an after-theatre nosh, now under renovation by new owners.

Masarykovo Nábřeží (Masaryk Embankment)

About 200 metres south of the National Theatre along Masarykovo nábřeží is a grand Art-Nouveau building at No 32, once the East German Embassy, now occupied by the **Goethe Institute**.

Opposite this is **Slovanský ostrov** (Slav Island), a sleepy, dog-eared sandbank with river views and gardens (see the Islands of Prague section later in this chapter). Opposite the south end of the island is the **Mánes Gallery**, established in the 1920s by a group of artists headed by painter Josef Mánes as an alternative to the Czech Academy of Arts, and still one of Prague's better displays of contemporary art.

Charles Square (Karlovo Náměstí)

At over seven hectares, this is Prague's biggest square, although it's more of a park. Presiding over it is **St Ignatius Church** (Kostel sv Ignáce), a 1660s Baroque *tour de force* by Carlo Lurago for the Jesuits, worth a look for its huge stone portal and lavish interior.

The square's historical focus is the **New Town Hall** (Novoměstská radnice) at the north end, built when the 'New Town' was new. From its windows two of Wenceslas IV's Catholic councillors were flung to their deaths in 1419 by followers of the Hussite preacher Jan Želivský, giving 'defenestration' (throwing out the window) a new political meaning and Czechs a new political tactic, and touching off the Hussite Wars. (The present tower, however, was only added 35 years later.)

The white edifice along the square's north end and up Spálená is the Municipal Courthouse. The Baroque palace at the south end is known as Faustův dům (Faust House) because of popular associations with Rudolf II's Irish court alchemist, Edward Kelley, who toiled here trying to convert lead into gold.

Resslova to the west, and Žitná and Ječná to the east, are central Prague's cross-town artery. The intersection of Resslova with the square is the city's nocturnal transport hub; all eight night-time tram routes pass through here (see the Getting Around chapter).

Resslova Ulice

The Baroque **Church of SS Cyril & Methodius** (Kostel sv Cyrila a Metoda), a 1730s work by Kilian Dientzenhofer and Paul Bayer at the corner of Resslova and Na Zderaze, was the hiding place of seven Czech paratroopers who took part in the assassination of Reinhard Heydrich, the Nazi governor of Bohemia and Moravia, in June 1942. During the German siege of the church, all were killed or committed suicide. In savage revenge the Germans obliterated the village of Lidice, west of Prague (see Lidice in the Excursions chapter).

Across Resslova is the 14th century Gothic **Church of St Wenceslas in Zderaz** (Kostel sv Václava na Zderaze), the former parish church of Zderaz, a village that predates Nové Město. On its west side are bits of a wall and windows from its 12th century Romanesque predecessor.

Rašínovo Nábřeží (Rašín Embankment)

President **Václav Havel's flat**, where he first chose to live in preference to Prague Castle, faces the river from the top floor of the nondescript building at Rašínovo nábřeží 78, on the corner with Resslova – surely the world's least pompous presidential residence. Today he lives in a house on the outskirts of Prague.

From here the Vltava is lined in both directions with *fin-de-siècle* apartment houses. Two blocks south, in Palackeho náměstí, is Stanislav Sucharda's extraordinary **monument to František Palacký** – an Art-Nouveau swarm of haunted bronze figures around a stodgy statue of the 19th century historian and giant of the Czech National Revival.

Emmaus Monastery (Klášter Emauzy)

A block inland from Palackého náměstí, at Vyšehradská 49, is the Emmaus Monastery, originally named the Monastery of the Slavs (Klášter Na Slovanech). It was completed in 1372 for a Slavic order of Benedictines by order of Charles IV, who persuaded the pope to allow the Old Church Slavonic liturgy here, possibly in hopes of undermining the Orthodox Church in neighbouring Slavic states. These un-Roman Catholic beginnings probably saved it from later Hussite plundering. Spanish Benedictines later renamed it Emmaus.

The monastery's Gothic **St Mary Church** (Kostel Panny Marie) was damaged by Allied bombs in February 1945. Though recently restored, it wears its scars proudly instead of being prettified. A few ceiling frescoes are still visible. The asymmetrical spires, added in the 1960s, look vaguely out of place.

The church is now a chilly concert and exhibition venue, and is open to the public from 10 am to 5 pm except Mondays, for 10 Kč. It's definitely worth 5 Kč more to see the attached cloisters with their fine, faded original frescoes, salted with bits of pagan symbolism.

Across Vyšehradská is the 1739 **Church of St John of Nepomuk on the Rock** (Kostel sv Jana Nepomuckého na Skalce), one of the city's most beautiful Dientzenhofer churches. Just south on Na slupi is a large, peaceful **botanical garden**, open every day.

East of Charles Square

Though full of hospitals, the area east of Charles Square and the botanical garden has a few delights. Wedged between Žitná and Ječná is the 14th century **St Stephen Church** (Kostel sv Štěpána), with a 15th century tower, 17th and 18th century chapels, and a neo-Gothic facelift by Josef Mocker in the 1870s.

Behind it on Na Rybníčku is one Prague's three surviving round Romanesque chapels, the **Rotunda of St Longinus** (Rotunda sv Longina), built in the early 12th century. It's unfortunately closed to the public.

The most striking building in the quiet neighbourhood south of Ječná, and one of the city's finest non-church Baroque structures, is the **Villa Amerika** at Ke Karlovu 20. This 1720, French-style summer house designed by (you guessed it) Kilian Dientzenhofer is now a museum dedicated to the composer Antonín Dvořák, open from 10 am to 5 pm except Mondays.

Around the corner at Na bojišti 12 is the **U kalicha** (At the Chalice) pub. Here the hapless Švejk is arrested at the beginning of Jaroslav Hašek's comic novel of WW I, *The Good Soldier Švejk* (which Hašek cranked out in instalments from his own local pub). U kalicha is milking the connection, as you'll see from the German tour buses outside.

At the southern end of Ke Karlovu is a little church with a big name, **Church of the Assumption of the Virgin Mary & Charlemagne** (Kostel Nanebevzetí Panny Marie a Karla Velikého), founded by Charles IV in 1350 and modelled on Charlemagne's burial chapel in

Aachen. In the 16th century it acquired its fabulous ribbed vault, whose revolutionary unsupported span was attributed by some to witchcraft. The monastery buildings next door house a humdrum **Police Museum**.

Below the church you can find some of Nové Město's original fortifications, and look out at the Nusle Bridge (Nuselský most) leaping the valley of the Botič River to Vyšehrad, with six lanes of traffic on top and the metro inside.

VYŠEHRAD

Archaeologists know that the early Slavic tribes set up camp near Hradčany, but *mythical* Prague was born at Vyšehrad ('High Castle'), a crag above the Vltava south of the Botič River valley (or Nusle valley, after the suburb through which it runs).

According to legend, the wise chieftain Krok built a castle here in the 7th century. Libuše, the cleverest of his three daughters, prophesied that a great city would rise here. Taking as her king a ploughman named Přemysl, she founded *Praha* and the Přemyslid line of Czech rulers.

Vyšehrad may in fact have been settled as early as the 9th century. Boleslav II (972-999) may have lived here for a time. There was a fortified town by the mid-11th century. Vratislav II (1061-92) moved here from Hradčany, beefing up the walls, adding a castle, the St Lawrence Basilica, the Church of SS Peter & Paul and the Rotunda of St Martin. His successors stayed until 1140, when Vladislav II returned to Hradčany.

Vyšehrad then faded away until Charles IV, aware of its symbolic importance, repaired the walls and joined them to his new town, Nové Město. He built a small palace, and decreed that coronations of the Bohemian kings should begin with a procession from here to Hradčany.

Nearly everything was wiped out during the Hussite Wars. The hill remained a ruin – except for a township of artisans and traders – until after the Thirty Years' War, when Leopold I re-fortified it.

The Czech National Revival generated new interest, both scholarly and romantic, in Vyšehrad as a symbol of Czech history. Painters painted it, poets sang about the old days, Smetana set his opera *Libuše* here. Many fortifications were dismantled in 1866, and the parish graveyard was converted into a national memorial cemetery.

Since the 1920s the old fortress has been a quiet park, with splendid views of the Vltava valley and a spot in

Czech hearts. It's a great place to stroll, shake off the urban blues, and catch a bit of Prague's mythical flavour.

The Vyšehrad Complex

Orientation From Vyšehrad metro station, head west past the Palace of Culture (Palác Kultury) to the Tábor Gate (Táborská brána). Inside are the remains of another gate, the Špičká brána, a café, and the Leopoldova brána, most elegant of the fort's gates. The Táborská and Leopoldova were erected, and the Gothic Špičká pulled down, in the course of re-fortification after the Thirty Years' War.

A steeper entrance is up from the No 18 or 24 tram on Na slupi or the No 7 tram on Svobodova, through the

Top : Church of SS Peter & Paul, Vyšehrad (RN)
Bottom : Cubist architecture, Vyšehrad (RN)

1842 Brick Gate (Cihelná brána, also called Pražská or Vyšehradská brána). Check the fine views into the Nusle valley from the north-east bastion.

A more demanding route is up the long stairs from tram No 3 or 17 on the riverside drive, directly to Vyšehrad Cemetery.

Rotunda of St Martin (Rotunda Sv Martina) Vratislav II's little chapel is Prague's oldest standing building. In the 18th century it was used as a powder magazine. The door and frescoes date from a renovation about 1880.

Nearby are a 1714 plague column and the Baroque St Mary Chapel in the Ramparts (Kaple Panny Marie v hradbách), dating from about 1750, and behind them the remains of the 14th century Church of the Beheading of John the Baptist (Kostel Stětí sv Jana Křtitele).

Museum Upstairs in the former New Archdeaconry at K rotundě 10 is a small museum about Vyšehrad, good value at 5 Kč, open daily from 9.30 am to 5.30 pm. A good booklet about Vyšehrad's buildings costs 10 Kč.

The cluster of three stone phalli in the park across the road, made of a stone not found in this region, may have been part of a prehistoric sundial or solstice marker.

Vyšehrad Cemetery (Vyšehradský Hřbitov) For Czechs this may be the hill's main attraction. In the 1880s and 1890s the parish graveyard was made into a memorial cemetery for the cultural good and great of the land. For the real heroes, an elaborate pantheon called the Slavín (loosely, 'Hall of Fame'), designed by Antonín Wiehl, was added along the north side in 1894.

The Slavín's 50 or so graves and some 600 in the rest of the cemetery include those of Smetana and Dvořák, writers Karel Čapek, Jan Neruda and Božena Němcová, painter Alfons Mucha and sculptor Josef Myslbek; a directory of big names is at the entrance. Some of the most beautiful headstones bear names few foreigners will recognise. It's open daily from 8 am to 7 pm in summer and 9 am to 5 pm in winter.

The Prague Spring music festival kicks off each 12 May, the anniversary of Smetana's death, with a procession from his grave to the Obecní dům.

Church of SS Peter & Paul (Kostel Sv Petra a Pavla) Vratislav II's church has been built and rebuilt over the centuries, culminating in neo-Gothic work-over by Josef Mocker in the 1880s. The towers were added in

1903, and most of its interior frescoes only in the 1920s. The only way to get beyond the entrance is probably to attend 9 am Sunday Mass, since archaeologists are still taking the place apart.

South of the church are the Vyšehrad Gardens (Vyšehradské sady), with four sculptures by Josef Myslbek, based on Czech legends. Libuše and Přemysl are in the north-west corner; in the south-east are Šárka and Ctirad. Šárka, one of a renegade army of women who fled across the Vltava after Libuše's death, was chosen as a decoy to trap Ctirad, captain of the men's army. Unfortunately she fell in love with him, and after her cohorts had done him in, she threw herself into the Šárka Valley in remorse (see North-West Outskirts later in this chapter). The women were slaughtered by the men of Hradčany in a final battle.

Casemates (Kasematy) Within Vyšehrad's ramparts are many vaulted casemates. At the Brick Gate, 5 Kč will buy you a guided tour through several of these chambers, now used for exhibitions and for storage of some original statues from the Charles Bridge (others are at the Lapidárium in Holešovice).

Other Attractions For a few crowns you can look at the foundations of the 11th century Romanesque **St Lawrence Basilica** (Bazilika sv Vavřince). Ask for the key in the snack bar by the Old Archdeaconry.

In front of the south-west bastion are the foundations of a small **palace** built by Charles IV, dismantled in 1655. Perched on the bastion is the **Galerie Vyšehrad**, with temporary exhibitions, open from 9.30 am to 5.30 pm except Mondays. Below the bastion are some ruined guard towers poetically named **'Libuše's Bath'**.

In the north-west corner, in the former **New Provost's House** (Nové proboštsví, 1874), you can catch a concert every Sunday at 3.30 pm in the high season (except July and August), ranging from jazz to chamber music.

Places to Eat There are mediocre *cafés* inside the Tábor Gate and by the St Lawrence Basilica. Marginally better is the *Warsteiner* 'snack bar' at the west end of the Palace of Culture, with pricey salads, light meals and beer.

Cubist Architecture

If you've taken the trouble to come out to Vyšehrad, don't miss a clutch of Prague's famous Cubist buildings in the streets north of the Brick Gate. Cubist architecture, with its eye-catching use of elementary geometric forms, is more or less unique to the Czech Republic, particularly Prague.

Best of the lot is a simple, striking façade by the dean of Czech Cubist architects, Josef Chochol, at Neklanova 30. Others by Chochol are at Libušina 3, and a villa on Rašínovo nábřeží, just before it tunnels beneath Vyšehrad rock. All date from around 1913. Other works by lesser lights are spotted around the neighbourhood.

HOLEŠOVICE

This patch of Prague in the Vltava's 'big bend' sprang from two old settlements, Holešovice and the fishing village of Bubny. Both remained small until the arrival of industry in the mid-19th century, along with the Hlávkův Bridge (1868) linking the area to Nové Město, a horse-drawn tram line, a river port and the Fairgrounds. The area became a part of Prague in 1884.

Fairgrounds (Výstaviště)

This vast exhibition area is the venue for spring and autumn fairs, when it's full of rides, candy floss and half of Prague having fun. Some older buildings, such as the Prague Pavilion (Pavilón hlavního města Prahy), which houses the Lapidárium, and the Palace of Industry (Průmuslový palác) were built for the 1891 Terrestrial Jubilee Exposition.

It's a popular weekend destination, if only for a sausage, a beer and some *dechovka* (Bohemian brass-band music). There is a 20-Kč admission charge in the warm months if the **Křižík Fountain** (Křižíkova fontána) is doing its thing – an hourly display to recorded music, Tuesday to Friday from 6 to 9 pm, weekends from 3 to 9 pm. It's best after sunset, all lit up with coloured lights.

Malá scéna is a children's theatre with regular weekend performances. **Laterna Animata** is a multimedia show similar to the Laterna Magika, with one performance nightly. The **Maroldovo Panorama** is an impressive 360° diorama of the Battle of Lipany in 1434, which the Hussites lost to imperial Catholic forces; it's open Tuesday to Friday from 1 to 5.30 pm, weekends from 10 am.

The **Lapidárium** is a repository of some 400 sculptures from the 11th to the 19th centuries, removed from Prague's streets and buildings to save them from demolition or pollution. They include bits of the Old Town Square's Marian column torn down by a mob in 1918, and several of Charles Bridge's original statues. It's open Tuesday to Friday from noon to 6 pm, weekends from 10 am to noon and 1 to 6 pm.

Get to the Fairgrounds on tram No 12 from Nádraží Holešovice metro station to the Výstaviště stop.

Stromovka Park

At over one million sq meters, Stromovka Park to the west of the Fairgrounds is Prague's largest park. In the Middle Ages it was a royal hunting preserve, and is sometimes referred to as Královská obora, the Royal Deer Park. Rudolf II had rare trees planted and several lakes dug (fed from the Vltava by a canal that still functions). You can cross the Vltava via Císařský ostrov.

Hanavský pavilón, Letná Gardens (RN)

Stromovka Park has a **Planetarium**, open Monday to Thursday from 8 am to noon and 1 to 6 pm, Friday from 8 to noon, weekends from 9.30 am to 5 pm, though it's not as good as the Štefánik Observatory on Petřín Hill.

National Technology Museum (Národní Technické Muzeum)

This good museum has a transport exhibit including airplanes, locomotives, Czech Škoda and Tatra cars from the 1920s and 1930s, and an impressive motorbike collection. You can take a tour down a mineshaft, or learn about photography, astronomy or timepieces. The museum, at Kostelní 42, is open Tuesday to Sunday from 9 am to 5 pm. From Vltavská metro station, take tram No 1 or 25 four stops to Letenské náměstí and walk down Nad štolou and Muzejní streets.

Letná

Letná is a vast open area above the Vltava between Hradčany and Holešovice, with an assembly area to the north and a park, the **Letná Gardens** (Letenské sady), to the south, and postcard views of the city and its Vltava bridges. In 1261 Přemysl Otakar II held his coronation celebrations here.

The present layout dates from the early 1950s, when a 30-metre-high, 14,000 tonne statue of Stalin, the biggest monument to the man in the Eastern bloc, was erected here by the Czechoslovak Communist party, only to be blown up in 1962 by the same sycophants when Stalin was no longer flavour of the decade. Today in its place stands a peculiar **giant metronome** sponsored by the Kotva department store. Skateboarders enjoy the area.

Letná used to be the site of May Day military parades similar to those in Moscow. In late 1989, some 750,000 people demonstrated here in support of what became known as the 'Velvet Revolution'. In 1990 Pope John Paul II said an open-air Mass here to over a million people.

The Hanavský pavilón in the south-western corner is a charming but pricey Art-Nouveau restaurant built by Otto Prieser for the 1891 Terrestrial Jubilee Exposition.

SMÍCHOV

Smíchov became part of Prague in 1838 as the suburb grew into an industrial quarter full of chimney stacks, railway yards and a large brewery known for the popular Staropramen beer.

Kinský Gardens (Zahrada Kinských)

In these peaceful gardens on the south side of Petřín Hill is an 18th century wooden church, the **Church of St Michael** (Kostel sv Michala), transferred here, log by log, from the village of Medveďov in Ukraine. Such structures are rare in Bohemia, though still common in Ukraine and north-eastern Slovakia.

The Pink Tank (Růžový Tank)

Smíchov meets Malá Strana at náměstí Kinských, formerly náměstí Sovětských tankistů (Square of Soviet Tank Drivers) in memory of Soviet soldiers who marched into Prague on 9 May 1945. Here stood tank No 23, allegedly the first to enter the city under General Lelyushenko (in fact the general had no such JS1 heavy tanks, and this one was a later donation to the city).

In 1991, artist David Černý decided that the tank, being a weapon of destruction, was an inappropriate monument to the Soviet soldiers, and painted it pink. The authorities had it painted green again, and charged Černý with a crime against the state. This infuriated many parliamentarians, and 12 of them painted the tank pink again. Their parliamentary immunity saved them from arrest and secured the release of Černý.

After complaints from the Soviet Union, the tank was removed. Only a grassy patch remains, where each 9 May a few diehard Communists celebrate their Liberation Day.

Bertramka

Mozart stayed at this elegant 17th century villa during his visits to Prague in 1787 and 1791, as guest of composer František Dušek. Here he finished his opera *Don Giovanni*. Today the house, at Mozartova 169, is a modest Mozart museum (☎ 54 38 93). Summer concerts and other events are also held here. It's open daily from 9.30 am to 6 pm, for 50 Kč. Take tram No 4, 7 or 9 from Anděl metro station.

TROJA

Facing the Vltava north of the 'big bend' is **Troja Castle** (Trojský zámek), a 17th century Baroque chateau with a mob of stone giants on the balustrade above its French gardens. On the walls and ceiling of the main hall is a vast, sycophantic mural depicting the Habsburgs in full transcendental glory. The chateau houses part of the

National Gallery's collection of 19th century Czech paintings. It's open from 10 am to 6 pm (gardens to 7 pm) except Mondays.

Across the road is the city **zoo**, on 60 hectares of wooded, hillside grounds. You may find the 2300 flea-bitten creatures depressing, but kids love them. Pride of place, at the top of the hill, goes to a herd of Przewalski's horses, little steppe-dwellers that still survive in the wilds of Mongolia and are successfully bred here. A rackety funicular climbs the hill for a few crowns in the summer. The zoo is open from 9 am to 6 pm every day. Outside the entrance are a restaurant (open to 10 pm) and an outdoor beer hall.

It's a short walk north to a branch of Prague's **botanical gardens**, open from 9 am to 6 pm daily, from April through October.

To get to Troja, take bus No 112 from Nádraží Holešovice metro station. Or, in summer (except Mondays), take the boat: excursions leave the pier by Palackého most at 9.30 am and 1.30 pm (Troja is the final stop) and return at 12.15 and 6.15 pm. The round trip is 20 Kč.

VINOHRADY

Vinohrady is south-east of the National Museum and main train station. The name refers to vineyards that grew here centuries ago; even 200 years ago there were few signs of urbanisation.

Náměstí Míru

Vinohrady's physical and commercial heart is náměstí Míru (Peace Square), dominated by the brick neo-Gothic **St Ludmilla Church** (Kostel sv Ludmily). Right behind

Vinohrady Theatre (RN)

it at No 9 is the neo-Renaissance **National House** (Národní dům, also called the Kulturní dům), with exhibit and concert halls and a good restaurant. On the north side of the square is the 1909 **Vinohrady Theatre** (Divadlo na Vinohradech), a popular drama theatre.

Though relatively close to the centre of Prague, the tree-shaded neighbourhood south from the square to Havlíčkovy sady, with genteel, turn-of-the-century mansions in every 'neo' style, makes a peaceful stroll.

Church of the Most Sacred Heart of Our Lord (Kostel Nejsvětějšího Srdce Páně)

With its perforated brickwork, outsize clock tower and ultra-simple interior, this is probably Prague's most original church, brash and lovely at the same time. Completed in 1932, it is the work of Josef Plečnik, the Slovenian architect who also raised a few eyebrows with his additions to Prague Castle. It's in náměstí Jiřího z Poděbrad, by the metro station of the same name.

St Wenceslas Church (Kostel Sv Václava)

Another surprise from the same period is Josef Gočár's 1930 Constructivist church, with its fragile-looking tower, climbing a hillside at náměstí Svatopluka Čecha (take tram No 4 or 22 from Karlovo náměstí, or walk the 800 metres east from Havlíčkovy sady).

ŽIŽKOV

Named for the one-eyed Hussite hero, General Jan Žižka, who whipped Emperor Sigismund of Luxembourg and his army on a hill here in 1420, Žižkov has always been a rough-and-ready neighbourhood, working-class and full of revolutionary fizz well before 1948. But the turn-of-the-century streets near the centre are now run-down and depressing. There's little for visitors except views from Žižkov Hill and Prague's futuristic TV Tower, and several melancholy cemeteries.

Žižkov (or Vítkov) Hill

The famous battle of 1420 took place on this long mound separating the Žižkov and Karlín districts. From beside the colossal 1950 equestrian statue of the general you can enjoy superior views across Staré Město to Prague Castle.

Behind you is the grandiose **National Memorial** (Národní památnik), completed around 1930 as a memorial to the Czechoslovak 'unknown soldier' but hijacked as a mausoleum for the Communist leader Klement Gottwald (whose body, mummified Lenin-style, is said to have been mostly latex by the time it was finally put in the ground). The memorial is now closed, weedy and neglected.

From Florenc or the main train station, walk along Husitská; after the first railway bridge, climb to the left up U památníku. Battle freaks may enjoy the **Military Museum** on the way up.

TV Tower (Televizní Věž)

Prague's tallest, ugliest landmark is the 216-metre TV Tower, erected in the 1970s. For 30 Kč you can ride a high-speed elevator up for views right out past the edges of the city. But you're actually *too* high to see the city skyline or much detail, so it's a bit of a disappointment.

The tower was built on the site of a **Jewish cemetery** that operated until 1890, after Josefov's was shut. What's left of the cemetery is just north of the tower. The area is called Mahlerovy sady (Mahler Park), though there are few things growing.

The tower's viewing area is open from 10 am to midnight, and the Restaurace Bohemia (at 63 metres) from 11 am to midnight. It's a few blocks north-east of the Jirího z Poděbrad metro station.

Olšany Cemetery & the Grave of Jan Palach

Jan Palach, the university student who set himself on fire in January 1969 after the Soviet invasion, was buried in Olšany Cemetery (Olšanské hřbitovy), Prague's main cemetery. When his grave became a focus for demonstrations, the remains were moved in 1974 to his home village, but were re-interred here in 1990.

The cemetery was founded in 1680 during a plague epidemic. Its oldest stones are in the north-west corner, near the 17th century **St Roch Chapel** (Kaple sv Rocha).

From Flora metro station, walk east on Vinohradská to the central entrance. Turn right and walk about 50 metres to Palach's grave. The cemetery is open from 8 am to 7 pm from May through September, to 6 pm in March and April, and from 9 am to 4 pm in winter.

New Jewish Cemetery

Franz Kafka is buried in this sad, overgrown graveyard, opened around 1890 when the previous Jewish cemetery – now at the foot of the TV Tower – was closed. The entrance is beside Želivského metro station, and the grave of Kafka and his parents is to the right, about two-thirds of the way along the front wall. Men should cover their heads (a handkerchief will do). The cemetery is closed on Fridays and Saturdays.

NORTH-WEST OUTSKIRTS

This area stretches from eastern Dejvice out to the vast, ugly housing estates in the north. It also takes in the green Šárka valley, the great battleground at Bílá hora (White Mountain), the Star Summer Palace and Břevnov Monastery.

Dejvice

Near the northern edge of Hradčany, at Mickiewiczova 1, is the striking **Bílkova Villa**, designed by the sculptor František Bílek in 1911 as his own home, and now a museum of his own unconventional stone and wood reliefs, religious works, drawings, ceramics and souvenirs. The villa is open Tuesday to Sunday from 10 am to 6 pm between 15 May and 15 October. Take tram No 18 one stop from Hradčanská metro station to Chotkovy sady.

Nearby at Tychonova ulice 4-6 are two houses designed by the Cubist architect **Josef Gočár** as his home.

In the north of Dejvice, the unusual villa suburb of **Baba** was a 1933-40 project by a team of Cubist artists and designers to build cheap, attractive single-family houses. A similar project was the **Hanspaulka** suburb to the south, built in 1925-30.

Šárka Valley

This valley of the Šárecký potok (Šárka stream) is one of Prague's best known and most valuable nature parks. It's named after the female warrior Šárka, who threw herself off a cliff here (see the earlier Vyšehrad section for more about this sad legend).

The most attractive area is among the rugged cliffs at **Divoká Šárka**, near the Džban Reservoir where the Šárka stream originates. You can swim in the reservoir.

It's about seven km, along the red-marked trail, from the terminus of the No 2 or 26 tram (from Dejvická metro station) to the suburb of Baba, where the Šárka stream empties into the Vltava. No matter where you stop along the valley, you can find a bus to get you back to central Prague.

White Mountain (Bílá Hora)

The 381-metre White Mountain, on the western outskirts of Prague, was the site of the 1620 Protestant defeat that ended Czech independence for almost 300 years. The

TV Tower (JK)

Top : Olšany Cemetery (RN)
Bottom : Grave of Jan Palach (JK)

only reminder today is a small monument in the middle of the field. Take tram No 8 from Hradčanská metro station or tram No 22 from Malostranská metro station, to the end of the line.

Star Summer Palace (Letohrádek Hvězda)

In 1530 Ferdinand I established a hunting reserve on a verdant hill east of the White Mountain. In 1556 one Archduke Ferdinand of Tyrol built a Renaissance summer palace here in the shape of a six-pointed star.

Inside is a museum dedicated to two leading lights of the Czech National Revival: Alois Jirásek (1851-1930), who wrote powerful stories based on Czech legends, and the artist Mikuláš Aleš (1852-1913). It's open Tuesday to Sunday from 10 am to 5 pm. Take the same trams as for the White Mountain, to the second-last stop, Malý Břevnov, past the petrol station on the right.

Břevnov Monastery (Břevnovský Klášter)

This is the oldest Benedictine monastery in the Czech Republic, established in 993 by Boleslav II and Bishop St Vojtěch Slavníkovec. The two men, from opposing and powerful families intent on dominating Bohemia, met at Vojtěška spring, each having had a dream that this was the place to establish a monastery. The name of the monastery comes from *břevno* (beam), for the beam laid across the spring where they met.

In 1993, the 1000th anniversary of the monastery's founding, the restored 1st floor, with its fine ceiling frescoes, and the crypt with the original foundations and a few skeletons were opened to the public for the first time. Restoration work is continuing. The monastery was a secret-police archive until 1990. It may not stay open; check with PIS.

The present monastery building and the nearby Baroque **Church of St Margaret** (Kostel sv Markéty) were completed in 1720 by Kristof Dientzenhofer.

Jan Patočka (1907-77), a leading figure of the Charter 77 movement, is buried in the **cemetery** behind the monastery. He died after interrogation by the secret police.

The best time to visit is from 10 am to 2 pm; at other times it may be closed for services. Take the same trams as for the White Mountain, but get off a few stops earlier at the Břevnovský klášter stop.

SOUTH-WEST OUTSKIRTS

This part of Prague has few accessible tourist sights, though the **Barrandov Cliffs** (Barrandovské skály) are a unique geological formation, named after the French geologist Joachim Barranda who explored the area. Nearby are the well-known Barrandov film studios.

Good for a pleasant hike are the scenic **Prokopské** and **Dalejské valleys** *(údolí)*, along the Dalejský potok between the suburbs of Hlubočepy and Jinonice. The eight-km trail starts from near the corner of Novoveská and Pod Vavřincem in southern Jinonice (from Jinonice metro station, take bus 130, 149 or 508 one stop to Sídliště Jinonice). It ends at Haladova Garden in Hlubočepy, from where you can catch bus No 104 or 120 from Hlubočepská to Smíchovské nádraží metro station.

Zbraslav

This town 10 km south of Prague was only incorporated into greater Prague recently, but the area was in use by 1268 when Přemysl Otakar II established a hunting lodge and a chapel here, later to be rebuilt as a Cistercian monastery. In 1784 the monastery was turned into a **castle** that today houses what may be the republic's best museum of 19th and 20th century Czech sculpture.

Enter its garden from Zbraslavské náměstí. The ground floor has exhibits of 19th century sculpture, including a large collection by Josef Myslbek, the country's leading sculptor at the turn of this century.

The museum is open Tuesday to Sunday from 10 am to 6 pm. Take bus No 129, 241, 243 or 255 from Smíchovské nádraží metro station.

SOUTH-EAST OUTSKIRTS

Several huge, unkempt woodlands lie at the edges of the city. One of the biggest is **Michelský les** and adjoining **Kunratický les**, straight out of Roztyly metro station. Michelský les has a mini-zoo and a snack bar with beer and sausages.

NORTH-EAST OUTSKIRTS

Out on the north-east edge of the city you can take a close look at a Russian MiG fighter plane. The **Museum of Aircraft & Space Exploration** (Muzeum letectví a kosmonautiky, ☎ 82 47 09), on Mladoboleslavská in the Kbely district (Prague 9), has a host of exhibits on aeronautics and space flight, including the exploits of

Church of St Margaret, Břevnov Monastery (RN)

Russian cosmonauts. It's open from 9.30 am to 4.30 pm except Mondays. Take bus No 185 or 259 from the Českomoravská metro station (end of the B line).

THE ISLANDS OF PRAGUE

Except for Kampa, Prague's Vltava islands are minor attractions but they make relaxing getaways.

Over the centuries islands appeared and disappeared as the Vltava deposited silt or washed it away. Today there are eight of them; since the river was dammed they have remained fairly stable. The remains of two others, Libeňský and Bohanský, between Holešovice and Libeň, are now joined to the mainland by industrial development.

Veslařský ostrov (Regatta Island), south of Vyšehrad, has been around since 1420. Once owned by (and named for) a wealthy German prince, the Communists renamed it in 1952. Today it has a sports ground and some club halls.

Císařská louka (Imperial Meadow) opposite Vyšehrad is a favourite place for picnics. It was once a royal playground (Wenceslas II held his coronation celebrations here), and in the 19th century gold was panned here. On the northern tip is a campsite with a majestic view of Vyšehrad.

Dětský ostrov, just north of Jiráskův most, is the smallest island. The name means Children's Island, and it includes a children's playground. It first appeared in 1355 and has disappeared and reappeared several times since.

Slovanský ostrov, south of the National Theatre, is the 'youngest' of the islands, first mentioned in 1610. Its banks were reinforced with stone in 1784. A spa and a dye works were established in the early 19th century. In 1841 Bohemia's first train had a demonstration run here, roaring down the island at 11 km/h. In 1925 it got its present name, which means Slav Island, after Slav conventions held here since 1848.

On a wharf facing the river is a café, from where you can tootle around between the two Vltava weirs for 45 minutes in a 12-seat cruise boat for 85 Kč, if there are enough people to fill it. If it's solitude you want, cross the island and hire a pedal-boat for about US$3 an hour, or a rowing boat for half that.

In the middle of the island is a 19th century meeting hall. At the south end is Šitovská věž, a 15th century water tower (once part of a mill) with an 18th century onion-dome roof.

Střelecký ostrov is crossed by Most Legií. The name means Shooting Island, from its 16th century use by the Prague garrison as a cannon and rifle target. Each summer a drama festival is held here.

Kampa lies off Malá Strana, across the Čertovka channel. It's the only island formed artificially, when ditches were dug to get the Vltava to run millwheels. Kampa was settled during the 16th century after it had been raised above flood levels. In 1939 the river was so low that Kampa was again joined to the mainland, and many coins and jewellery were found in the channel. For more on Kampa, see the earlier section on Malá Strana.

Ostrov Štvanice, between Holešovice and Karlín, was first mentioned in 1118. The name means Chase Island, for a wooden corral where Prague's citizens were once entertained by bull, bear and boar chases. Czechoslovakia's first artificial ice-skating rink in was built here in 1930-32. The Prague Tennis Open is held annually on the courts here, and the Davis Cup has also been played here. Beneath Hlávkův most, the bridge linking the island to Nové Město, are river locks through which excursion boats pass now and then. Take tram No 3 from Wenceslas Square.

Císařský ostrov, between Troja and Bubeneč, is the northernmost island and the largest, 1250 metres long. The name, Imperial Island, refers to an imperial pheasantry kept here by Rudolf II. There are no attractions now.

MUSEUMS & GALLERIES

If you're pursuing special interests, the following listings of museums and galleries will help you on your way.

Museums

Museum admission charges are typically 15 to 20 Kč, except where noted. Often youth, student and senior discounts are available for the asking.

Dvořák Museum, Villa Amerika, Ke Karlovu 20, Nové Město (☎ 29 82 14) – 10 am to 5 pm except Monday

Kafka Exhibition, corner Maislova and Old Town Square – Tuesday to Friday from 10 am to 6 pm, Saturday to 5 pm, closed Sunday and Monday

Komenský (Comenius) Museum, Wallenstein Palace, Valdštejnské náměstí, Malá Strana – 10 am to noon and 1 to 5 pm

Lapidárium, Výstaviště (Fairgrounds), Holešovice – Tuesday to Friday from noon to 6 pm, weekends from 10 am to noon and 1 to 6 pm

Military Museum (history from WW I), U památníku 2, Žižkov – 8.30 am to 5 pm except Monday

Mozart Museum at Bertramka, Mozartova 2/169, Smíchov (☎ 54 38 93) – daily from 9.30 am to 6 pm; 50 Kč

Museum of Czech History (until 1848), Lobkovic Palace, Jiřská 3, Prague Castle – 9 am to 4.30 pm except Monday

Museum of Czech Literature, Strahov Monastery, Hradčany – 9 am to 12.30 pm and 1 to 5 pm except Monday

Museum of Decorative Arts, 17.listopadu 2, Josefov – 10 am to 6 pm except Mondays and holidays; 10 Kč

Museum of Military History (pre-WW I), Schwarzenberg Palace, Hradčanské náměstí 2, Hradčany – 9.30 am to 4.30 pm except Monday

Museum of Musical Instruments, Lázeňská 2 (near Maltézské náměstí), Malá Strana (☎ 53 08 43)
Museum of Physical Education & Sport, Tyršův dům, Újezd 40, Malá Strana – 9 am to 5 pm except Monday
Museum of the City of Prague, Na poříčí 52, Prague 3 – 10 am to 6 pm except Monday; 10 Kč
Náprstek Museum of Asian, African & American Cultures, Betlémské náměstí, Prague 1 – 9 am to noon and 12.45 to 5.30 pm except Monday
National Museum, Wenceslas Square 68 – 9 am to 5 pm except Tuesday (Monday and Friday to 4 pm), free on the first Monday of each month
National Technology Museum, Kostelní 42, Holešovice – 9 am to 5 pm except Monday
Postage Stamp Museum, Nové mlýny 2, Nové Město – 9 am to 5 pm except Monday
Smetana Museum, Novotného lávka 1, Staré Město (☎ 26 53 71) – 10 am to 5 pm except Tuesday
State Jewish Museum (Old Jewish Cemetery, synagogues and other buildings in Josefov) – 9.30 am to 6 pm except Saturday; 30 Kč ticket at High Synagogue for that and Old-New Synagogue, 80 Kč ticket at Klaus Synagogue for that, cemetery and Maisel and Pinkas synagogues
Vyšehrad Museum, K rotundě 10, Vyšehrad – 9.30 am to 5.30 pm daily; 5 Kč

State-Run Galleries

National Gallery venues cost about 40 Kč, though at least some (eg St Agnes) are only 10 Kč for students, and free to all on the first Sunday of each month.

City Library, Mariánské náměstí – occasional exhibitions of contemporary Czech art
National Gallery, changing exhibitions: Kinský Palace, Old Town Square 12, Staré Město (☎ 231 51 35); Rudolfinum, Jan Palach Square, Josefov; Riding School, U Prašného mostu 55, Prague Castle; in addition, some of the permanent venues (see next entry) also have exhibition halls
National Gallery, permanent collections, all 10 am to 6 pm except Monday. The main collection is at the Šternberk Palace, Hradčanské náměstí 15, Hradčany (☎ 35 24 41) – 14th to 20th century (and especially 19th and 20th century) European art. Others are at the Convent of St Agnes, U milosrdných 17, Staré Město (☎ 231 42 51 ext 47) – 19th century Czech painting and sculpture; the Convent of St George, Prague Castle (☎ 53 52 46 ext 11) – Czech Gothic and Renaissance art; and Zbraslav Castle, Zbraslav – 19th and 20th century Czech sculpture
Prague Municipal Gallery. Venues include the House at the Stone Bell, Old Town Square 13 (☎ 231 02 72); Old Town Hall on Old Town Square; and Troja Castle (19th century Czech painting), Troja, 10 am to 6 pm except Monday

Private Galleries

These include both exhibition and sales galleries. Some may close for weeks at a time, so call ahead to the more remote ones. Lots of other small galleries come and go.

Behémot Gallery, Elišky Krásnohorské 6, Josefov (☎ 231 78 29) – 10 am to 6 pm daily, Czech avant-garde art

Central Bohemian Gallery and Central European Gallery, Husova 19-21, Staré Město (☎ 236 07 00); and associated Centre for Czech Graphic Art, Husova 10 (☎ 232 79 40) – all open from 10 am to 6 pm daily

Gambra Surrealist Gallery, Černinská 5, Hradčany – noon to 6 pm except Monday and Tuesday

Hollar Gallery, Smetanovo nábřeží 6, Staré Město – 10 am to 1 pm and 2 to 6 pm except Monday, contemporary Czech graphics

Jednorožec s Harfou (Unicorn with a Harp), Průchodní 4, Staré Město – 11 am to 10 pm daily, art by the physically and mentally disabled

Karolinum, Ovocný trh 3, Staré Město – 10 am to 6 pm except Monday

Loreto Gallery, Loretánská 23, Hradčany – 10 am to 6 pm daily

MXM Gallery, Nosticova 6, Malá Strana (☎ 53 15 64) – noon to 6 pm except Monday

Mánes Gallery, Masarykovo nábřeží 250, Nové Město (☎ 29 55 77) – 10 am to 6 pm except Monday, contemporary Czech art

Nová síň, Voršilská 3, Nové Město – 10 am to 1 pm and 2 to 6 pm except Monday, contemporary Czech art

Pallas Gallery, Náprstkova 10, Staré Město (☎ 26 08 15) – 10 am to 6 pm daily, 20th century Czech art

Prague House of Photography, Husova 23, Staré Město (☎ 22 93 49) – 11 am to 6 pm daily

Topič Salon, Národní 9 (☎ 232 09 24, ext 214) – contemporary art

U prstenu Gallery, Jilská 14, Staré Město (☎ 26 28 58) – 11 am to 6 pm daily, 'Grotesque Humour and Fantastic Art'

Václav Špála Gallery, Národní 30 (☎ 22 47 09) – 10 am to 1 pm and 2 to 6 pm except Monday, contemporary Czech art

Via Art Gallery, Resslova 6, Nové Město (☎ 29 25 70) – 11 am to 5 pm except Monday

National Theatre (RN)

PRAGUE WALKS

Walk 1: The Royal Way (Královská Cesta)

(To start this walk, refer to the Staré Město & Josefov map.)
The Royal Way is the ancient coronation route to Prague Castle. The part of it through Staré Město and Malá Strana takes you past some of the city's most inspiring sights. From Wenceslas Square, walk up Na příkopě to náměstí Republiky, from where this tour starts.

Facing náměstí Republiky is the Art-Nouveau façade of Prague's most delicious building, the Municipal House (Obecní dům, 86, pp 156-157). It also has several good restaurants, a rip-roaring club, and a pub (see the Places to Eat and Entertainment chapters). Next door, swathed in scaffolding as it has been for years, is the 15th century Powder Tower (Prašná brána, 87, p 156).

Go under the tower and west into Celetná. On the corner with Ovocný trh, the Old Fruit Market, is one of the earliest Cubist façades in a city famous for Cubist façades, on the House at the Black Madonna (96, p 156). Westwards towards Old Town Square, Celetná is a virtual open-air museum of pastel Baroque façades.

But backtrack a bit and turn off the Royal Way, north into Králodvorská. This area, the Králův dvůr or Royal Court, was once a royal stables. On U Obecního domu is the Art-Nouveau Hotel Paříž, built in 1907 and recently restored.

Just before reaching the Kotva department store, turn left into Jakubská. At the west end of Jakubská, facing Malá Štupartská, is St James Church (71, pp 152-154), famous for its pipe organ and acoustics. The entire block across from the church was once a medieval inn, the Týn Court (69, p 152). Turn right and go around it by way of the quiet Týnská passage.

Admire the beautiful north door of the Týn Church (67, p 152) and turn left behind it to emerge back into Celetná and the Royal Way. Pass No 3, Franz Kafka's boyhood home from 1896 to 1907, and No 2, where his family lived in 1888-89, and you're in Old Town Square (pp 144-152). See Walk 2 for a tour round the square.

Left and beyond the Old Town Hall tower, the corner building covered in Renaissance sgraffito is the Dům U minuty (62, p 146), another Kafka house. Beyond this is Little Square (Malé náměstí), with a Renaissance fountain and some fine Baroque and neo-Renaissance façades.

Bear left, then right, into Karlova. At No 18 is the House at the Golden Snake (119, p 155), site of Prague's first coffee house. From here, all along the right side of Karlova, is the Klementinum (59, pp 154-155), once a Jesuit college and now part of the Czech National Library. Along the wall are three churches: the Orthodox St Clement Church, the little Assumption Chapel and the grand Church of the Holy Saviour, facing the Vltava; see p 154 for more on these churches.

You're now looking at the Old Town tower of Charles Bridge (pp 139-144). Cross the bridge, through the crowds of tourists, hawkers and pickpockets and the rows of Baroque statues, and drink in the views of Prague Castle.

(From here on, refer to the Hradčany & Malá Strana map.)

The western end of Charles Bridge crosses Kampa island (p 131, 193), separated from Malá Strana by the Čertovka channel. Just before the Malá Strana bridge towers, look right to the hotel and restaurant U tří pštrosů, one of Prague's more luxurious establishments; the 16th century house still has traces of its painted façade.

Walk beneath the towers and you're in Mostecká. The upper façades of some of the houses are worth noting, especially the Rococo Kounický Palace at No 277, now the Yugoslav Embassy.

At the top of Mostecká is Malostranské náměstí, bisected by trams and centred on one of Prague's finest Baroque structures, St Nicholas Church (58, p 127). Detour south to see Prague's most famous religious icon, the *Infant of Prague*, in the Church of Our Lady Victorious on Karmelitská (97, p 130).

Return and cross the square to Nerudova, one of Prague's most picturesque streets, named after the poet Jan Neruda, who lived in the House of Two Suns (42). On many of the street's mostly Baroque façades are colourful emblems that have given these buildings their popular names. On the right at No 2 is the House of the Cat *(kocoura)*, now a restaurant (49). At No 4 is the House at the Golden Anchor, which proudly displays its emblem: the devil's head. At No 6 is the House at the Red Eagle, with a richly decorated entrance above which two angels hold a painting of a red eagle.

Continue along Úvoz to the Strahov Monastery (34, pp 124-125), and return via Loretánská to Hradčanské náměstí (alternatively, short-cut up Nerudova on Ke Hradu). Facing the square is the entrance to Prague Castle. Before entering, admire the magnificent view of the city from the corner of the square. On your right is Petřín Hill, below you the rooftops of Malá Strana. Looking across the Vltava to Staré Město, it is easy to see why Czechs call Prague the 'city of 100 spires'. For a description of the castle, see pp 110-122.

Walk 2: Wenceslas Square To Old Town Square

(To start this walk, refer to the Southern Nové Město map.)
This tour starts at Prague's most media-famous landmark, the equestrian statue of St Wenceslas, the 10th century 'good King Wenceslas' of the Christmas carol (87, p 170). Just below it is a modest memorial to those who died for their resistance to Communism, including Jan Palach (88, p 170). Looming above the statue is the neo-Renaissance National Museum (86, p 167).

Below the statue stretches Wenceslas Square (pp 167-170), a focal point of Czech history since the 19th century. In 1918 the new Czechoslovak Republic was celebrated here, and on 24 November 1989 the obituary of Czech Communism was pronounced by Alexander Dubček and Václav Havel from the balcony of the Melantrich building at No 36, on the west side (74). Among the square's turn-of-the-century buildings, the finest is probably the 1906 Art-Nouveau Grand Hotel Evropa at No 25 (27).

Two-thirds of the way down, Jindřišská ulice, a major tram thoroughfare, enters from the east. Visible at the end of the street is the Jindřišská Tower (19, p 166), a 15th century watchtower.

At the bottom of Wenceslas Square is the 'Golden Cross', the intersection with Na příkopě, one of the city's premier shopping streets; it marks part of the ancient ditch around Staré Město, the Old Town.

Take a little detour, west from the intersection, around the metro entrance to Jungmannovo náměstí and the beautiful 14th century Church of Our Lady of the Snows (37, p 171). By its Gothic north door is a bizarre Cubist street lamp.

(From here on, refer to the Staré Město & Josefov map.)

Back at the 'Golden Cross', the onward extension of Wenceslas Square is Na můstku, where a footbridge once crossed the moat into Staré Město. A block along at No 7 is the American Hospitality Center (147), a cheerful source of maps, books and advice.

Na můstku ends at Rytířská, and a one-block detour eastward takes you to Prague's oldest theatre and finest neo-Classical building, the Tyl or Estates Theatre (93, p 161), where Mozart's opera *Don Giovanni* premiered in

Buildings (RN)

Buildings (RN)

1787. Next door is the Karolinum (94, pp 159-161), birthplace of central Europe's oldest university.

Na můstku then crosses Prague's most central open-air market on Havelská (p 159). Now squeeze on into Melantrichova. If you're feeling peckish, pause at Prague's primo vegetarian stand-up eatery, *Country Life*, at No 15 (105).

Then emerge into pastel-painted Old Town Square (pp 144-152) and join the crowd waiting for the hourly performance of the Astronomical Clock (pp 150-151) on the 14th century Old Town Hall (63, p 146); climb the tower for postcard views of the city. Just to your right is the best source of general tourist information and help, the Prague Information Service (PIS).

The square's centrepiece is the Art-Nouveau bronze Statue of Jan Hus (64). Across to the right (east) is the spiky-topped Gothic Týn Church (67, p 152), and next to it, behind Jan Hus, is the Kinský Palace (65), probably the city's finest Rococo façade. In the north-west corner of the square is the wedding-cake Baroque St Nicholas Church (46, pp 146-150).

Walk 3: Josefov

(Refer to the Staré Město & Josefov map.)

Prague's Jewish community was confined to a walled ghetto in Staré Město in about the 13th century, and it was not until 1848 that the walls came down. A drastic clearance at the turn of the century brought the ghetto to an end as a community. For a fuller look at Josefov and its history, turn to pp 134-139.

At the bottom of Maiselova, on Old Town Square's north-west corner, is the birthplace of Franz Kafka (45, p 147, 150), though the building itself is new since then; beside it is a private Kafka Exhibition. Maiselova runs north into the heart of Josefov. In the second block is the neo-Gothic Maisel Synagogue (41). Beyond the pink Jewish Town Hall (12) in the third block is the Old-New Synagogue (10), Europe's oldest active synagogue, completed about 1270. Beside it is the 16th century High Synagogue (11).

Left down U starého hřbitova are the walls of the melancholy Old Jewish Cemetery (pp 137-138), Europe's oldest surviving Jewish burial ground – spared, ironically, by a Nazi plan for a memorial to an 'extinguished race'. Continuing along the cemetery wall, a left turn into Břehová brings you to 17.listopadu ulice, across which is the Charles University Law Faculty. The street's name ('17 November') refers to students killed in a 1939 anti-Nazi demonstration, and to the clubbing of students 50 years later that triggered the fall of Czechoslovakia's Communist government.

Turn left to reach No 2, the Museum of Decorative Arts (7, pp 138-139), with a trove of eye-popping 16th to 19th century furnishings (and a good coffee shop). Across the road is the Rudolfinum (6, p 139), interwar seat of the Czechoslovak Parliament and now home of the Czech Philharmonic.

From náměstí Jana Palacha (Jan Palach Square, p 139) beside the Rudolfinum you will catch your first views of Prague Castle. Turn left (east) into Široká, where the 16th century Pinkas Synagogue (8, p 137) is now a memorial to the Bohemian and Moravian victims of the Nazis. The eponymous 'hero' of Bruce Chatwin's *Utz* had his fictional home in this street, overlooking the cemetery.

Two blocks on, in a sudden change of atmosphere, you come to Pařížská třída (p 138), testament to Prague's turn-of-the-century infatuation with Art-Nouveau architecture. Turn left and look across the river to the Letná Gardens, where a gigantic metronome slowly bobs, on the spot once occupied by a 14,000-tonne statue of Stalin (p 182). One block on, turn right into Bilkova. A block along, at Elišky Krásnohorské 10 and 12, is Prague's last purely Cubist façade (5).

If your feet are sore, take the second right into Dušní and head back to Old Town Square. If you're game for a bit more, continue to the end of Bílkova, left into Kozí and right into U milosrdných, to Prague's oldest Gothic structure, the former Convent of St Agnes (17, pp 161-163), now housing the National Gallery's collection of 19th century Czech art.

Return to Old Town Square via Haštalské náměstí, Kozí and Dlouhá.

Walk 4: Vltava & Petřín Hill

(Refer to the Hradčany & Malá Strana map.)
A convenient place to start this walk is Malostranská metro station. Head south along Klárov and right into Letenská to the Wallenstein Garden (70, p 130). Returning to Klárov, continue south to where it divides into Cihelná and U lužického semináře. Left of Cihelná is a small park facing the Vltava, with good views of Charles Bridge and the Old Town, as swans float by and beg for food.

Return to U lužického semináře, where on the right is the pleasant Vojan Park (p 130). Head towards Kampa island on a small bridge beneath the Charles Bridge, with a good view of Prague's most photographed water wheel. Continue to Na Kampě, once a pottery market.

Take one of the little lanes on the right and cross the Čertovka channel to Velkopřerovské náměstí and the John Lennon Wall (91, p 131).

Return to Kampa, where you continue southwards either through the park or along the river, enjoying the views of the Old Town. Pass the popular Rybářský klub fish restaurant, whose surrounding walls are covered in colourful graffiti.

Leave the island on Říční, passing the Church of St John at the Laundry (110, p 131). Continue along Všehrdova to Újezd. To the right is the Museum of Physical Education & Sport (105, p 131); turn left and then right into U lanové dráhy for your ascent of Petřín Hill, on foot through lush gardens or by cable car (p 132).

From Petřín Hill, cross the Strahov Gardens towards the Strahov Monastery (34, pp 124-125), enjoying the fine views of Hradčany, Malá Strana and the Old Town. Climb Petřín Tower (117, p 132) for the best views of all.

From the Strahov Monastery, continue on the final stretch of the Royal Way walk to Prague Castle, or catch a tram or bus at Pohořelec.

ACTIVITIES

For a full list of Prague's sports halls and complexes, contact PIS or see *Přehled* magazine.

Prague Marathon

The Prague Marathon, started in 1989, is now an annual event, attracting far more foreigners than Czechs. It's normally run in late June. The end of the race is usually celebrated with a late-night bash at Obecní dům. Entries may be accepted right up until the day before the race. The entry fee in 1993 was US$37 for foreigners and 150 Kč for Czechs.

Swimming

You can take a swim at the Plavecký stadión (Swimming Stadium) sports complex in Podolí (Prague 4). An Olympic-size outdoor pool is open weekdays from 6 am to 10 pm and weekends from 8 am to 8 pm; an indoor pool is open at least on weekends, year-round. Non-Czechs pay about US$1 for the day from May through September, and about 50 US cents an *hour* in winter. A two-hour sauna session is about US$1.50.

The complex, with restaurant and snack bar, is on Podolské nábřeží. Take the No 3 tram from Wenceslas Square to the Dvorce stop, from where it's a five-minute walk. Take flip-flops (thongs) for the grotty shower. Theft is a problem, even from lockers, so leave your valuables at the desk.

Tennis *(Tenis)*

Among many places to play tennis is the prestigious Štvanice club (TJ Slavoj Praha, ☎ 231 84 63) on Ostrov Štvanice (Štvanice Island); take tram No 3 from Wenceslas Square. The cheaper Tenis areál Strahov is in Strahov (Prague 6); take bus No 149 or 217 from Dejvická metro station to the Koleje Strahov stop.

Cycling & Rowing

See the Getting Around chapter for details on where to hire bicycles and rowing boats.

Ice Skating *(Bruslení)*

There are many places to skate in winter. When it's below zero, parts of certain parks are sprayed with water and turned into ice rinks. Or try the rinks *(zimní stadióny)* at HC Konstruktiva (☎ 49 62 09), Mikuleckého 1441, Braník (Prague 4), open on weekends from 1 to 3 pm; or Štvanice (☎ 37 67 55) in the winter-sports complex on Ostrov Štvanice, Holešovice, open Friday from 7.30 to 10 pm, Saturday from 1 to 3.30 pm and Sunday from 7.30 to 10 am.

It is also possible to skate on the ice rink at the Sparta Sport Hall next to the Fairgrounds in Bubeneč. If you're a guest at the Hotel Hasa in Vinohrady, you can use the adjacent rink free of charge.

Other Activities

Before 1989 the Czech Republic had no casinos; now it has the highest casino-per-capita ratio of the world's large cities (one casino per 210,000 people). Tourists and business people started the boom, though it's doubtful whether all the casinos will last. A few have already gone bankrupt and others are being sold.

There is a cheap billiards and pool hall at the Spartakiadni stadium complex, open daily from 11 am to 11 pm.

A year-round horse-riding facility is at Jezdecké středisko (Riding Centre) Zmrzlík (☎ 54 87 47), Zmrzlík 3 in Řeporyje (Prague 5); take bus No 256 from Nové Butovice metro station to the Zmrzlík stop.

There are many fitness centres around Prague with pools, saunas, massage, weight-lifting rooms and tennis courts; see PIS for a list of centres and opening times.

One of the largest is Sportovní areál Masopol (☎ 471 08 31) at Libušská 320, Prague 4 (take bus No 113 or 171 from Kačerov metro station).

Places to Stay

You can find something habitable in Prague without booking ahead, in any season. But in the high season – roughly April through October, plus the Christmas/New Year and Easter holidays – you cannot count on space in a top-end hotel (nor in some mid-range places) without booking ahead at least a few weeks.

To minimise the effects of inflation, we have given prices in US dollars – although for the time being, with government-controlled exchange rates, dollar prices are likely to rise too.

TYPES OF ACCOMMODATION

Campsites

Don't expect wide-open spaces. They're cheek-by-jowl, and differ mainly in attitude and amenities. Prices include a per-person rate (US$3 to US$4, with discounts for kids) plus charges per car (about US$3), van (around US$6), caravan (US$4 to US$6), big tent (US$3 to US$6), small tent (about US$2.50) and electrical hook-up (US$2 to US$5). Some campsites have unheated huts or bungalows at US$5 to US$7 per bed.

All have showers (with hot water unless stated) and most have communal kitchens and at least a snack bar. Most are in the outskirts of the city, and are open from March through October.

Hostels

A 'hostel' can be anything from a zed-bed dorm in a gymnasium to a double room with shower – the common factor being that filling the other beds is up to them, not you. Some operate throughout the year; others are sports clubs and student dormitories that only have beds in the summer. We have indicated the year-round ones. Most sports clubs have TJ (*Tělovychovní jednota*, physical education association) in their names. Student hostels with *kolej* (college) in the name are usually to a decent standard, and some have mini-suites (see the following information on Hotels).

The number of hostel beds explodes from late June through August when school is out. Typical per-bed prices are US$7 to US$10, but they can be as low as US$4 and as high as US$25. Few have places to eat on the premises. Except where noted, most don't have curfews.

Pensions

Once upon a time, a pension *(penzion)* meant a boarding house – a home or apartment block fitted out with locking doors, washbasins, extra toilets, sometimes a café. But the word has been adopted by high-rise hotels that want to sound homy. Real pensions are a nice compromise between hotel comforts and the personal touches of a private home. But they're not cheap, and are often out on the fringes of the city.

Private Rooms

A booming sector of small-scale capitalism is the renting of rooms in private homes. Touts swarm on the arrival platforms of the main and Holešovice train stations; most are honest amateurs with good deals. But check the map and the transportation: some are right out in the suburbs.

The easiest way to find a private room is through an accommodation agency (see further). Or, if you fancy a particular neighbourhood, look for *Zimmer frei* ('room for rent') signs and make your own arrangements.

Away from the city centre, prices for a double room with bath and toilet shared with the family are about US$25 to US$35 per night; a double room or flat with its own facilities and entrance will be at least US$60. For something near the centre, you pay 15% to 30% more. Many people offer discounts for longer stays, but put their prices up for Easter, Christmas and some European holidays.

Hotels

We organise hotels by the price of their most basic double in the high season. 'Bottom end' means less than about US$50 per double; 'middle' is US$50 to about US$100; and 'top end' is everything above that. Some places have lower rates in the off-season.

Unless noted, prices are for a room with attached shower and toilet. If they say they're full, ask if there's anything with shared facilities. In addition to being cheaper, these can be quite grand: the 'common bath' down the hall is often a private room with a bathtub. Some refurbished hotels have mini-suites, with two or three rooms (each with its own lock) sharing toilet and shower.

Nearly all hotels at mid-range and above have a restaurant, and usually a snack bar, night bar or café as well. Prices given here are without breakfast, unless noted.

Prices separated by a slash are for single/double or single/double/triple rooms. Hotels usually have few singles, but the ones they have are often available even when larger rooms aren't. Major credit cards are accepted by all top-end hotels; the few mid-range hotels that take them are noted.

'Hotel Garni'

You may see this in some hotel names. It means they're equipped only for a simple breakfast – a 'B&B hotel'.

ACCOMMODATION AGENCIES

Following are some reputable agencies. Most can arrange private rooms, and many can get cheaper rooms in pensions and hotels. Some have offices at the airport and the main train station:

American Express (☎ 26 17 47), Wenceslas Square 56 – hotel rooms from US$35

Ave, with offices at the main train station (☎ 236 25 60, fax 236 29 56), Holešovice train station, the airport and on several highways into Prague – open from 6 or 7 am to 10 or 11 pm daily, efficient and helpful, offering private, hostel and hotel rooms

Bohemiatour (☎ 231 39 17, fax 231 38 06), Zlatnická 7, Nové Město – pensions and private rooms

CKM (☎ 26 85 07), Jindřišská 28, Staré Město – open from 9 am to 1 pm and 2 to 5 pm weekdays, to noon Saturdays, with youth-oriented accommodation in hostels (20% IYHF/HI discount), cheaper hotels and some private homes

CKM (☎ 20 54 46, 29 99 41), Žitná 12, Nové Město – open weekdays from 8 am to 6 pm, with a hostel upstairs

ČD, main train station – open from 7.30 am to 12.30 pm and 1 to 3 pm weekdays, glum and unhelpful; also has an office in Holešovice station

Čedok (☎ 212 75 52/56), Panská 5, Staré Město – private rooms and pricier hotels

Hello (☎/fax 22 42 83), Senovažné náměstí 3 – open from 9 am to 9 pm daily; an eager, helpful outfit with private rooms, hostels and pricier pension and hotel beds; also has good advice for drivers; accepts credit cards

Intercity (☎ 216 150 66), Masarykovo train station – open from 9 am to 6 pm weekdays only, mostly private rooms

PIS (☎ 22 44 52/53), Old Town Square 22 – mainly pensions and private homes

Pragotur (☎ 232 22 05, fax 232 22 16), U Obecního domu 2 off náměstí Republiky – open in summer from 8 am to 9 pm weekdays, 9 am to 8 pm Saturdays and to 3 pm Sundays, mainly private homes

Prague Suites, Melantrichova 8, Staré Město – rooms and apartments in private homes

Stop City (☎ 236 13 68 or 25 78 40), Vinohradská 24, Vinohrady – open from 10 am to 9 pm, private apartments only

Top Tour (☎ 232 10 77 or 269 65 26, fax 232 08 60), Rybná 3, Staré Město – private homes and summer hostels

Universitas Tour (☎ 22 35 50, fax 22 35 43), Opletalova 38, near the main train station – open daily from 9 am to 8 pm in summer, Monday through Saturday to 6 pm the rest of the year; a recommended stop if you're after a summer hostel (there's one upstairs); also some private, pension and hotel rooms

Wasteels (☎ 216 150 54), main train station – cheaper hotels, hostels, private homes

Vesta (☎ 236 81 28, 236 81 92), main train station – hostels and its own Hotel Kafka in Žižkov

Small agencies operating from abroad can set you up with a room before you even leave home, at elevated prices. Some are listed in the Tours section of the Getting There & Away chapter.

WHERE TO STAY

Hradčany & Malá Strana

What little accommodation there is on this side of the river tends to be pricey. Hostels and private rooms are the cheapest options.

Hostels The *ESTEC Hostel* (☎ 52 73 44) at Spartakiádní block 5, Strahov, and the *Strahov Hostel* in block 11, both year-round, have beds in doubles for about US$8, with shared showers and toilets. Reception at the latter is only from 8 am to 1 pm weekdays, to noon on weekends. From Dejvická metro station, take bus No 143, 149 or 217 south to the Kolej Strahov stop.

The quiet *Kolej J A Komenského*, Parléřova 6, a 10-minute walk west of Prague Castle, has rooms in various combinations for around US$21/33 with breakfast. They're best booked through the Universitas Tour agency in Nové Město. Take bus No 108, 174 or 235 from Hradčanská metro station two stops west to the Hládkov stop.

Hotels – bottom end & middle Near the southern end of Kampa is *Privat U Kiliána* (☎ 561 81 40) at

Všehrdova 13, where rooms cost US$36/54. Opposite at No 16 is *Hotel Kampa* (☎ 245 111 77, fax 53 28 15), with rooms at US$61/100 with breakfast.

Hotels – top end The pleasant, small but popular *Pension U raka* (☎ 35 14 53, fax 35 30 74) at Černínská 10/93 has US$120 doubles with breakfast, and a snack bar serving light meals. Book ahead.

Hotel U tří pštrosů (☎ 53 61 51), Dražického náměstí 12/76, is opposite the tall Malá Strana tower of Charles Bridge. Overpriced rooms with splendid views start at US$114/155, breakfast included. Nearby is the small, deluxe *Hotel U Páva* (☎ 53 22 51, fax 53 33 79) at U Lužického semináře 32, with doubles for US$159, some with magical views of Prague Castle.

At Pod Bruskou 9, Klárov, is the new, Czech-built and owned *Hotel Hoffmeister* (☎ 53 83 80, fax 53 09 59). Rooms have air-con and there's an underground garage.

Staré Město & Josefov

Hotels – bottom end Highly recommended is the *Unitas Penzion* (☎ 232 77 00, fax 232 77 09) at Bartolomějská 9, in space rented from a convent that was once a Czech secret police jail. Václav Havel was held here for a day, and if it's available you can stay in the very room (No P6). Quiet doubles and triples with common toilet and showers are about US$20 per bed with breakfast; book ahead if you can.

Hotels – middle A three-star hotel with a one-star exterior is the *Central* (☎ 232 43 51, fax 232 84 04) at Rybná 8. Clean rooms are US$67/81 with breakfast. Visa cards are accepted.

Hotels – top end The splendid Art-Nouveau *Hotel Paříž* (☎ 236 08 20, fax 236 74 48) at U Obecního domu 1 is now a historic monument. Even if you can't afford it (US$150/210 and up, with breakfast), have a look. In the Týnský dvůr, a medieval caravanserai, is the *Hotel Ungelt* (☎ 232 04 70/1, fax 231 95 05), Štupartská 1, with eight elegant suites (double US$200, quad US$250).

At the north end of Pařížská, at náměstí Curieových 5/43, the five-star *Hotel Inter-Continental Praha* (☎ 280 01 11, fax 231 05 00) has rooms from US$234/277. Behind it, facing the river at No 100, is the four-star *President Hotel* (☎ 231 48 12, fax 231 87 56), for US$165/210. In a former life as the Hotel Budovatel, this was a favourite of party and trade-union bigwigs.

Northern Nové Město

These listings include a few places east of Wilsonova in Karlín (Prague 8), which are near Florenc and most easily reached from northern Nové Město.

Hostels The ageing *Kolej Jednota* (☎ 22 35 50), Opletalova 38, has beds for about US$10 with breakfast, in summer; ISIC cards get a 25% discount. In the lobby is the Universitas Tour agency, who can also book you into several other hostels. One is *Kolej Petrská* (☎ 231 51 89) at Petrská 3, a dreary neighbourhood but near trams and food on Na poříčí; a single/double in a mini-suite is US$23/42 with breakfast.

If you're on a rock-bottom budget, try the year-round *Raketa Hostel* (☎ 216 170 14); Na Florenci 2, inside the rail yard at Masarykovo station. Basic but fairly clean rooms with shared facilities are US$9 per bed. You can also book this with the Vesta agency in the main train station.

If this isn't cheap enough, try *TJ Sokol Karlín* (☎ 22 20 09), Malého 1 in Karlín, a truly down-and-out place just east of Florenc bus station. Beds range from US$3.50 to US$8. You must clear out from 8 am to 6 pm.

Hotels – bottom end At Senovažné náměstí 21 is the *Tour Hotel* (☎ 235 99 17), poor value at US$13 per hostel bed or US$20/30 with shared facilities.

Hotels – middle A recommended mid-range place is the faded *Hotel Opera* (☎ 231 56 09, fax 231 25 23) at Těšnov 13/1743, lonely but near Florenc. Threadbare but clean doubles are US$54 without shower or WC, US$72 with shower, US$85 for both, with breakfast. Walk-in odds look good, and credit cards are accepted.

A good off-season bargain is the floating hotel, *Botel Albatros* (☎ 231 36 00, fax 231 97 84), on nábřeží Ludvika Svobody. Spartan cabins with tiny shower and toilet are US$70/88 in summer, discounted to US$35/47 in the off season. It has a restaurant and café, and connections by tram No 3 to Wenceslas Square.

Na poříčí, though noisy, has tram connections and plenty of food. Two group-oriented hotels there have the occasional spare room. The pleasant *Atlantic* (☎ 231 85 12, fax 232 60 77) at No 9 has rooms with TV for US$90/115, including rooms for disabled visitors, and it accepts credit cards. The plain *Axa* at No 40 is US$55/90/120, though some US$50 doubles without bath may be available through Top Tour. It also has a pool and sauna.

Hotels – top end Central Europe's biggest hotel is the 788-room *Atrium* (☎ 232 25 51, fax 232 35 95), Pobřežní 3, Karlín, with glass roof, swimming pool, four restaurants – the lot. Rooms start at US$200/225. Opposite Masarykovo train station is the *Penta* (☎ 231 24 22, fax 231 31 33), V celnici 1, starting at US$225/250, chiefly for groups and business people.

A nice place for the money is the modest *Hotel Harmony* (☎ 232 00 16) at Na poříčí 31, with huge, clean doubles for US$120 (the quieter ones face Biskupská) and a pleasant restaurant. Rooms with TV and bath at the friendly *Hotel Meteor* (☎ 235 85 17, fax 22 47 15), Hybernská 6, are somewhat overpriced at US$87/

Hotel Evropa, Wenceslas Square (RN)

122/140 with breakfast. It's booked solid with groups on weekends but often has space on weekdays.

Southern Nové Město & Vyšehrad

Hostels & Cheap Hotels A recommended hostel is the quiet *Hlávkova kolej* (☎ 29 00 98) at Jenštejnská 1, two blocks from Karlovo náměstí metro station. Mini-suites are US$25/50 in July and August, including breakfast.

A cheaper hostel is east of Karlovo náměstí along dreary Žitná: the *CKM Hostel*, upstairs from CKM's accommodation agency at No 12. It's about US$10 per bed, with a 20% IYHF/HI discount. Don't confuse this with the *CKM Juniorhotel* (☎ 29 29 84) at Žitná 10, which has doubles with toilet, shower and TV for about US$45 with breakfast, but is usually booked out with youth groups. *TJ Praha*, at No 42, is just a gymnasium full of US$4 beds in July and August; reception is open until midday and after 5 pm.

Hotels – middle One of Prague's architectural gems, the Art-Nouveau *Grand Hotel Evropa* at Wenceslas Square 25, actually has some mid-range rooms without bath for US$40/65/82, and with bath for US$62/82/102. You'd probably have to book well ahead. The tatty *Hotel Juliš* (☎ 235 28 85/7, fax 235 52 47) across the road at No 22 is US$73/104 with a coffee-shop breakfast; there's no restaurant.

In a run-down lane south of Národní is the *Hotel Koruna* (☎ 29 39 33, fax 29 24 92) at Opatovická 16, with restaurant, café and rooms for US$50/85/115.

Hotels – top end A block off Wenceslas Square at Panská 12, the Art-Nouveau *Hotel Palace* (☎ 236 00 08, fax 235 93 73) is aimed at business people. In addition to the good-value Delicatesse Buffet (see Places to Eat) it has two pricier restaurants. Rooms start at US$260/310 with breakfast – or how about the Presidential Apartment at US$1000?

On Wenceslas Square are more top-end places. At No 5-7, the *Ambassador* and *Zlatá Husa* (☎ 214 31 11, fax 236 31 72) form a single four-star establishment with lots of restaurants, and US$158/205 rooms, mainly for groups. Rooms at the snooty, five-star *Hotel Jalta* (☎ 26 45 97, fax 22 20 87) at No 45 are US$180/200 in summer, with breakfast. Across the square, the renovated *Adria* (☎ 242 165 43, fax 242 110 25) at No 26 has rooms with bath and satellite TV for US$105/130 with breakfast, a flash vinárna and a café.

At Washingtonova 19 opposite the Opera House, the five-star *Hotel Esplanade* (☎ 22 60 56/8, fax 26 58 97) looks like an embassy. Rooms start at US$175/225.

Near the river, the spiffy *City Hotel Morán* (☎ 29 42 51, fax 29 75 33), Na Moráni 15, right by trams and the metro, has rooms with bath, toilet, fridge and satellite TV for US$170/200 (high season) or US$95/125 (off season), with breakfast – plus a cheeky 8% service charge.

Sandwiched between lanes of raging traffic at Fügnerovo náměstí (off Legerova) is the *Hotel Patty* (☎ 29 00 52/5, fax 29 21 97), with rooms for US$102/115.

Just below Vyšehrad is the *Hotel Union* (☎ 692 75 06, fax 692 72 98), Ostrčilovo náměstí 4. Plain, clean rooms are US$100/120. It's on the No 24 tram line to Wenceslas Square. The cloistered, high-rise *Hotel Forum* (☎ 41 02 38, fax 49 94 80), right beside Vyšehrad metro station and the Palace of Culture (and not much else), has European-class service, US$195/220 rooms and US$1.50 beers.

Bubeneč & Holešovice

Hostels In north-east Holešovice, near Nádraží Holešovice metro station, is the year-round, very basic *Youth Hostel B&B*, Jankovcova 163A. The doors are closed between 10 am and 6 pm. It's about US$9 a bed with breakfast.

Hotels – middle Rooms at the quiet *Hotel Splendid* (☎ 37 33 51/9, fax 38 23 12), Ovenecká 115, are US$65/92 with breakfast. From Vltavská metro station, take tram No 25 two stops to Letenské náměstí.

The pleasant *Hotel Belveder* (☎ 37 47 41/9, fax 37 03 55), Milady Horákové 19, has rooms with breakfast for US$78/102. Take tram No 1 two stops from Vltavská metro station.

Hotels – top end Overpriced rooms – US$110/135 with breakfast – at the prefab *Parkhotel* (☎ 380 71 11, fax 38 20 10) at Veletržní 20 reflect its proximity to the Fairgrounds. From metro station Nádraží Holešovice, take tram No 12 to the third stop. The newly renovated *Schweigerov Gardens Hotel* (☎ 32 00 05, fax 32 02 25) at Schweigerova 3 has rooms with all the extras from US$118/145, with breakfast.

Smíchov

Campsites The *Císařská Louka Campsite* (☎ 54 09 25, fax 54 33 05), at the tip of the island of the same name, has fine views across to Vyšehrad. From Anděl metro station, take tram No 12 four stops to Lihovar; it's a 20-minute walk from there.

Hotels – bottom end Near Anděl metro station at třída Svornosti 28 is *Hotel Balkán* (☎ 54 01 11). Basic rooms are US$19/31 without bath, US$26/35 with.

In the quiet streets above Bertramka is *Hotel U Blaženky* (☎ 53 82 66), U Blaženky 1, with US$27/54 rooms and a good, cheap restaurant. From Anděl metro station, take bus No 137 or 508 four stops to the Malvazinky stop.

Hotels – middle The new *Hotel Kavalír* (☎/fax 52 44 23), Plzeňská 177, has clean rooms for US$56/73 with breakfast. From metro station Anděl, take tram No 4, 7 or 9 west to the fourth stop.

Smíchov has two floating hotels, with rooms for about US$60/75: *Botel Admirál* (☎ 54 74 45), Hořejší nábřeží near Palackého bridge, and *Trans Botel Vodník* (☎/fax 54 11 04), below Smíchov Stadium on Strakonická, a five-minute walk from Smíchovské nádraží metro station.

At the north end of Smíchov is the modern-looking *Hotel Mepro* (☎ 56 18 121), Viktora Huga 3, with rooms from US$63/96.

Hotels – top end On the hill beside the Kinský gardens is the four-star *Hotel Vaníček* (☎ 35 07 14, fax 35 06 19) at Na Hřebenkách 60. Rooms cost US$134/149. Take bus No 143 from Dejvická metro station.

Troja & Kobylisy

Campsites Along Trojská in Troja (Prague 7) are four campsites, all less than 10 minutes from Nádraží Holešovice metro station on bus No 112: *Dana* at No 129 (Trojská bus stop), *Hájek* (☎ 84 10 08) at No 149 and *Autocamp Trojská* (☎ 84 88 05) at No 157 (Kazanka bus stop), and the treeless *TJ Sokol Troja* (☎ 84 28 33) at No 171a (Čechova Škola bus stop). All but the last are family-run.

The best choice is *Autocamp Trojská*, with a grassy site, ISIC discounts, satellite TV and a security guard. It also has bungalows, and rooms in the house for US$12 per bed. There are also pensions in the neighbourhood.

Hostels The *TJ Sokol Kobylisy*, U školské zahrady 9 in a residential neighbourhood of Kobylisy, is managed with military zeal by the lady at No 11 (☎ 84 15 16, no English).

Beds are US$4 to US$6, with an IYHF/HI discount if she likes your face. She also has US$9 beds in her own home. But you can check in to either place only between 6 and 10 pm. Take tram No 12 or 24 from Palmovka metro station to the Střelničná stop, walk up Náhorní, turn left, then right to the end of the block.

Hotels – bottom end Good value and friendly (but noisy) is *Hotelový dům Kobylisy* (☎ 84 38 94) at Střelničná 8 in Kobylisy. Very plain doubles/triples with shared toilet and shower are US$21/26. It's opposite the Střelničná stop on tram No 12 or 24 from Palmovka metro station. There are no restaurants nearby.

Hotels – middle A recommended mid-range place is the quiet *Hotel Stírka* pension (☎ 84 37 67, fax 84 74 88) at Ke Stírce 11/78, Kobylisy. Rooms with WC, shower and TV are US$46/74/93, and less than half that in the off season; credit cards are accepted. Book directly or through the Ave agency. Take tram No 25 from Nádraži Holešovice metro station, or tram No 12 or 24 from Palmovka metro station, to the Ke Stírce stop.

Karlín & Libeň

Hotels – bottom end The *Botel Neptun* (☎ 683 12 26, fax 683 61 88) is a floating hotel at U Českých loděnic in Libeň (Prague 8). Little cabins with toilet, shower and fridge are US$35/48 in the high season and US$25/35 other times, with breakfast. There are eateries in the neighbourhood. From Palmovka metro station, walk five minutes north on Zenklova, turn left at Elznicovo náměstí and follow the channel.

Hotels – middle The *Hotel Brno* (☎ 232 35 35, fax 231 27 67) at Thámova 26, beside the Křižíkova metro station, is a pretty good deal at US$40/60/63 (credit cards accepted). It has a small restaurant.

At Šaldova 9/54, a strange building on the east side of the block is the well-run *Hotel Karl-Inn* (☎ 232 25 51/2, fax 232 80 30). Very comfortable rooms are US$70/85 from mid-March to early November, US$40/53 the rest of the year, and cards are accepted. You can also book through Čedok or Top Tour.

A five-minute walk from Invalidovna metro station is the small *Hotel Čechie* (☎ 684 91 57/60, fax 683 01 37), U Sluncové 618, Karlín, with good walk-in odds. Rooms are US$38/73 with breakfast (less in winter), but the restaurant is very overpriced.

Hotels – top end Beside Invalidovna metro station are the posh, four-star *Olympik* (☎ 81 91 11, fax 683 64 12) at Sokolovská 138, US$82/120 in the high season; and behind it, the *Olympik II* (or *Olympik-Garni*, ☎ 684 55 01), U Sluncové 14, which costs about 20% less. Both are mainly for groups.

Vinohrady & Žižkov

Hostels A recommended, backpacker-friendly place in Žižkov is the year-round *TJ Tesla Žižkov* (also known as *TJ Sokol Žižkov*, ☎ 27 53 22, fax 27 48 42) at Koněvova 19. Throw your own bag on the gym floor for US$4 or take a bed in a smaller room for US$7 to US$8; breakfast is extra. There's also a sauna. The neighbourhood has a few adequate restaurants. Take bus No 133 or 207 from Florenc metro station, or bus No 168 from the main train station, two stops to Tachovské náměstí.

The *Šehlova kolej* (627 50 02, 627 50 18), Slavíkova 22 in Žižkov, is a run-down, cranky place but just US$4.50 per bed. It's only open in summer.

At the *TJ Kovo Praha* (☎ 77 07 37, fax 781 67 40), Nad Třebešínem III in Vackov (Prague 10), bunk beds in mini-suites are US$11 (US$9 in winter) with breakfast. It also has hotel-style rooms at US$30/55, and a restaurant with hotel prices (there's nowhere else to eat). The hostel is a 15-minute walk from Želivského metro station in a web of residential streets that all have *Třebešín* in their names – go east along the Jewish Cemetery, take the first left and second right into Na Třebešíně for a block, go diagonally across a park and one block east.

Hotels – bottom end Good value in Vinohrady is the *Bulharský Klub* (☎ 25 25 15) at Americká 28, an ageing but cheerful hotel for Bulgarians and other visitors. Doubles and triples with shower and WC are US$16 per bed; bigger rooms with shared facilities are about US$11 per bed. It has a small restaurant, and is close to the trams. It can also be booked through CKM.

Another good place is the *Hotel Kafka*, Cimburkova 24 in Žižkov, with scrupulously clean rooms for US$31/42/52 in summer (but oddly about 20% higher in August), and a winter bargain at US$20/30/44. Call via the Vesta agency (☎ 236 81 92), which owns it. It's in a dreary neighbourhood, but near the trams (eg No 9 to Wenceslas Square).

South of Havlíčkovy park is *Hotel Hasa* (☎ 72 37 51/2, fax 72 37 53) at Sámova 1, Vinohrady. Comfortable rooms are US$27/47/63. It's 15 minutes by tram No 24 from Wenceslas Square.

Hotels – middle A good deal in dreary inner Žižkov is the *Hotel Bílý Lev* (☎ 27 11 26, fax 27 32 71) at Cimburkova 20, where a double with breakfast is US$81. A few blocks west is another bright spot, the small *Hotel Ostaš* (☎/fax 627 93 86) at Orebitská 8, with a good restaurant and pleasant rooms for US$47/86/101 with breakfast. Take tram No 5, 9 or 26 from the main train station or bus No 133 or 207 from Florenc.

The *Olšanka Hotel* (☎ 27 84 33, fax 27 33 86), Táboritská 23 (enter at the rear), shares a building with the Central European University (CEU). Rooms with shower, WC and TV are overpriced at US$45/60 with breakfast. From the same lobby, *CEU* (☎ 27 23 35) offers the same kind of room for more money and without the TV. Walk-in odds at both are poor.

The *Hotel Vítkov* (☎ 27 93 41/9, fax 2793 57), Koněvova 114 in Žižkov, has overpriced, threadbare rooms for US$62/84 with breakfast; credit cards are accepted. It's 15 minutes from Wenceslas Square on tram No 9.

Another five minutes out on the No 9 line (at the Chmelnice stop) is the friendly *Hotel Jarov* (☎/fax 82 15 70) at Koněvova 204, where rooms with WC, shower and fridge are US$38/62/69 (breakfast included). American Express cards are accepted. You can book through Bohemiatour (and get a discount!) or Top Tour. But there are no restaurants within walking distance.

TJ Kovo Praga also has hotel-style rooms; see the earlier Hostels section.

In Vinohrady, a recommended place is the well-run *Pension City* (☎/fax 691 13 34), Belgická 10, in a quiet neighbourhood two blocks from náměstí Míru metro station. Plain rooms with bathtubs are US$40/61 with breakfast. It has no restaurant but there are some nearby. This can also be booked through Top Tour. Just east of náměstí Míru at Blanická 10, the *Hotel Juventas* (☎ 25 51 51/52, fax 25 51 53) has US$60 rooms full of tram noise. A rumoured renovation may drive prices up.

North-West Outskirts

Campsites The year-round *Kemp Džbán* (☎ 36 90 06/7, fax 36 13 65), Nad lávkou 3, Vokovice, is part of the Aritma sport complex (and some 200 metres on from the sports ground). Facilities also include huts and bungalows.

Hostels The year-round *TJ Aritma* (☎ 36 85 51, fax 36 13 65), at the same address as Kemp Džbán, has beds in doubles and five-bed rooms for US$7, and a restaurant.

At the year-round *TJ Motorlet Praga* (☎ 52 61 42) at Podbělohorská 97, Císařka (Prague 5), quads are US$7.50 per bed. From Anděl metro station, take bus No 191 to the fourth stop – about 20 minutes from the main train station.

The small *TJ Hvězda Praha* (☎ 316 51 04) at Za lány, Střešovice (Prague 6), has beds for US$7. You can book through Agentura 22 (☎ 312 33 38). From Dejvická metro station, take tram No 2, 20 or 26, four stops to Horoměřická.

In Dejvice's Šárka valley, the very basic *Tour Hotel* (☎ 312 10 88), V Šáreckém údolí 84, has beds in clean rooms for US$8.30, common shower and toilet, a lounge, and a swimming pool. Take bus No 116 eight stops to the Šatovka stop from Dejvická metro station.

Hotels – bottom end Rooms with bath and toilet at *Hotel Vaza* (☎/fax 35 46 17), Na Petynce 45, Střešovice, are US$24 per person, with breakfast. Take bus No 108 or 174 three stops to Kajetánka from Hradčanská metro station.

The helpful, family-run *Pension BoB* (☎/fax 311 78 35) at Kovárenská 2, Lysolaje (Prague 6), has rooms with two or more beds, shower and toilet for US$21 per person, with breakfast. There's a bar and secure parking. Take bus No 160 from metro station Dejvická to the Žákovská stop.

Hotels – middle The *Hotel Coubertin* (☎ 35 28 54, fax 35 40 69) is on Atletická in Strahov, next to the Spartakiádní stadión. Rooms with breakfast are US$57/76. Take bus No 143 from Dejvická metro station. Beyond Hradčany is *Hotel Pyramida* (☎ 311 32 41, fax 311 32 96), Bělohorská 24 in Strahov, with comfortable rooms for US$55/100 with breakfast.

Hotels out towards Ruzyně Airport, in the suburb of Veleslavín, are the *Krystal* (☎ 316 52 26, fax 316 42 15) at José Martiho, with rooms for US$48/66 with breakfast (bus No 119 from Dejvická metro station), and the *Obora* (☎ 36 77 79, fax 316 71 25) at Libocká 271/1, with rooms for US$66/83 with breakfast. *Hotel Ekypa* (☎ 36 80 87, fax 316 62 61) at Na rovni 34 has rooms from US$34/42.

Hotels – top end The *Hotel Spiritka* (☎ 53 66 58, fax 53 64 22) at Atletická 115, Strahov, has rooms for US$123/132.

In Dejvice, the tower with a star on top is on the Soviet-style *International Hotel* (☎ 331 91 11, fax 311 60 31) at Koulova 15, built for the army in 1952-57. Rooms start at US$94/133 with breakfast. Dejvice's two top-quality hotels are the *Diplomat* (☎ 331 41 11, fax 331 42 15) at Evropská 15, with rooms from US$226/258, and the *Praha* (☎ 333 81 11, fax 312 17 57) at Sušická 20, starting at US$184/203.

South-West Outskirts

Campsites *Caravancamp Motol* (☎ 52 47 14) is on Plzeňská in Motol, below the Hotel Golf. From Anděl metro station, take tram No 4, 7 or 9 seven stops to Hotel Golf. Pension *Eva* in Zličín has an adjacent campsite (see the following section).

Hotels – bottom end The big *Hotel Tourist* (☎ 529 622 90) at Peroutkova 531/81, Košíře, has basic rooms for US$12/13, with shared shower and toilet. From Anděl metro station, take bus No 137 to the end of the line and walk back several hundred metres. The *Hotel Viator* (☎ 52 55 50, fax 52 25 01) at Radlická 113, Jinonice, has doubles for US$49. It's a five-minute walk from Nové Butovice metro station.

A clean cheapie on the edge of Prague is *Motel Stop* (☎ 52 56 48) at Jeremiášova 974, Zličín, with rooms with shared facilities for US$12 a bed, and a restaurant. From Nové Butovice metro station, take bus No 164 or 184 to Konstruktiva.

Pension *Eva* (☎ 301 92 13), Strojírenská 78 in Zličín (Prague 5), has rooms for about US$15 per bed, and an adjacent campsite. From Wenceslas Square, take tram No 9 to the end of the line, then bus No 164 to the third stop, a total of about 25 minutes.

Hotels – middle The drab but friendly *Hotel Golf* (☎ 52 32 51/9, fax 52 21 53) at Plzeňská 215a, Motol, has rooms for US$53/80/98.

South-East Outskirts

Campsites A peaceful campsite with a view across the Vltava is *Intercamp Kotva Braník* (☎ 46 17 12, fax 46 61 10) at the end of the tram lines in Braník (Prague 4), 25 minutes south of the city centre.

Sky Club Brumlovka (☎/fax 42 35 19), Vyskočilovna 2, Michle (Prague 4), is right off 5.května (Highway E50/65), and half a km east of Budějovická metro station (take bus No 118 or 178 one stop). It takes telephone bookings and offers student discounts.

Hotels – bottom end A recommended place along the river is *Pension Bohemians* (☎/fax 43 08 34) at Modřanská 51 in Podolí (Prague 4). Doubles with hot breakfast are US$50 (less in winter), and walk-in prospects are good. There are a few mediocre restaurants nearby. Take tram No 3 for 10 minutes from Wenceslas Square, walk around the back and go to the top floor.

Another good but distant cheapie is *Hotel Fasádostav* (☎ 43 12 44, fax 43 20 33), Jemnická 4 in Michle (Prague 4). Very basic mini-suites are US$12 per bed in the high season. There's a mediocre restaurant next door, but little else. It's usually full, so try to book ahead. From Budějovická metro station, take bus No 118, 124 or 178 east to the Na Roli stop and walk round to the inner courtyard.

Near Háje metro station (20 minutes from the city centre), the glum *Hotel Kupa* (☎ 791 00 41, fax 791 02 16) at Kupeckého 842 has rooms for US$28/37.

Hotels – middle The *Botel Racek* (☎ 42 60 51/54, fax 42 60 55) is a quiet floating hotel at Na Dvorecké louce in Podolí (Prague 4), with restaurant, café and spartan cabins with shower and toilet for US$68/86 with breakfast (US$40/50 in the off season). Walk-in prospects are good on weekdays, and credit cards are accepted. It's a five-minute walk from the No 3 or 17 tram stop, 10 minutes from the city centre.

The business-oriented *Hotel ILF* (☎ 43 35 53, fax 42 36 92), Budějovická 15, Michle (Prague 4), has plain, carpeted rooms from US$37/62 with breakfast; the cheapest ones can be booked through Top Tour. There's a dining room, and a smokey pivnice down the road. It's a block from Budějovická metro station.

The small, well-kept *Hotel Kačerov* (☎/fax 42 62 82), Na úlehli 1200, Kačerov (Prague 4), has rooms for US$30/50 with breakfast, good walk-in odds, a fairly good restaurant and a shifty, overpriced bar. It's a 10-minute walk (or bus No 106, 139 or 182) under the highway from Kačerov metro station.

The *Slavia Hotel* (☎ 74 49 51, fax 74 49 50) at Vladivostocká 10 in Vršovice (Prague 10) has spiffy rooms for US$51/74 with breakfast, and a restaurant; cards are accepted. From Strašnická metro station, take tram No 7 west for two stops, or tram No 19 to the terminus; the hotel is to the right of the sports complex at the No 19 terminus.

On the edge of the Michelský woodlands in Prague 4 is CKM's smartly run *Hotel Globus* (☎ 792 77 00, fax 792 00 95), Gregorova 2115, Roztyly. Doubles with bath and TV are US$90 with breakfast, good value in this price range; some are outfitted for disabled guests. The hotel has a restaurant, pivnice and nightclub. Credit cards are accepted. Walk-in odds are good. It's five minutes from Roztyly metro; walk up left of the trees, then right on Gregorova.

A pair of hotels sits on the edge of a housing estate near Opatov metro station (about 20 minutes from the centre). Walk east from the station towards two brown tower blocks. On the left is the *Hotel Opatov* (☎ 795 14 40, fax 791 48 48), Jonášova 2141. A one-plus-two mini-suite is US$45 with breakfast, a great bargain for three. This can also be booked through Top Tour. The other is the less appealing *Hotel Sandra* (☎ 795 16 21/22, fax 791 98 66), Bardounova 2/2140, with doubles for US$43.

Hotels – top end Rooms in the high-rise *Interhotel Panorama* (☎ 41 61 11, fax 42 62 63) at Milevská 7, Pankrác (Prague 4), are US$151/177 with breakfast. It's around the corner from Pankrác metro station.

The small *Villa Voyta* (☎ 472 55 11, fax 472 94 26), in a fine Art-Nouveau house at K Novému dvoru 54/124, Lhotka (Prague 4, past the southern edge of our Greater Prague map), has elegant rooms targetted at business people for US$170/205 with breakfast, and a very good restaurant. Take bus No 113, 171, 189 or 215 south from Kačerov metro station to the Sídliště Krk stop, and walk three blocks west on Na Větrově.

North-East Outskirts

Campsites There are more campsites in this quadrant of the city than anywhere else, many out past the edge of our Greater Prague map.

One that's relatively close is the *Siesta* (☎ 82 14 23), Pod Šancemi 51 in Vysočany (Prague 9), half an hour out – from Českomoravská metro station, take tram No 3 or bus No 277 one stop. On the fringes of Prague 9 is *Autocamp Sokol* (☎ 72 75 01), on Nad Rybníkem in Dolní Počernice, 45 minutes out – from Palmovka metro station, take bus No 250 or 261 to the Dolní Počernice stop, plus a five to 10-minute walk.

Two campsites north of the centre in Prague 8 can be reached from the terminus of the No 12 tram line from Palmovka metro station. *Vlachovka* (☎ 84 12 90) in Kobylisy is about 100 metres up the hill from the terminus. Northward in Březiněves is *Bušek* (☎ 859 18 52, fax

22 36 17), U parku 6 – from the No 12 terminus, take bus No 258 to the end of the line.

Also in Prague 8 is *Triocamp* (☎ 84 28 39), Obslužná 043 in Dolní Chabry, about 40 minutes from the city centre – from Nádraží Holešovice metro station, take bus No 175 to Kobyliské náměstí, change to bus No 162 and go four stops.

Hostels The year-round *TJ Praga* hostel (☎ 683 82 70) is at U lidového domu 11 in Vysočany. From the Českomoravská metro station, walk 700 metres east on Ocelařská and cross Freyova. A bed is about US$13.

Hotels – bottom end The *Siesta Hotel* (☎ 82 14 23), Pod Šancemi 51 in Vysočany (Prague 9), has rooms with shared WC and shower for US$13 per bed, and a campsite – see the previous Campsites section for directions. Book through Top Tour.

In Staré Strašnice (Prague 10), the uninspiring, high-rise *Hotel Rhea* (☎ 77 90 41/8, fax 77 06 23) on V úžlabině has mini-suites for US$22/44, but there's little food in the neighbourhood. From Želivského metro station, take tram No 11 to the Zborov stop.

Places to Eat

FOOD IN PRAGUE

Czech cuisine is typically central European, with German, Austrian, Polish and Hungarian influences. It's very filling, with meat, large portions of dumplings, potato or rice topped with a heavy sauce, and usually served with a vegetable or sauerkraut.

The standard meal, offered in just about every restaurant, is *'knedlo, zelo, vepřo'* (bread dumpling, sauerkraut and roast pork). Caraway seed, salt and bacon are the most common flavourings – most Czech chefs are rather generous with salt. Everything is washed down with alcohol, mainly beer. It's no diet food.

Prague's restaurant situation is changing fast, with new ethnic and international restaurants as well as fast-food outlets like McDonald's. Chinese restaurants now seem to be around every corner. These 'imported' places rarely seem to fill up as they're too expensive for the average Czech (and often the average budget traveller).

Breakfast *(Snídaně)*

A typical Czech breakfast is *chléb* (bread) or *rohlík* (bread roll) with butter, cheese, eggs, ham or sausage, jam or yoghurt, and tea or coffee. Some Czechs eat at *bufets* that open between 6 and 8 am – typically soups or frankfurters washed down with coffee or beer.

Hotel breakfast is typically a cold plate or buffet with cheese, sausage or meat, bread, butter, jam, yoghurt, coffee or tea. Some also offer cereal and milk, pastries, fruit and cakes. Only at top-end hotels and a few restaurants can you get an American or English-style fry-up. Some eateries serving Western-style breakfasts are noted later in this chapter.

You can also go to a *pekárna* or *pekařství* (bakery), or one of the French and Viennese bakeries now appearing in Prague, for *loupáčky*, like croissants but smaller and heavier. Czech bread, especially rye, is excellent and varied.

Lunch *(Oběd)* & Dinner *(Večeře)*

Lunch is the main meal, but except on Sunday it's a hurried affair. Because Czechs are early risers, they may sit down to lunch as early as 11.30 am, though latecomers can still find leftovers in many restaurants at 3 pm. Even many of the grungiest spots are non-smoking until lunch is over. Dinner might only be a cold platter with bread.

Bufet and *samoobsluha* are self-service buffets – sit-down or stand-up – for lunch on the run. Common items are *chlebíčky* (open sandwiches), *klobásy* (spicy sausages), *buřt* (mild pork sausages), *párky* (frankfurters), *guláš* (goulash), and good old *knedlo, zelo, vepřo.*

Most *hospoda* and *hostinec* (pubs), *vinárna* (wine bars) and *restaurace* (restaurants) serve sit-down meals with several courses until at least 8 or 9 pm. Some stay open until midnight.

Czechs start their meal with soup *(polévka)*. Other common starters are sausage, the famous Prague ham, and open sandwiches. Salads and condiments may be extra. The most common main meal is dumplings *(knedlíky)*, made from potato *(bramborové knedlíky)* or bread *(houskové knedlíky)*, served with pork and sauerkraut. Roast beef may be served with dumplings and comes with a sauce – eg goulash *(guláš)*, dill cream sauce *(koprová omáčka)* or mushroom sauce *(houbová omáčka)*. A delicious Czech speciality is *svíčková* – roast beef and bread dumplings covered in sour cream sauce, served with lemon and cranberries. Another speciality is fruit dumplings *(ovocné knedlíky)*.

Fish is common, mainly carp *(kapr)*, and sometimes trout *(pstruh)*. Pike *(štika)* and eel *(úhoř)* are on more specialised menus. Seafood is found only in a handful of restaurants. Note that for a meal with a whole fish, the menu price is not for the whole fish but per 100 grams. Ask how much the trout weighs before you order it!

Poultry is common, either roasted or as *kuře na paprice*, chicken in spicy paprika cream sauce. Duck *(kachna)*, goose *(husa)* and turkey *(krůta)* usually come roasted with dumplings and sauerkraut. Turkey is the traditional Christmas-day lunch.

A few restaurants specialise in game. Most common are venison *(jelení)*, pheasant *(bažant)*, hare *(zajíc)* and boar *(kanec)* – fried and served in a mushroom sauce.

What is it? Many meals come with names that don't offer a clue as to what's in them. One that all Czechs know is *Španělský ptáčky*, literally 'Spanish Birds' – veal rolled up with sausage and gherkin, served with rice and a sauce. Another is *Moravský vrabec*, 'Moravian Sparrow', a fist-sized piece of roast pork.

But even Czechs may have to ask about *Meč krále Jiřího* (King George's Sword – beef and pork roasted on a skewer), *Tajemství Petra Voka* (Peter Voka's Mystery – carp with sauce), *Bašta nadlesního Karáska* (Ranger

Karásek's Meal) and *Kotlík rytíře Řimbaby* (The Kettle of Řimbaba the Knight).

Vegetarian Meals 'Meatless' dishes are available on most menus, but some may be cooked in animal fat or even with pieces of ham or bacon! If you ask, most chefs can whip up something genuinely vegetarian. Useful phrases include:

I am a vegetarian	*Jsem vegetarián*
I don't eat meat	*Nejím maso*
I don't eat chicken/fish/ham	*Nejím kuře/rybu/šunku*

Some common vegetarian dishes are:

Knedlíky s vejci – Fried dumplings with egg
Omeleta se sýrem a bramborem – Cheese and potato omelette
Smažené žampiony – Fried mushrooms with potatoes
Smažený květák – Fried cauliflower with egg and onion
Smažený sýr – Fried cheese with potatoes and tartar sauce.

Dessert *(Moučník)*

Most restaurants have little in the way of cakes and pastries, pubs even less. It's better to go to a café *(kavárna)* or cake shop *(cukrárna)*. Most desserts consist of canned/preserved fruit *(kompot)*, either on its own or *pohár* – in a cup with ice cream *(zmrzlina)* and whipped cream. Pancakes *(palačinky* or *lívance)* are also very common. Other desserts you're likely to encounter are *jablkový závin* (apple strudel), *makový koláč* (poppy-seed cake), and *ovocné koláče* (fruit slices).

Snacks

The most popular Czech snacks are *buřt* or *vuřt* (thick sausages, usually pork) and *klobása* (spicy pork or beef sausages), fried or boiled, served with mustard on rye bread or a roll. Other snacks are *párky* (hot dogs), *langoše* (a Hungarian snack of fried pastry coated with garlic, cheese, butter or jam), *bramborák* (a potato cake from strips of raw potato and garlic) and *hranolky* (chips, French fries).

Locally produced *bílý jogurt* – natural white yoghurt – is so popular that local manufacturers cannot keep up with demand, and it's often sold out by 11 am. In autumn, street vendors offer roasted chestnuts *(kaštany)*.

FOOD GLOSSARY

Food & Condiments

biftek	beefsteak
brambory	potato
česnek	garlic
chléb	bread
cibule	onion
citrón	lemon
cukr	sugar
džem	jam
fazole	beans
hořčice	mustard
houby	mushrooms
hovězí (maso)	beef
hranolky	chips, French fries
hrášek	peas
játra	liver
karbanátek	hamburger
kmín	caraway
knedlíky	dumplings
kotleta	cutlet, chop
křen	horseradish
kuře	chicken
květák	cauliflower
máslo	butter
maso	meat
med	honey
mrkev	carrot
okurka	cucumber or pickle
ovoce	fruit
paprika	capsicum
pepř	pepper
rajče	tomato
řízek	cutlet
ryba	fish
rýže	rice
smetana	cream
špenát	spinach
sterelizované zelí/zelenina	pickled cabbage/ vegetables
sůl	salt
šunka	ham
sýr	cheese
telecí (maso)	veal
těstoviny	pasta
tvaroh	cottage cheese

vejce	egg
míchaná vejce	scrambled egg
omeleta	omelette
smažená vejce	fried egg
vejce na měkko	hard-boiled egg
vejce na tvrdo	soft-boiled egg
vejce se slaninou	egg with bacon
vepřové (maso)	pork
žampiony	mushrooms
zelenina	vegetables
zelí	sauerkraut

Cooking Terms

čerstvý	fresh
domácí	home-made
dušený	steamed
grilovaný	grilled or on the spit
pečený	roasted or baked
roštěná or *na roštu*	broiled
sladký	sweet
smažený	fried
uzený	smoked
vařený	boiled

Utensils

ashtray	*popelník*
drink	*pití*
fork	*vidlička*
glass	*sklenice*
knife	*nůž*
plate	*talíř*
spoon	*lžíce*
toothpick	*párátko*

Phrases

bon appétit	*dobrou chuť*
cheers	*nazdraví*
Table for ..., please.	*Stůl pro ... osob, prosím.*
May I have the menu please?	*Jídelní lístek, prosím.*
What is today's special?	*Jaká je specialita dne?*
The bill, please.	*Účet, prosím*

The date stamp on most perishable Czech foods is the date of manufacture, not the use-by date.

DRINK IN PRAGUE

Coffee & Tea

Coffee *(káva* or *kafe)* and tea *(čaj)* are very popular. Basic coffee is *turecká* (Turkish) – hot water poured over ground beans that end up as sludge at the bottom of your cup. *Espreso* is sometimes a fair equivalent of the Italian version. Viennese coffee *(Vídeňská káva)* comes closer to its Austrian counterpart. Tea tends to be weak and is usually served with a slice of lemon; if you want it with milk, ask for *čaj s mlékem*.

Non-Alcoholic Drinks

In Prague it's hard to find any soft drinks *(limonády)* other than Western imports. Mineral water is widely available, as many Czechs themselves don't like the chlorine taste of tap water. 'Juices' are widely available, but aren't always 100% juice.

Remember that most glass bottles can be returned to the point of purchase for a 2-Kč refund.

Beer *(Pivo)*

Czech beer is among the best in the world. Brewing traditions go back to the 13th century. The world's first lager was brewed in Plzeň (Pilsen) in West Bohemia. Czechoslovakia had the world's second-largest per capita beer consumption after Germany, but by itself the Czech Republic may now be No 1 in that category. Beer is served almost everywhere; even cafeterias and breakfast *bufets* have a tap. Most pubs close at 10 or 11 pm, but some bars and nightclubs stay open until 6 am.

Most Czech beers are lagers, naturally brewed from hand-picked hops. Czechs like their beer at cellar temperature with a creamy, thick head. Americans and Australians may find this a bit warm. When ordering draught beer, ask for *malé pivo* (0.3 litre) or *pivo* (0.5 litre).

Most beer is either *dvanáctka* (12-degree) or *desítka* (10-degree). This local indicator of its 'gravity' doesn't correspond to alcohol percentage. Most beers are between 3% and 6% alcohol, regardless of the degrees.

The best known Czech beer is Plzeň's Pilsner Urquell, exported worldwide. Many Czechs prefer Gambrinus, also from Plzeň. The largest Czech beer exporter is Budvar – Budweiser in German, a name also adopted by an American brewer for an unrelated brew. Budvar's mild, slightly bitter brew is popular in Austria, Germany and Scandinavia. Prague's major local brand is Smíchovský Staropramen.

Some pubs brew their own beer; best known is the strong, dark brew served at *U Fleků* in Nové Město.

Pub Etiquette Always ask if a chair is free before sitting down – *Je tu volno?* (Is it free?). Service is normally quick, but if it's slow, chasing the waiter is a sure way to guarantee that you'll be ignored. Your tab is run on a slip of paper left at your table. Tipping is as in a restaurant, ie 5% to 10%, and the bill is usually rounded up to the next crown.

Wine *(Víno)*

Wine is not as popular as beer, but widely available in wine bars *(vinárny)*, restaurants and pubs – though not in many beer halls.

Reasonable local wines are available in Prague shops, but the best ones are bought straight from the vineyards. Bohemia's largest wine-growing area is around Mělník, though the wine doesn't measure up to Moravia's. The best label is Vavřinec, a red from south-east Moravia; another good red is Frankovka. A good dry white is Tramín. Rulandské bílé is a semi-dry white, Rulandské červené a medium red.

Czechs seem to prefer sweeter whites. A popular summer drink is *vinný střik*, white wine and soda water with ice. In winter mulled wine is also popular.

Spirits *(Lihoviny)*

Probably the most unique Czech spirit is Becherovka, from the spa town of Karlovy Vary, with its 'cough-medicine' taste. Another popular bitter spirit is Fernet. A good brandy-type spirit is Myslivecká.

Slivovice (plum brandy), fiery and potent, is said to have originated in Moravia, where the best brands still come from. A good Slovak slivovice is Jelínek. If you have a sweet tooth, try Griotka cherry liqueur. Others include Meruňkovice apricot brandy and pine-flavoured Borovička.

Spirits are drunk neat, and usually cold. They're available in all restaurants and most pubs and wine bars. Western spirits are widely available in Prague.

Drawing beer in the Old Town Square (JK)

WHERE TO EAT

There's no shortage of places to eat in Prague. If you like meat and dumplings you'll have no problems, though you may soon begin craving something else. The last few years have seen a boom in good restaurants serving more exotic cuisine, though the selection is constantly changing. Use this book as a guide, but have a look also at *Prognosis* and the *Prague Post* for current lists and reviews.

Opening hours are volatile, so don't be surprised if they're different from what we found. Most restaurants seem to stay open on national holidays. Main courses may stop being served well before the advertised closing time, with only snacks and drinks after that.

Prices soar as you approach Old Town Square and Malostranské náměstí. We list price ranges for the main *hotová jídla* (ready-to-serve courses) and *jídla na objednávku* (courses to order). Expect to pay half to two-thirds *more* than this if you order side dishes and drinks.

As with accommodation, we quote prices in US dollars to minimise the effects of inflation – although for the time being, with government-controlled exchange rates, dollar prices are likely to rise too.

Types of Eateries *Restaurace* (restaurant) is a catch-all term. A *vinárna* (wine bar) may have anything from snacks to a full-blown menu. A *pivnice, hospoda* or *hostinec* is a pub or beer hall, many of which serve basic meals. The occasional *kavárna* (coffee shop) has a full menu but most only serve snacks. A *bufet* is a cafeteria-style place with zero atmosphere but cheap soups and stodge.

Reservations In the high season an advance booking is essential for dinner at upper-end restaurants; for places near the city centre you may have to plan up to a week ahead. It's not unusual to find a restaurant entirely 'reserved' – say, for a coach party – and at dinner time there are always a few desperate tourists marching up and down in search of a meal. That said, in three months of Prague research, we did just fine without making any reservations at all. The higher your standards, the more trouble you'll have.

Most places that see tourists have someone who can speak English, but if you'd rather dispense with bookings, try eating at odd hours, eg lunch by 11.30 am, dinner by 6 pm (but note that many places run out of food after 3 pm and after 10 pm). Many pubs will serve you meat and dumplings at any time of the day. Don't overlook the many cheap stand-up bufets, some tucked to the side of *potraviny* (food shops).

Tipping A tip of 5% to 10% is reasonable in all but the cheapies, but don't just leave it on the table. The usual protocol is for them to show you the total for food, and you to reply with what you intend to pay – food plus tip.

Hazards Prague's restaurants are notorious for overcharging. A survey by the Czech Commercial Inspectorate found that some 70% of meals eaten by

Czechs are overcharged, so you can imagine what happens with foreigners. Some restaurants in tourist areas have two menus – one in Czech, and one in German, English or French with higher prices. You might be charged considerably more for Wiener schnitzel than for *smažená vepřová kotleta*, which is the same thing.

If there's no menu, go elsewhere. If the menu has no prices, ask for them. Don't be intimidated by the language barrier; know exactly what you're ordering. When the waiter says 'rice or potatoes?' it may well cost you extra; learn how to say 'does it cost extra?' *(platí se zato zvlášť?)*. If something's not available and the waiter suggests an alternative, ask the price of that. Return anything you didn't order and don't want, eg bread, butter or side dishes; don't just leave it to one side.

Finally, check your bill; better yet, estimate it before you let go of the menu. If you pay with a credit card, be sure the date and the price have been clearly and correctly entered, and keep in mind that unscrupulous proprietors may make several imprints of your card and copy your signature – try not to lose sight of it.

Many restaurants have a cover charge *(couvert)*, typically 10 to 20 Kč, though some bury it so deep in the menu you'll never find it. In some places condiments like ketchup and mustard are not free, but if they charge you when you haven't used them, politely decline.

Self-Catering There are *potraviny* (food shops) everywhere, the best and most expensive being near the city centre – eg in the basement of the glitzy Krone on Wenceslas Square, or in the Kotva department store off náměstí Republiky.

There aren't many open-air produce markets in the city. The biggest one near the centre is the daily market along Havelská, south of Old Town Square. Others are in Dejvice (from Dejvická metro station, walk south-east on Dejvická towards the railway line); at Bubenské nábřeží in southern Holešovice (closed Sunday); and a small one at Arbesovo náměstí in southern Malá Strana.

Where to Find Breakfast Plenty of bufets are open by 8 am, but you may not fancy soup and sausage at that time of day. Most restaurants that can cope with a Western-style fry-up don't open until 10 or 11 am.

But there's help for early risers. The kavárna at the rear of the *Paris-Praha* shop at Jindřišská 7 does scrambled eggs and omelettes for US$1 to US$2; it's open daily in summer from 8.30 am. *New York Pizza* (☎ 26 81 34), Na perštýně 4, does greasy eggs, hash-browns, meat, toast, juice and 'bottomless' coffee or tea for US$2.50.

The *Galerie Café* (☎ 26 26 37), on the 1st floor of the Adria Palace on Jungmannovo náměstí, is said to do Western breakfast from 8 am. *U Královské louky*, U Královské louky 6 near Smíchov train station, does ham-and-egg breakfast from 9 am to 1 pm.

Hradčany & Malá Strana

Prague Castle There might be room among the group tourists at *Vikárka*, Vikářská 39, where main courses are US$6 to US$11. A cheaper place is the passable upstairs bufet *U Kanovníků* on Vikářská (but check your bill closely). For cake and coffee, or a meal from US$5 to US$7, try *Café Poet* on Na baště, left of the castle's main gate.

Hradčany Loretánská is lined with places serving Czech and international meals. *U staré radnice* at Loretánská 2, in the former Hradčany town hall, has a mock-medieval atmosphere but blasé service. A place with expensive but big baguette sandwiches is *Potraviny U Loretánské* at Loretánská 5. Out of the way at Nový svět 3 is *U zlaté hrušky*, with courses from US$3 to US$7. A good pub serving hot snacks and the cheapest beer in Hradčany is *Pivnice U Černého vola* on Loretánské náměstí.

Towards Strahov at Pohořelec 3 is the *Sate indonéské speciality* restaurant, with very good Indonesian dishes from US$1 to US$2. In the Strahov Monastery (Strahovské nádvoří 1/130) is the up-market *Peklo* restaurant (☎ 53 32 77). The name means 'hell', not for the atmosphere but because monks use to do penance here. The food is Italian and Czech, with many pasta dishes and even duck, for US$10 to US$15; the bar and a disco stay open until 4 am.

Nerudova & Malostranské Náměstí On Nerudova are several places aimed at tourists. *Hostinec U kocoura* (☎ 53 89 62) at No 2 offers Czech dishes for US$2 to US$3. *U tří housliček* at No 12 has a varied menu of Czech, meat, fish and vegetarian dishes from US$5 to US$10. At No 19, *U zeleného čaje* (☎ 53 26 83) serves and sells teas from around the world.

If you feel like Greek food, try *Restaurant Faros* (☎ 53 34 82) at Šporkova 2. Of course it has souvlaki and moussaka, at US$4 to US$6. In the same area is the pricey but popular *Lobkovická Vinárna* (☎ 53 01 85), Vlašská 17, with main courses from US$4 to US$15. It's open from noon to 3 pm and 6.30 pm to midnight.

U sněděného krámu at Lazeňská 19 has a Czech/international menu with main courses from US$4 to US$8, and old-Prague décor. At Mostecká 18 is an excellent and well-priced bakery, the *Mostecká pekárna*, where everything is baked in traditional ovens. The cukrárna and café *U tří bílých jehňátek* on Josefská is pleasant but a bit pricey.

On Malostranské náměstí, the *Malostranská beseda* (☎ 53 85 68) offers good Czech meals from US$3 to US$5, and expensive beer. Also on the square, *Restaurant U Mecenáše* (☎ 53 38 81) at No 10 serves international dishes from US$5 to US$8, from 5 to 11.30 pm. Next door at No 8 is the similarly priced *U tří zlatých hvězd*, with a US$6 four-course special lunch (from 11.30 am to 4 pm).

At No 7 is *Jo's Bar*, a cheerful place serving sandwiches and Mexican food to young expats from noon to 2 am. Salad, soup and a sandwich is about US$3. It has a two-beers-for-one happy hour weekdays from 5 to 6 pm, and a Sunday Mexican brunch.

A wonderful food shop off the square is *J+J Mašek & Zemanova* at Karmelitská 30. At No 20 is the pricey *Grand Restaurant Regent*, with international and Czech dishes, as well as fresh salads and fondue; courses are US$3 to US$11.

Pivnice U sv Tomáše at Letenská 12 has standard Czech meals at US$4 to US$6 per course, plus a few vegetarian dishes. Another different place to eat near Malostranské náměstí is *Valdštejnská hospoda*, on the corner of Valdštejnské náměstí and Tomášská. The international menu includes deer and wild pig at US$6 to US$14 per course, as well as a vegetarian plate.

Near Charles Bridge *U tří pštrosů* (☎ 53 61 51) in the hotel of the same name at Blažeckého náměstí 12 is popular with tourists, so standard Czech dishes are pricier than usual, from US$9 to US$12. Nearby is the *Charlie Pub* (☎ 53 38 75) at Míšenská 10, with main courses from US$4 to US$6, and good but overpriced fresh salads. *Vinárna Gaudium* at Míšenská 12 is a cheap, cosy wine bar.

Opposite Kampa island is *Vinárna Čertovka* (☎ 53 88 53) at Cihelná 24, OK for a meal or a drink, though its main attraction is the view of Charles Bridge and Staré Město. Small main courses are US$4 to US$13. Not far away is *Bistro Tkalcovský dvůr* on the corner of Cihelná and U cihelného semináře, with light meals for around US$3, and expensive beers.

Kampa & Southern Malá Strana Around Na Kampě square are several restaurants and bistros. *Bar Art Club Galerie* at No 5 is good for snacks, and the walls are covered with paintings for sale. Next door at No 6 is *U zlatých nůžek* (☎ 53 08 10), with salads and Czech dishes for US$3 to US$4. A good place is *Restaurace Kampa Club* at No 14, where main courses are US$4 to US$11. At the southern end of Kampa is a good fish restaurant, the *Rybářský klub* (☎ 53 02 23) at U sovových mlýnů. Main courses are US$2 to US$7.

At Maltézské náměstí 11 is one of Prague's best (and most expensive) restaurants, the *Mazlova vinárna U malířů* (Mazl Artists' Wine Bar, ☎ 53 18 83). The menu offers French cuisine with typical main courses around US$30. It's open daily until 2 am.

Snack U Kiliána (☎ 561 81 40) at Všehrdova 13 is good for soup, sausages or goulash. Nearby is *Canto Club* on Besední, where you can enjoy dinner before a concert or a play in the club. Main courses cost US$2 to US$5, but the good deals are on the midday *(polední)* menu, at around US$1.50. The *Steak House* (☎ 53 05 02) at Újezd 16, with a Wild-West atmosphere, has steaks for US$4 to US$11 without the extras.

Nearby is the funicular railway up Petřín Hill. At the first stop, at the *Nebozízek Restaurant* (☎ 53 79 05), Petřínské sady 411, courses on the balcony are cheaper than those inside, from US$4 to US$7. The salads are good and the views are great.

Staré Město & Josefov

Josefov *Kavárna Hogo Fogo* (☎ 231 70 23), Salvátorská 4 near Pařížská, is great for a hit of coffee and pastry, or for lunch, and the music's good. A big list of vegetarian dishes are righteously priced from US$1 to US$2. It's open Sunday to Thursday from noon to midnight, Friday and Saturday to 2 am.

Vinárna U Golema (☎ 232 81 65) and *Vinárna U Rudolfa* (☎ 232 26 71) are similar-looking places across Maiselova from one another, at Nos 8 and 5. U Golema is a quiet wine bar with not-too-overpriced fish, poultry and meat dishes (US$3 to US$5), open daily from 11 am to 10 pm. The smaller U Rudolfa is probably better, a *gril* with fine meat dishes at similar prices, from 10 am to 10 pm.

Shalom (☎ 231 89 96), in the Jewish Town Hall at Maiselova 18, is Prague's only kosher restaurant, with set lunch (noon to 3 pm) and dinner (6 to 8.30 pm), each at US$13.

The cavernous restaurant at the rear of *Klub novinařů* (Press Club) at Pařížská 9 has an interesting menu of chicken, rabbit, trout and meat dishes from under US$5, and is open from 10 am to 11 pm.

Inside the Museum of Decorative Arts at 17.listopadu 2 is an excellent (but smokey) *coffee house* with good coffee and light meals, and good music. It's open from 10.30 am to 10.30 pm on weekdays, to 6 pm on weekends.

The smokey, unpretentious *Česká hospoda* pub (☎ 231 73 30), Vězeňská 9 on the corner of Kozí, serves Czech food at Czech prices (courses from US$2 to US$3), though food and service are uneven. It's closed on Sundays.

Around Old Town Square Restaurants around Old Town Square tend to be predatory, but the food can be splendid. *Restaurace U Supa*, at the site of a very old pub at Celetná 22, offers Czech and international dishes for US$5 to US$8, though you're likely to pay more.

Around Dlouhá A very good bakery at Dlouhá 1, *Michelské pekařství*, is open weekdays from 6.30 am to 6.30 pm, Saturday 7 am to noon, Sunday 3.30 to 7 pm. A cheap bargain is *US Burger* (☎ 239 59 83) at Masná 2, open from 10 am to 10 pm every day with hamburgers, fishburgers, good chicken dishes and Mexican food; nothing costs more than about US$1.50. *Caffé Zlatá ulička* at Masná 9 is done up to look like Prague Castle's Golden Lane. Ho-hum main dishes are US$2 to US$3, served daily from 10 am to midnight.

Restaurace U Dlouhé (☎ 231 61 25), Dlouhá 35, serves tasty, reasonably priced Czech food daily from 11 am to 11 pm. At Benediktská 16 is a better-than-average pizza joint, *Mikulka's Pizzeria* (☎ 231 57 27), open from 11.30 am to at least 10 pm, with pizzas for US$2 to US$3 per person.

Across the street at Benedisktská 11 is the crisp *U Benediktská* restaurant (☎ 231 15 27), with salads, a few vegetable dishes and a menu of un-greasy poultry, fish, steak and game dishes for US$2 to US$5. It's open from 10 am to midnight.

Around Náměstí Republiky *Red, Hot & Blues* (☎ 231 46 39), Jakubská 12, offers nachos, burgers and hot chilli for about US$2, and New Orleans specials like shrimp creole for up to US$7, plus wicked desserts and a 'bottomless' cup of coffee. It's open from 11 am to about midnight, with traditional jazz on the box and the occasional live gig.

Restaurace U králova dvora (☎ 232 11 83), U prašné brány 3, is heavy on meat but has a big fish selection.

Main dishes range from US$3 to US$7. It's open from 9 am to midnight every day. Around the block at Celetná 29, and under the same management, is *Kavárna U zlatých andělů* (☎ 232 82 37).

Municipal House (Obecní Dům) The Obecní dům at náměstí Republiky 5 provides an unmatched Art-Nouveau setting for some good food and drink. As you enter, to the left is *Café Nouveau* (☎ 231 80 84), with pastries and coffee from 11 am to 5 pm, then passable pasta, salads and gooey desserts until late. The food doesn't live up to the prices (US$4 to US$5 per course), but the live music and beautiful surroundings are free. The *Martini Bar* on the balcony is open from 6 pm to midnight.

To the right of the entrance is *Brasserie Mozart* (☎ 231 80 29), with a Swedish chef, fresh Scandinavian seafood and French cuisine for US$5 to US$7 per course. It's open from 11 am to 2 am daily, with a two-drinks-for-one happy hour Thursday from 4 to 6 pm.

In the basement is the all-night *Repre Klub* (see the Entertainment chapter), and around the back on U Obecního domu, open daily to 2 am, is a first-rate beer hall, the *Thirsty Dog*.

Around Havelská *Country Life*, Melantrichova 15, is Prague's finest stand-up joint – a health-food shop with a vegetarian salad-and-sandwich bar (pizza and goulash too) where you can fill up on wholesome, fresh food for under US$2. It's densely crowded at lunch time, so go early or ask for a takeaway. It's open Sunday from noon to 6 pm, Monday to Thursday from 8.30 am to 7 pm, Friday to 2.30 pm and closed Saturday. If you'd like to sit down, go to the other branch on Jungmannova.

The quiet Vietnamese *Club-Bar Que Húóng* (☎ 22 55 84) is behind what was once the Vietnamese cultural information office at Havelská 29. The food is unexceptional and the servings smallish, but it's a refreshing change from Bohemian stodge. Main courses are US$3 to US$6. It's open daily except Sunday from 11 am to only 8 pm.

From behind the market stalls at Havelská 12, the stand-up *Queenz Grill Bar* (☎ 26 00 95) serves felafel, gyros (döner kebab) and other Middle-Eastern goodies in pitta sandwiches for about US$1 a hit, plus good vegetable salads, from 10 am to 10 pm.

A quiet setting for good coffee, drinks or a light meal is *Caffe Antik* (☎ 26 29 56), upstairs at Provaznická 1, near the bottom of Wenceslas Square.

Around Betlemské Náměstí The *Hospoda U Vejvodů* (☎ 22 06 86) is a traditional pub serving Czech stodge for US$2 to US$4, in an ancient building at Jilská 4. Service is unhurried, though you'll have a beer before you sit down. It's open daily from 11 am to 10 pm.

At *Pivnice ve Skořepce* (☎ 22 80 81), Skořepka 3, the house special is an enormous leg of pork, but nearly everything looks good. Try Rabinova kapsa ('Rabbi's Pocket'), a chicken fillet stuffed with Roquefort cheese and ham; there are also some vegetarian courses. Main courses are US$3 to US$7, and service is snappy. It's open from 11.30 am to 10.30 pm daily.

North of Národní Třída The *Restaurace U medvídků* (☎ 235 89 04), at Na Perštýně 5-7 just off Národní, is a beer hall plus wine bar plus no-smoking restaurant (all day) plus outdoor garden, all with the same meaty menu. Czech standard meals are good but pricey for a beer hall (main courses from US$3 to US$6). It's open daily except Sunday, from noon to 11 pm.

Across the road at No 4, *New York Pizza* (☎ 26 81 34) serves so-so pizza (US$3 will fill you up) and American-style breakfasts. It's open Monday to Thursday from 8 am to midnight, Friday to 1 am, Saturday from 11 am to 1 am, Sunday from noon to midnight.

Northern Nové Město

If you're craving something exotic, *Restaurace U Bílého slona* (White Elephant, ☎ 231 17 67) at Soukenická 4 has a Thai menu with shrimp and fish, curries and poultry for US$5 to US$10 per course, and a cheaper Czech menu. Prices are lower downstairs. It's open daily from 11 am to 11 pm. Up the street at No 2, *Café Four* offers pizza, trout, salads and apple pie.

At Truhlářská 4 is the vaguely rustic *Restaurace M D Rettigové* (☎ 231 44 83), named after Magdalena Dobromila Rettigová, a 19th century exponent of a culinary Czech National Revival. The menu is serious (poultry and meat for US$4 to US$7, specials like roast goose and frog legs to US$10) and the food is pretty good.

Pizzeria Mamma Mia (☎ 231 47 26), Na poříčí 13, rustles up very good pizzas in a wood-fired oven at US$3 to US$6 for two people. It's open daily from 11 am to 11 pm (Sunday from 3 pm).

If you're stuck out in this neighbourhood in the wee hours, the snack bar at the *Hotel Opera* at Těšnov 13/1743 (near Florenc) is open until 3 am.

Southern Nové Město

Main Train Station The old part (level 4) of the station has two restaurants, one a cafeteria with no redeeming features, and the other a cavernous place with Art-Nouveau tile work and very cheap (US$1.50 a plate) Czech meals.

Around Wenceslas Square The square is lined with atmospheric places where you generally pay over the odds, but there are some good exceptions.

One of the best is the *Delicatesse Buffet* in the Hotel Palace at Panská 12, on the corner with Jindřišská, open daily from 10 am to 10 pm with a US$1.50 salad bar and a few meat dishes – very good value. Don't walk into the hotel's pricey restaurant instead!

Another excellent place is the *Mayur Indický Snack Bar* (☎ 236 99 22), off the other side of the square at Štěpanská 63. Deprived spice-heads will weep for joy over the curries and tandoori meats (about US$4), soups, salads and fresh tandoori bread; there are also vegetarian dishes. It's open every day from noon to 11 pm. Next door is the *Mayur Indický Restaurant*, with bigger main courses at bigger prices, during the same hours.

On the square, the stand-up *Bonal Café* at No 57 has good sandwiches, pastries and coffee; two doors down it also has a patisserie. Another stand-up place is the *Galaxy mléčné lahůdky* (Galaxy Milk Bar) at No 49. In the *Melantrich building* at No 36 is a sausage shop with a popular bufet serving soups, goulash and chicken, weekdays from 7.30 am to 7 pm, Saturday 8 am to 6 pm and Sunday 10 am to 4.30 pm.

West of Wenceslas Square At Vodičkova 9 you can sample the unique salsa-hot cuisine of the Texas-Mexico border at *Buffalo Bill's Tex-Mex Bar & Grille* (☎ 242 154 79), open from 11 am to 11 pm. At Vodičkova 26, the unpretentious restaurant and beer hall *U Purkmistra* (☎ 26 00 05) has a very meaty but good-value Czech menu (main courses from US$3 to US$6) and cheap beer. It's open from 11 am to 11 pm daily.

Country Life, Jungmannova 1 on the corner with Vodičkova, has fresh vegetarian salads, sandwiches, pizza and goulash at great prices (fill up for less than US$2), cafeteria-style. It's crowded at lunch time, so try for early or late; it's open Monday to Thursday from 8.30 am to 6.30 pm, Friday to 3 pm and closed weekends.

At Ve Smečkách 26, *Smečky dietní restaurace* serves boring, low-calorie lunches in a manic atmosphere, for less than US$1 per course, weekdays only from 10 am to 2.30 pm. It has some vegetarian dishes, and even a macrobiotic menu. At No 3, the plain *Pohádka* pub (☎ 236 27 69) has cheap Gambrinus beer and all-night hours (daily from noon to 6 am).

Around the block at Krakovská 20, the good *V Krakovské* pub serves plain Czech food (with light or dark Braník beer) for US$1 to US$3 per serving. It's open daily from 10 am to 11 pm; it gets crowded, so it might be wise to book ahead.

Národní Třída The modest *Café Národní* (☎ 26 75 19) at Národní 21 has Czech standard courses for around US$3.50. The pseudo Art-Nouveau *Café-Bar Evropa* (☎ 26 20 80) at No 23 has snacks downstairs from 8 am, and a pricey international restaurant upstairs (US$5 to US$25 per course), open from noon to midnight daily.

Across the road, on the 1st floor at No 22, is a kavárna called *Gany's*, open from 8 am to 11 pm; though it was closed when we saw it, the menu looks good, with Czech courses from US$3 to US$5 and some vegetarian dishes.

In the Viola Building at Národní 7 are the *Restaurace Trattoria* (☎ 26 67 32), open from noon to midnight with good Italian main courses from US$3 to US$13, and the *snack bar* of the Viola Jazz Club, with US$3.50 pizzas and US$2 to US$10 main courses.

South of Národní Třída *Restaurace U Mázlů* (☎ 26 12 72), Jungmannova 26, offers Czech dishes plus more interesting fare including trout and venison; main dishes are US$2 to US$7. Try the spicey pork goulash called 'Slovakian Good Grub'. Service is quick and there's an English menu. It's open daily from noon to midnight.

An excellent bakery for a sugar-and-caffeine hit is the *Cukrárna U Tety Stejskalový*, down an alley at Národní 32. It's open daily from 9 am to 7 pm (Sunday from 11 am).

The *Kavárna Velryba* (☎ 20 39 91) is an arty café-bar serving good coffee and heaps of tasty, mainly vegetarian food at ridiculously good prices (US$1 to US$2 per dish). Service is absent-minded but the music is interesting. It's at Opatovická 24 and is open daily from 11 am to 2 am.

Pizzeria Kmotra (☎ 20 35 64) makes good, non-greasy pizzas from scratch in the basement at V jirchářích 12. There's lots of cheap beer to wash it down. Hours are 11 am to 1 am; by 8 pm crowd control is the biggest problem, so go early.

The jolly warren of drinking and eating rooms at the *U Fleků* beer hall, Křemencová 11, is a Prague institution, increasingly clogged with tour groups high on oompah music and the tavern's own 13° black beer. Purists grumble and go anyway, because everybody has a good time, though the locals can hardly afford it any more (prices are shamelessly touristic). You might still find an empty seat at 7 pm on a weekday. It's open from 9 am to 11 pm every day.

Pivnice U zpěváčků on the corner of Vojtěšská and Šítkova is a good, cheap pub if you like mixing it with young drop-outs; it gets very crowded.

On the west side of Slovansky ostrov is an unexceptional *café* with exceptional views to accompany an afternoon beer or snack.

South of Ječná Shamelessly milking the *Good Soldier Švejk* connection (this is where Jaroslav Jašek's comic novel of WW I opens) is the *Hostinec U Kalicha* (☎ 29 07 01) at Na bojišti 12. It's a short walk south-west of the I P Pavlova metro station and open from 11 am to 11 pm. You may not want to spend the evening with the coach-loads of tourists that usually front up here.

Karlovo Náměstí The *Pizza Taxi* Italian restaurant (☎ 29 57 62), Karlovo náměstí 28, has a huge menu of pizzas and pasta (eg pizza for one from US$3 to US$9). It's open from 11 am to 11 pm daily. *Vinárna U Čížků* (☎ 29 88 91) at No 34 serves Czech dishes for US$5 to US$8; it's open from noon to 3.30 pm and 5 to 10 pm daily. Both are a few minutes from Karlovo náměstí metro station, or tram No 24 from Wenceslas Square.

Near the Vltava All these places are within a few blocks of Karlovo náměstí metro station, and close to tram No 3 from Wenceslas Square.

The small but popular fish restaurant *Na Rybárně* (☎ 29 97 95) at Gorazdova 17 is open daily from noon to midnight. Evenings get booked out days ahead, often by groups, so lunch is a better bet.

Down the road at No 10, the friendly *Snek Bar* café (☎ 29 73 21) offers 'Chinese' food and meaty variants on Czech dishes for a modest US$2 each, between 11 am and about 11 pm (from 2 pm to midnight on Sundays). At No 1, *Restaurace U Pomníku* serves meat and fish dishes for US$1 to US$2 at lunch, US$2 to US$4 at dinner.

At the central quay, from where river cruise boats leave, *Restaurant Vltava* (☎ 29 49 64) serves decent fish dishes for about US$2, and meat for US$2 to US$5, from 11 am to 10 pm. It's great on a warm evening, but sunlight off the river on a bright summer day turns it into a solar oven.

South of Karlovo Náměstí *U Činského labužníka* (☎ 20 28 61), Vyšehradská 37-39, offers authentic and very good Chinese dishes for about US$3 to US$7, and several vegetarian dishes. It's open from 11 am to 3 pm and 6 to 11 pm daily. Take tram No 24 from Wenceslas Square.

Vyšehrad

The *Warsteiner* 'snack bar' at the west end of the Palace of Culture is a restaurant, with meaty main courses somewhat overpriced at US$4 to US$6, plus salads. Within the Vyšehrad complex there's a café between the Tábor and Leopold gates, and a snack bar beside the remains of the St Lawrence Basilica.

Holešovice

At U Uranie 20 is a classy Mexican restaurant, the *Acapulco Club* (☎ 87 73 10), open Monday to Friday from 11 am to 11 pm. Reservations are recommended. Opposite the Fairgrounds, on the corner of Dukelských hrdinů and Strojnická, is the *Pražský hostinec*, a pub with a choice of South-Bohemian dishes for only about US$1. At Dukelských hrdinů 48 is the Vietnamese restaurant *Thang Long* (☎ 80 65 41). Most courses are US$4 to US$11, and it's open from 11.30 am to 11 pm. For all of these establishments, take the No 12 tram east from Nádraží Holešovice metro station.

Hong Kong Chinese restaurant (☎ 37 13 70) at Letenské náměstí 5 has main courses under US$5; it's open from 11 am to 3 pm and 6 to 11 pm. In a quiet, tree-lined street is the good Indonesian restaurant *Bali* (☎ 37 03 42) at Čechova 9; main courses are US$3 to US$7. For either of these places, take tram No 25 or 26 from Vltavská metro station to the Letenské náměstí stop.

The *Hanavský pavilon* at Letenské sady was built for the 1891 Prague Exposition. Though ordinary main courses are US$7 to US$17, the attractions are the seafood dishes (US$43 to US$54) and the views of Prague and the Vltava. In summer you can dine outside. Take tram No 16 or 22 from Malostranská metro station one stop to Chotkovy sady.

Smíchov

At the north end of Smíchov is the relaxing *Café Classique* at Vítězná 5, for a drink or a US$3 to US$4 meal. *Diana Snack bar vinárna* (☎ 53 17 35) at Elišky Peškové 17 has vegetarian courses to US$3 and meaty dishes to US$4.

Vinárna U Mikuláše Dačického at Viktora Huga 2, open weekdays from 4 pm to 1 am, weekends from 6 pm, has basic dishes from US$2 to US$4, and a variety of salads. *Snack bar Angelika* at Štefánikova 25 has good dishes and salads from US$3 to US$4.

At Kořenského 3 is *Pizzeria Mačedonia* with pizzas and pastas from US$2 to US$4. At náměstí 14.října 16 is *Secese* (☎ 54 72 01), a place with a good reputation and a big choice of dishes from US$2 to US$11. It's open daily from 11 am to midnight.

Restaurant Penguins (☎ 54 56 60) at Zborovská 5 has Czech and international dishes for US$3 to US$5, plus vegetarian items and cheap salads. At No 6 is *Taverna P Club* (☎ 54 76 81), with Czech, Italian and Chinese dishes and fish and chicken courses, cheap at US$2 to US$4. Near Anděl metro station, *U bílého lva* at Na bělidle 30 serves good Czech pub grub.

Above the Mozart Museum at Bertramka is *Restaurant U Blaženky* (☎ 53 82 66), U Blaženky 1 in the hotel of the same name. The food is good, with main courses from US$2 to US$9. Take bus No 137 from Anděl metro station to the Malvazinky stop.

U Královské louky, U Královské louky 6 near Smíchov train station, is an American-style café good for a ham-and-egg breakfast (until 1 pm) or a drink, open from from 9 am to 11 pm.

For a taste of Ireland, try the *Irish Rover Pub* (☎ 54 76 14) at Holečkova 123, with Guinness and Irish whiskies, open Tuesday to Sunday from 8 pm to 2 am. From Anděl metro station, take tram No 4, 7 or 9 two stops to the U Znovnu stop.

Libeň

A refuge for vegetarians and paupers is the *Góvinda Vegetarian Club* (or *U Góvindy*, ☎ 683 72 26) at Na hrázi 5, just north of Palmovka metro station. For a 'donation' of at least US$1 you get a generous, imaginatively seasoned set meal of hot vegetable, soup, salad, rice, cake and herbal tea. It's run by Hare Krishnas but nobody's preaching. It's only open on weekdays, from noon to 6 pm.

Žižkov

The *Restaurace U koleje* (☎ 627 41 63), Slavíkova 24, is an unpretentious vinárna with carefully prepared Czech dishes and good prices (all dishes US$2 to US$3). It's four blocks north of Jiřího z Poděbrad metro station, and is open daily from 11 am to 10 pm (Sunday from noon to 5 pm).

Restaurace Asia (☎ 27 50 26), Seifertova 18 on the corner of Přibyslavská, is a quiet Chinese place with attentive service and generous helpings at US$3 to US$7 per course (seafood to US$14). It's open from 11 am to 3 pm and 5 to 11 pm every day.

Vinárna pod kostelem sv Prokopa at Miličova 1 is, as the name says, across Seifertova from St Procopius Church in inner Žižkov. Meaty Czech standard dishes are mostly US$2 to US$5. They're a bit cheaper at *Restaurace Viktoria* (☎ 27 63 60), two blocks north at Prokopovo náměstí. Both places are open from 11 am to 11 pm daily. Take the No 9 tram from Wenceslas Square.

South of Olšaný Cemetery is a good Italian restaurant, the *Restaurace Venezia* (☎ 73 17 61) at Vinohradská 142 opposite Flora metro station. Good risottos are less than US$2, pasta and pizza under US$3, seafood to US$4, meat dishes to US$7. It's open from 11 am to 11 pm daily.

Vinohrady

In addition to some odd décor, the *FX Café* at Bělehradská 120 has great salads, imaginative vegetarian dishes and California-style soups, pitta sandwiches and cakes, and stays open from 11.30 am to at least 4 am every day. It's part of the Club Radost complex (see the Entertainment chapter), two blocks east of the I P Pavlova metro station, or a 10-minute walk from the top of Wenceslas Square

A Chinese restaurant in the same area is *Zlatý Drak* (☎ 235 45 93) at Anglická 6, open Monday to Saturday from 11.30 am to 3 pm and 6.30 to 10.30 pm, Sunday from 6.30 to 11.30 pm. Main dishes are pricey at around US$5.

In Národní dům (Korunní 1) by the náměstí Míru metro station, the *Elité Restaurace* is a complex with an Italian restaurant (good dishes from US$3 to US$6), international restaurant, café-bar and kavárna. It's open daily from 11 am to 11 pm. At Francouzská 30, south-east from náměstí Míru, *Restaurace Pravěky* offers duck, venison and wild boar for US$3 to US$4 per course, plus beer and wine.

Down where Vinohrady spills into the Nusle valley is *Restaurace Na Zvonařce* (☎ 691 13 11), in a quiet residential area at Šafaříkova 1. The patio commands a wide view across the valley, and the 'Plzeň-style' Czech dishes are good value at US$2 to US$3. It's open from 10 am to 11 pm daily. Get there by tram No 6 from I P Pavlova metro station, or on foot in 10 minutes from náměstí Míru metro station.

North-West Outskirts

Dejvice has a few interesting spots near Vítězné náměstí. *U Cedru* (☎ 312 29 74), Národní obrany 27, is a Lebanese restaurant with dishes such as chopped lamb, tabouli salad and stuffed vine leaves, from US$1 to US$5.

Popular with locals and foreigners, *Budvarka* on the corner of Wachterlova and Svatovítská is good for a drink or something from the varied Italian, Chinese and Czech menu for US$2 to US$4.

The *Bar restaurant Harlekin* at Jugoslávských partyzánů 7 serves specialities such as fondue for up to US$4. *Pivnice U Švejka*, on the corner of Nikoly Tesly 1 and Jugoslávských partyáznů, is a popular pub with good grub for under US$2.

The uninspiring *Lama Restaurant* at Dejvická 20 is good for a US$2 to US$3 meal while your wash is going around at Laundry Kings, two doors down.

More unusual is *U zlatého ražně* (☎ 312 10 32) at Československé armády 22, with Icelandic, Czech, Chinese and Russian dishes from US$3 to US$17. The house speciality is Peking smoked pork tongue.

Near the Slovak Embassy is *Hostinec U vozovny* at Na Ořechovce 15, with basic pub food; take tram No 2 from Dejvická metro station. The *Restaurant Schweigerov Gardens* (☎ 32 00 05), in the hotel of the same name at Schweigerova 3, Bubeneč, has an international menu with courses from US$5 to US$12.

Banquet restaurant *U Rudolfa* (☎ 301 67 51) at Bělohorská 151/259 in Motol recreates 17th century meat dishes in a matching setting; try the gingerbread chicken.

South-West Outskirts

On a cliff above the Vltava near the Barrandov film studios is *Terasy na Barrandově* (☎ 54 53 09), Barrandovská 1. The views of Prague are great, especially in summer when you can sit outside, but things could change under the new ownership. Take bus No 105 or 128 from Smíchovské Nádraží metro station to the Terasy stop.

South-East Outskirts

The *Dlouhá Zeď* (Great Wall) Chinese restaurant (☎ 692 23 74), Pujmanové 10/1218 in Pankrác (Prague 4), a five-minute walk from Pankrác metro station, is worth the trip for its calm atmosphere and good food. It's open from 11 am to 3 pm and 5.30 to 11 pm except Mondays.

If you feel like splashing out, the elegant restaurant in the *Villa Voyta* hotel (☎ 472 55 11), a restored Art-Nouveau house at K Novému dvoru 54/124, Lhotka (Prague 4, past the southern border of our Greater Prague map), offers game at US$4 to US$10 per course, and meaty international selections from US$6 to US$20. Take bus No 113, 171, 189 or 215 south from Kačerov metro station to the Sídliště Krk stop, and walk three blocks west on Na Větrově.

The *Restaurace Eureka* (☎ 76 11 15), Roztylské náměstí 2 (Prague 4), has excellent Czech and international dishes with good prices (US$1 to US$4) and big portions, and several kinds of salad. From Roztyly metro station, take bus No 118 to the Roztylské stop, a few minutes' walk from the restaurant.

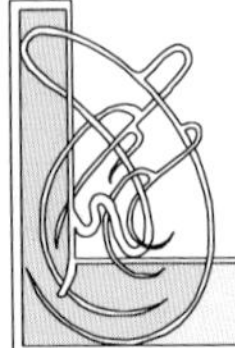

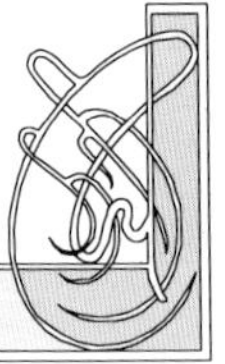

Entertainment

Across the spectrum from jazz to rock, ballet to bluegrass, highbrow drama to ice hockey, there's a bewildering array of entertainment in this eclectic city. Prague is now as much a European centre for jazz, rock and post-rock as for classical music.

It's a changing scene too. These listings will probably be out of date by the time you read them. For reviews, an up-to-the-minute directory of venues, and day-by-day listings, consult the 'Night & Day' section of the *Prague Post* or the '17 Nights' section of *Prognosis*. There are other listings magazines, including the weekly *Pro/Gram* and the monthly *Přehled*, but they're in Czech. Even these publications don't catch everything, so keep an eye on the posters and bulletin boards.

Theatre poster (RN)

If you're not into music, you could catch a game of ice hockey in winter or the Czech Open tennis tournament in summer. You could also spend a few merry hours tasting the excellent beer and meeting Czechs; see the Places to Eat chapter for some of the better pubs.

Tickets

For classical music, opera, ballet, theatre and some rock concerts – even the most thoroughly 'sold-out' events – you can often find a ticket or two on sale at the box office during the half-hour or so before concert time.

If you can't be bothered, or you want a sure seat, Prague is awash in ticket agencies. Their advantage is convenience: most are computerised and quick, and accept credit cards. Their drawback is the extra cost: tickets are always cheapest straight from the box office. Touts will sell you a ticket at the door, but avoid them unless all other avenues have been exhausted.

Many places have discounts for students and seniors, and sometimes for the disabled. At the box office, non-Czechs normally pay the same price as Czechs.

Following are some reliable agencies. The main 'wholesalers' are BTI, FOK, IfB and PIS. The others are apt to get their tickets from them:

American Express, Wenceslas Square 56 (☎ 26 17 47)
American Hospitality Center, Na můstku 7, Staré Město (☎ 26 15 74)
BTI, Na příkopě 16, Staré Město (☎ 22 87 38); Karlova 8, Staré Město (☎ 26 13 50)
Čedok, Na příkopě 18, Staré Město (☎ 212 73 50); Bílkova 6, Josefov (☎ 231 82 55); Rytířská 16, Staré Město (☎ 26 36 97)
FOK, U Prašné brány 1, Staré Město – mainly Prague Symphony (☎ 232 25 01)
IfB, Grand Hotel Evropa, Wenceslas Square 25 (☎ 26 37 47)
Pragotur, U Obecního domu 2, Staré Město (☎ 232 22 05, fax 232 22 16)
PIS, Old Town Square 22, Staré Město; Na příkopě 20, Staré Město

For rock and jazz clubs, just front up at the door.

CLASSICAL MUSIC, OPERA & BALLET

Don't believe anyone who says it's impossible to get tickets. There are half a dozen concerts of one kind or another almost every day in summer, a fine soundtrack to the city's visual delights. Many are chamber concerts by aspiring musicians in the city's churches – gorgeous but chilly (take an extra layer, even on a summer day) and not always with the finest of acoustics.

Following are some major venues:

Hradčany

St George Basilica, Prague Castle

Lobkovic Palace, Prague Castle

St Vitus Cathedral, Prague Castle

Wallenstein Palace, Valdštejnské náměstí

Malá Strana

St Nicholas Church, Malostranské náměstí

Nostitz Palace, Maltézské náměstí 1

Nové Město

State Opera Theatre (☎ 26 53 53), Wilsonova 4 – mainly opera and ballet; box office open from 10 am to 5.30 pm (weekends closed noon to 1 pm)

Villa Amerika (Dvořák Museum), Ke Karlovu 20 – special Dvořák concerts

Vyšehrad

New Provost's House – 3.30 pm Sunday afternoon concerts in summer

Palace of Culture, 5.května 65 by Vyšehrad metro station – recitals, chamber concerts, pop concerts

Holešovice

Fairgrounds (Výstaviště)

Smíchov

Villa Bertramka (Mozart Museum, ☎ 54 38 93), Mozartova 2/169 – special Mozart concerts

Staré Město & Josefov

House at the Stone Bell, Old Town Square 13

Rudolfinum (☎ 286 03 52), 17.listopadu – box office open from 10 am to 12.30 pm and 1.30 to 6 pm, and for one hour before performances

Convent of St Agnes, U milosrdných 17

Church of Our Lady Before Týn, Old Town Square

Church of St Francis Seraphinus, Křižovnická náměstí

National Theatre (☎ 20 53 64), Národní 2 – mainly opera and ballet; box office at the Nová Scéna at Národní 4, open weekdays from 10 am to 6 pm, weekends from noon

Opera Mozart Theatre (☎ 22 82 34), Novotného lávka 1 – chamber concerts, opera and Sunday jazz; box office open from 1 to about 6 pm, or until performances begin

Smetana Hall, Obecní dům, náměstí Republiky 5

Tyl (Estates) Theatre (☎ 22 86 58), Železná 11 – opera as well as drama; is equipped for the hearing-impaired, has wheelchair access, and wheelchair-bound people can book up to five days in advance; for bookings, go round the corner to the Kolowrat Theatre, or to the National Theatre box office at Národní 4 (the one here is open only half an hour before performances)

Chapel of Mirrors, Klementinum

Prague Spring (Pražské Jaro)

This is the Czech Republic's best known annual cultural event, and now a major tourist event too. It begins on 12 May, the anniversary of Smetana's death, with a procession from his grave at Vyšehrad to the Obecní dům, and a performance there of his *Má vlast* song cycle. It runs until 2 June. The calibre of most performances is not much higher than many other programmes you can catch in April-June and September-October. The beautiful venues are as big a draw as the music.

If you want a guaranteed seat at a Prague Spring concert, book it by mid-March. Write to Prague Spring (MHF Pražské jaro), Hellichova 18, Malá Strana, 118 00 Praha 1, or fax +42-2-53 60 40. Ballet and opera performances during the same period are handled by BTI, Salvátorská 6, Josefov, 110 00 Praha 1, or fax +42-2-231 22 71.

Occasional seats may be available as late as the end of May – watch the papers. The cheapest tickets are at the official box office at Hellichova 18, off Karmelitská in Malá Strana, open weekdays from 10 am to 6 pm during the run-up to the Festival.

JAZZ

The following clubs all have a cover charge of about US$1 to US$2 except as noted, and some double as restaurants:

Malá Strana

Malostranská beseda (☎ 53 90 24), Malostranské náměstí 21 – jazz on Mondays at 8 pm

Staré Město

Café Nouveau, Obecní dům, náměstí Republiky 5 – Italian restaurant with traditional jazz in the evenings

Opera Mozart Theatre (☎ 22 82 34), Novotného lávka 1 – box office open from 1 pm to about 6 pm, or until performances begin; jazz on Sundays

Red, Hot & Blues (☎ 231 46 39), Jakubská 12 – a restaurant with traditional American jazz on the box, and occasional live gigs (check the board outside)

Viola Jazz Club (☎ 235 87 79), Národní 7 – Saturdays at 8.30 pm, plus other days

Southern Nové Město

Reduta Jazz Club (☎ 20 38 25), Národní 22 – one of the city's older clubs, with live jazz daily from 9 pm to whenever, and a stiff cover charge of about US$3; advance bookings can be made here from 3 pm

AghaRTA Jazz Centrum (☎ 22 45 58), Krakovská 5 – nightly jazz, open weekdays from 3 pm to 1 am, weekends from 7 pm; also has a café and a music shop

ROCK & POST-ROCK

Prague has a high-energy club scene, with plenty of rock, metal, punk, rap and uncategorisable soundz at over three dozen legitimate DJ and live-music venues. There are also a few unlicensed places with mutating addresses, which tend to be grotty, structurally unsound and/or dodgy. The clubs listed here are at least semi-reputable.

For current listings and reviews, see the entertainment pages of *Prognosis* or the *Prague Post* – and watch the posters. Except as noted, the following clubs have a bar and usually a dance floor, and a cover charge of about US$1 to US$1.50:

Staré Město & Josefov

Classic Club, Pařížská 4, Josefov – a dance club open from midnight to 3 am daily

Exodus Club, Národní 25 – DJ reggae, ragga and more, daily from 8 pm to 5 am

Klub U zoufalců, Celetná 12, Staré Město – 9 pm to 3 am; a grungy spot with occasional live gigs followed by DJ music, and a cover charge as high as US$3

Repre Klub (☎ 248 110 57), in the Art-Nouveau basement of Obecní dům, náměstí Republiky 5 – 9 *am* to 5 am every day, with all-night DJ and occasional live music (including imported bands)

Rock Café, Národní 22 – open weekdays from 10 am to 3 am, weekends from noon, with DJ and live rock, and a café downstairs

Northern Nové Město

RC Bunkr, Lodecká 2 near Petrské náměstí – DJ and live music (local and international), raucous dancing and excessive drinking from 6 pm to 5 am daily (music from 9 pm), with a café upstairs; increasingly tourist-laden

Southern Nové Město

Euroclub (☎ 22 25 09), Opletalova 5 near Muzeum metro station – everything from jazz to folk-rock

Big Pohoda Club, Opletalova 38 – daily from 9 pm to 1 am

Vinohrady & Žižkov

Club Radost, Bělehradská 120, Vinohrady, near I P Pavlova metro station – DJ and occasional live music daily from 9 pm to 6 am, plus early-evening fixtures from 6 to 9 pm (eg Sunday poetry night, open-mike acoustic music every other Wednesday); *FX Café* until 4 am

Belmondo Revival Club (☎ 755 10 81), Slavíkova 22, Žižkov – a dance club with local bands, open daily from 7 pm to 1 am

Holešovice

Disco Štvanice, in the Winter-Sports Stadium on Ostrov Štvanice (tram No 3 from Wenceslas Square) – open daily from 9 pm to 5 am, with a minuscule cover charge

Smíchov

Futurum, Zborovská 7 – DJ and occasional live heavy metal, open nightly from 9 pm to 5 am (to 8 am Friday and Saturday)

Penguin Club, náměstí 14.října – open daily from 7 pm to 2 am, a nightclub with disco or dance-type music

Hradčany & Malá Strana

African Safari Night Club, corner of Petřínská and Zborovská, southern Malá Strana – open daily from 7 pm to 5 am

Borát (also called *Újezd) Rock Club*, Újezd 18, Malá Strana – live bands daily (except Monday) from 9 pm to at least 2 am (to 6 am on Friday and Saturday nights) in a sweaty, graffiti-covered space full of locals and tourists; the club opens at 6 pm

Club America, Petřínská 5 in southern Malá Strana – open Monday to Thursday from 8.30 pm to 4 am, Friday to Sunday to 5 am; a straight/gay dance club with rap, techno and metal, and a US$2 cover charge

Malostranská beseda (☎ 53 90 24), Malostranské náměstí 21 – open from 7 pm to 1 am daily (music from 8 pm); one of Prague's larger venues, a sit-down place with anything from hard rock to jazz and bluegrass

Peklo ('Hell'), part of the restaurant of the same name at Strahovské nádvoří 1/130, in the Strahov Monastery – open from 8 pm to 4 am

Strahov 007, in the student dormitory complex east across the road from the Spartakiádní stadium (take bus No 217 from either Dejvická or Anděl metro station to Strahov) – cheap beer and raw music from up-and-coming Bohemian bands, daily from 7 to 11 pm

THEATRE

Probably Prague's most famous theatre is the Laterna Magika (Magic Lantern), a multimedia show interweaving dance, opera, music and film, which caused a stir when it premiered in 1958 at the Brussels World Fair. Since moving from its birthplace in the basement of the Adria Palace into Nová Scéna, the 'New National Theatre' building at Národní 4, it has evolved very little, and is now just clever, expensive, mainstream entertainment, mainly for tourists.

Čedok may tell you it's booked out, but you may bag a leftover seat at the box office on the day before a performance, or a no-show half an hour beforehand. Tickets are about US$16 (or US$20 from Čedok). The box office (☎ 20 62 60) is open from 10 am to 8 pm on weekdays, from 3 pm on weekends.

A big theatre event is 'Island Theatre', a drama festival held on Střelecký ostrov since 1985. It was expanded in 1993 from two weeks to three months, mid-June to mid-

September. A daily charge of about US$1.50 admits you to a programme of events from 2 pm until late in the evening, and an arts and crafts fair.

Other venues, including for drama, experimental theatre, musicals and revues, are:

Staré Město & Josefov

Theatre on the Balustrade (Divadlo Na zábradlí, ☎ 236 04 49), Anenské náměstí 5 – box office open from 1 to 8.30 pm on performance days

Gag Studio (☎ 26 54 36), in the passage at Národní 25 – comedy

Kolowrat Theatre, Ovocný trh 6 – box office open from 10 am to 6 pm on weekdays, plus weekend performance days from noon to 1 pm and 2.30 to 6 pm (or go to the National Theatre box office at Národní 4)

National Marionette Theatre, Žatecká 1 – the old Říše Loutek (Marionette Kingdom) theatre where the Kladno puppet troupe does sell-out performances of Mozart's *Don Giovanni* at US$15 a ticket

Tyl (or *Estates*) *Theatre* (☎ 22 86 58), Železná 11 – drama and opera; some plays include simultaneous translation on headphones; for advance bookings, go around to the Kolowrat Theatre, or to the National Theatre box office at Národní 4, since the box office here is only open half an hour before performances; has wheelchair access (wheelchair-bound people can book up to five days ahead) and is equipped for the hearing-impaired

Theatre Image, Classic Club, Pařížská 4, Josefov – black-light and mime theatre

Viola Jazz Club (☎ 235 87 79), Národní 7 – sometimes offers short plays, including children's plays (in Czech) on Saturdays at 4 pm

Southern Nové Město

Divadlo za Branou II (☎ 26 67 65), Adria Palace, Národní 40 – box office open daily from 10 am to 8 pm, with 50% off for students, disabled and seniors

Dramatic Club (Činoherní Klub, ☎ 235 23 70), Ve Smečkách 26

Lucerna Bar, Lucerna Passage, Štěpánská 61 – revues

Reduta Theatre (☎ 20 38 25), Národní 22 – part of the jazz club of the same name, but with drama performances at 7.30 pm on selected evenings

Holešovice

Laterna Animata, Fairgrounds (Výstaviště) – similar to Laterna Magika; nightly performances for about US$11 at the box office

Vinohrady

Vinohrady Theatre (☎ 25 24 52), náměstí Míru 7 – box office open weekdays from 10 am to 7 pm

Karlín

Karlín Music Theatre (Karlín hudební divadlo, ☎ 22 08 95), Křižíkova 10, near Florenc – musicals and operettas

CINEMA

Prague has about 45 movie theatres (*kino* in Czech), some showing first-run Western films, some with Czech films. Admission is typically 40 Kč. See the *Prague Post* and *Prognosis* for reviews and a list of cinemas.

SPECTATOR SPORTS

Ice Hockey *(Lední Hokej)*

The Czech ice hockey team always finishes near the top in the European and world championships, and has won the European title 17 times and the world title six times.

One of the best national teams in recent years has been Sparta Praha. You can see them play in winter at the ice rink of the Sparta Sport Hall next to the Fairgrounds in Bubeneč (take tram 12 one stop from Nádraží Holešovice metro station). Other games are played at the winter stadium of the Stadión SK Slavia Praha complex on Na hroudě in Vršovice. The season runs from September until early April, and cheap tickets are available from the ice rinks for Tuesday, Friday and Sunday games.

Tennis *(Tenis)*

When it comes to Czech sport stars, most Westerners think of tennis. But you won't run into Lendl or Navrátilová here: they're now US citizens. Tennis tournaments can be seen on Ostrov Štvanice (tram No 3 from Wenceslas Square). The Škoda Czech Open is usually played here in early August.

Soccer *(Fotbal)*

Sparta Praha has been one of the leading teams in the national league, along with the army team, Dukla Praha, and Slavia Praha. Each has its own stadium where you can see matches, mostly on Sunday afternoons. The season runs from September to December and March to June.

The Sparta Praha Stadium is at Milady Horákové in Bubeneč; take tram No 25 or 26 from Hradčanská metro station. The Slavia Praha Stadium is on Vladivostocká in Vršovice (Prague 10); take tram No 4 or 22 from Karlovo náměstí. The Dukla Praha Stadium is on Na Julisce in Dejvice (Prague 6); take tram No 20 or 25 to the end of the line from Dejvická metro station.

Horse Racing *(Dostihy)*

Check this at the Chuchle závodiště (racecourse) on Radotínská in Velká Chuchle (Prague 5); take bus No 453 or 172 from Smíchovské Nádraží metro station. Races usually start after 2 pm on Tuesdays and Sundays, from May to October. Contact PIS about other venues and events, as these constantly change. Tickets are cheap and usually available at the grounds.

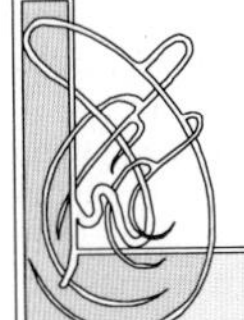
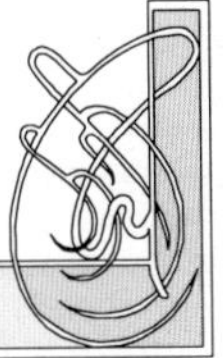

Shopping

In Communist days the shops in Prague, though drab, usually had most of the basic goods most of the time, though supplies were erratic and goods were of poor quality. The privatisation of retailing since 1989 has radically changed Prague's shopping scene. Consumer goods are easily obtainable and mostly of good quality. Imports carry Western European prices, but Czech products are affordable for Czechs and cheap for Westerners.

For special needs, try looking in the *Zlaté stránky* (Gold Pages) of the telephone book, or ask your hotel receptionist or the people at PIS.

WHERE TO SHOP

The main shopping streets are Wenceslas Square and three streets around the edge of Staré Město: Na příkopě, 28.října and Národní třída. Here you should be able to find almost anything you need.

Department Stores

The city's major department stores are:

- Bílá Labuť, Na poříčí 23, Nové Město
- Dětský dům, Na příkopě 15, Staré Město
- Kotva, náměstí Republiky 8, Staré Město
- Krone, corner of Wenceslas Square and Jindřišská
- Máj, Národní 26, Nové Město

Kotva is the best of the Czech stores, now with patisserie, photo supplies and processing, a photocopy shop and groceries along with the traditional stuff. Krone is a German joint venture, with German prices.

Open-Air Markets

Along Havelská and V kotcích, south of Old Town Square, is a daily market with fruit, vegetables, clothing and souvenirs. Another is at Bubenské nábřeží, on the south side of Holešovice, open daily except Sunday.

One in Dejvice (from Dejvická metro station, walk south-east on Dejvická towards the railway line) has fruit and vegetables, other foodstuffs and cheap clothing. There's also a small one at Arbesovo náměstí in southern Malá Strana.

Tuzex Shops

In Communist days, state-run Tuzex shops in tourist centres (at least 16 in Prague) sold imported or export-quality clothing, jewellery, cosmetics, glass and porcelain, food, alcohol, cigarettes, cameras, electronics and even cars for hard currency, at duty-free Western prices. There are still some Tuzex shops about, and now you can pay in crowns too; but with the growth of European joint-venture shops, Tuzex is increasingly obsolete.

WHAT TO BUY

Antiques & Artwork

If you have bought what you think is a genuine antique or a piece of museum-quality art that may cause trouble at customs on the way out, you'd be wise to follow official procedures – see the Customs section in the Facts for the Visitor chapter (also for information on which goods are dutiable). In general, anything made before 1920 (among other things) is apt to be non-exportable.

Books

Books are an easy gift or souvenir, and many shops stock reference books and good-quality coffee-table books on Prague and the Czech Republic. Refer to Books & Maps in the Facts for the Visitor chapter for a list of worthwhile bookshops.

Glass & Crystal

One of Prague's best buys is Bohemian crystal, from simple glassware to stupendous works of art, sold at some three dozen high-toned places in the shopping streets. Prices aren't radically different from shop to shop, though they are highest in the city centre.

The city's most exclusive (and expensive) crystal shop is Moser, worth a browse for the décor as well as the goods. It's in an originally Gothic building called House at the Black Rose (Dům U černé růže) at Na příkopě 12.

Some shops around Jungmannovo náměstí and Národní advertise that they will ship abroad. If you want to do it yourself, you will have to take your parcel, unsealed, to the customs post office (see Customs in the Facts for the Visitor chapter).

Top : Painter on Charles Bridge (RN)
Bottom : Na příkopé ulice (JK)

Junk

You may not need a door knob, rusty bed springs or a cracked teapot, but drop in anyway at Dlouhá 32 and look around the wonderful old hardware/household-equipment shop of Eduard Čapek, founded before WW I and doing a roaring trade ever since.

Music

Good buys are classical CDs of the works of Czech composers, eg Smetana, Dvořák, Janáček and Martinů, as well as folk music – even *dechovka* (brass-band 'polka' music) if you are into that sort of thing.

There are almost as many CD and tape shops as bookshops. A good one for classical music is in the basement of the Rudolfinum in Josefov. The AghaRTA Club has its own jazz music shop at Krakovská 5, Nové Město, open weekdays from 3 pm to midnight, weekends from 7 pm. The Albatros bookshop at Národní 29 has a big selection of rock CDs and tapes, and its branch on the corner of Havelská and Melantrichova has classical CDs.

If you have problems finding anything specific, try Popron at Jungmannova 30 in Nové Město, or Suprafon a few doors down.

Souvenirs

There is a vast array of souvenirs for sale, with some quality work among the junk. Look for painted Easter eggs, marionettes, wood and straw toys, wooden utensils, ceramic ware with traditional designs, linen with traditional stitching, and Bohemian lacework. You'll find many stores selling these items along the heavily touristed Royal Way and Wenceslas Square. A large shop full of wooden toys and ceramics is L&L at Husova 8.

Stalls are everywhere in Wenceslas Square, Na můstku and Old Town Square, on Charles Bridge, and along the steps to Prague Castle. Once a source of good drawings, paintings and photographs of the city, many have now descended into kitsch.

A few stalls still sell Soviet military paraphernalia and *matryoshka* dolls (look inside: some don't have all the dolls they should).

Sporting Goods

Good tents and camping equipment are hard to find. Sokol, on Újezd next to the Museum of Physical Education & Sport in Malá Strana, has some. Dům Sportu at

Jungmannova 28, Nové Město, has general sports equipment, as do the big department stores. A good place for bags, backpacks and ice-hockey equipment is Opus, Vodíčkova 7 off Wenceslas Square. Locally manufactured equipment is moderately priced.

Excursions

The Central Bohemian countryside within an hour's train or bus ride from Prague is rich in fine landscapes, good walks and interesting architecture, often in the middle of nowhere. Following are a few interesting day or overnight trips you can do on your own.

Top of the line, for our money, are Křivoklát castle and the Berounka River valley, photogenic Karlštejn castle, the silver-mining town of Kutná Hora, and the park at Průhonice, barely outside the city limits. Be ready for summer crowds at Karlštejn and Konopiště castle. Staying the night lets you see a place in a kinder light, when the tour buses have gone back to Prague.

Castles & Chateaux

Křivoklát and Karlštejn are open year-round, but the others close from November to March. All the sights in this chapter are closed on Monday except the Lidice memorial and Mělník chateau.

The risk of theft has prompted castles and chateaux to admit visitors only in guided groups, though most will let you pay the Czech price (typically less than 30 Kč) and lend you a written English narrative. If you want to catch every detail, be prepared to fork out 60 to 100 Kč for an English-language tour.

Walks

Only a few walks are noted in this chapter, but there are over 50 itineraries described (only in Czech) on Kartografie Praha's excellent map, *Výlety do okolí Prahy* (Excursions to the Outskirts of Prague). Trails are well marked, with the same colours shown on the map.

Tours

If you don't want to do it yourself, Čedok and other operators have a range of all-day excursions in the high season, with lunch included. See Tours in the Getting Around chapter for more information.

MĚLNÍK

Mělník, on a prominent hill above the confluence of the Vltava and Labe (Elbe), began as a 9th century Slavic settlement. Mělník chateau was the second home of Bohemia's queens from the 13th century until the time of George of Poděbrady. A solidly Hussite town, it was demolished by Swedish troops in the Thirty Years' War, and the castle gave way to the present chateau.

Mělník is the centre of Bohemia's small wine-growing region. The best of the area's vineyards are descended from Burgundy vines imported by Charles IV.

This is an easy day trip, good for lazy strolling and wine-tasting.

Orientation

From the bus station, climb west up Jaroše or Krombholcova. Beyond the old gate tower, bear right into náměstí Míru, an arcaded square lined with pastel-tinted Renaissance and Baroque façades. Take the first left along Svatováclavská to the chateau and church.

Chateau

The Renaissance chateau was acquired by the Lobkovic family in 1739. Since getting it back from the state in 1990, they've opened it to the public (from 10 am to 6 pm, seven days a week).

On the hour, for 50 Kč (students 30 Kč), you can take a tour through the **former living quarters** on the top floor, crowded with the family's rich collection of Baroque furniture and 17th and 18th century paintings. Additional rooms are given over to changing exhibits of modern works.

At half-past each hour you can look at the 13th century **wine cellars** for 20 Kč or indulge in various wine-tasting programmes for 60 to 125 Kč. A shop in the courtyard sells the chateau's own label.

Independent of the family's operations is a dreary **regional museum** on the 1st floor (10 am to 6 pm in summer, 9 am to 4 pm in May and September, closed Monday).

Church of SS Peter & Paul (Kostel Sv Petra a Pavla)

This 15th century Gothic church, with Baroque furnishings and tower, is worth a look. Remnants of its Romanesque predecessor have been incorporated into the rear of the building, south of the bell tower.

The old **crypt** is now an ossuary, packed with the bones of some 10,000 people dug up to make room for 16th century plague victims, and arranged in macabre patterns. It's open to the public from 9.45 am to 3.45 pm except Monday, with an unintentionally hilarious hourly show. Tickets and information are at the snack bar across the street.

Viewpoint & Walks

The view from behind the chateau takes in the confluence of the Vltava and Labe, and a once busy 10-km canal from upstream on the Vltava. The big bump on the horizon to the north-west is a hill called Říp where, legends say, the brothers Čech and Lech stopped on a journey from the East; the former stayed and founded the Czech nation, the latter went on to sire the Poles.

Lobkovic vineyards carpet the wedge of land between the Vltava and the canal. To the right of the canal is thickly wooded Hořínský Park, to which you could descend for some pleasant walking, with a look at the ruins of Hořín, the old Lobkovic family home, and the canal lock, still in use.

Places to Eat

The best local red and white wines are both called Ludmila, after the saint and grandmother of St Wenceslas. The best place to taste them is probably in the chateau. On the ground floor are the *Zámecká* restaurant, with a smashing view and very good food (main dishes are about US$4, plus vegetarian items for less), and a pricier *vinárna*, both open from 10 am to midnight.

The snug *Stará Škola* vinárna behind the church has views to rival the chateau's, and modest prices. A pricier alternative is *U Svatého Václava*, outside the chateau gate at Svatováclavská 22. For cheap eats, try *U Tomaše* at Svatováclavská 3, or *Pivnice U Karla* on Palackého, a block south of náměstí Míru.

Getting There & Away

Buses run to Mělník from Florenc bus station and Holešovice metro station at least hourly, taking about 45 minutes.

LIDICE

When British-trained Czech paratroops assassinated Reichsprotektor Reinhard Heydrich in June 1942, the Nazis took a savage revenge. Picking – apparently at random – the mining and foundry village of Lidice, north-west of Prague, they proceeded on 10 June to obliterate it from the face of the earth. All its men were shot, all the women and most children shipped to the Ravensbrück concentration camp, and the remaining children farmed out to German foster homes. The village was systematically burned and bulldozed so that no trace remained. Of its 500 inhabitants, 192 men, 60 women and 88 children eventually died.

But the act backfired, electrifying the world and triggering a campaign to preserve the village's memory and create a kind of symbolic Lidice. The site is now a green field, eloquent in its silence, dotted with a few memorials and the reconstructed foundations of a farm where most of the men were shot and buried.

Nearby is a museum that recreates the village in photographs and text, along with chilling SS film footage of its destruction. It's opposite the Prague-Kladno bus stop, and is open from 8 am to 5 pm every day.

Places to Stay & Eat

If you're caught out, or want to explore the region more, the dreary smokestack town of Kladno is not far and has some cheap accommodation. The *Hotel Kladno* (☎ 6241), where a double is about US$50, is at náměstí Sítná on the Prague-Kladno bus line, two stops before Kladno station. *Pension Tonička* (☎ 2759), Bendlova 2037, has suites with shared toilet for US$12 a bed, with breakfast; from the Hotel Kladno, cross the bridge, turn left and it's a block in.

Year-round hostel accommodation is available for US$3.50 a bed at *Domov mládeže*, 5.května 1879. From the Hotel Kladno, cross the street and walk 1½ block. In summer, Ču Tour agency (☎ 2306) on Vrbenského, beside the bus station, can arrange a student *dorm bed* for US$5.

Two adequate *restaurants* are just off náměstí Starosty Pavla near the Kladno bus station, and the *Hotel Kladno's* eatery is not too pricey.

Getting There & Away

Lidice is on the bus line to Kladno, half an hour from Prague. Buses go from Dejvická metro station every 30 to 60 minutes, and a few go from Florenc. *Přímý spoj* (direct) buses to Kladno don't stop at Lidice, but anything serving Buštěhrad does.

BEROUN

Though of little interest itself, Beroun is a good jumping-off point for Křivoklát and Karlštejn castles, the Koněprusy Caves and hikes in the beautiful Berounka River basin.

Orientation & Information

The main square, Husovo náměstí, is a 10-minute walk straight out (north) of the train station. There's a bank on the square, and the bus station is east of the square, across the river. The Beroun telephone code is 0311.

Places to Stay & Eat

The *Hotel Český dvůr* (☎ 214 11), Husovo náměstí 86, has basic rooms with toilet and shower for US$9 a bed. The *Hotel Barbora* (☎ 254 42) has clean rooms with shared facilities for US$14 a bed; from the train station, turn right beyond the highway. At the *Hotel U Blažků* (☎ 213 76), north off the square at Česká 176, a double room with breakfast is US$35. The place on Havlíčkova with the illuminated 'hotel' sign is the *Hotel Litava* (☎ 252 65), where doubles are about US$50.

The *Restaurace U Mlýnaře*, on the road to the bus station, has pasta and Chinese dishes along with Czech items. *Hotel U Blažků* serves big helpings of Czech standards. Both charge US$2 to US$4 per course, and stay open until 10 pm.

Getting There & Away

Beroun is a beautiful 50-minute ride along the Berounka River by express trains that go about every three hours from Prague's main train station, or local trains hourly from Smíchov station. An unreserved seat is 10 Kč.

KONĚPRUSY CAVES

The tour through these impressive limestone caves (known as the Koněprusy Jeskyně in Czech), six km south of Beroun and 600 metres deep, reveals colourful formations, the bones of humans and a woolly rhinoceros, and a 15th century underground forge used to make counterfeit coins.

Buses run at odd intervals from Beroun's train station to Koněprusy village below the caves. Go by midday to be sure of a bus back; the caves office will know the times. It's open May to September from 8 am to 4 pm daily (to 5 pm on weekends from June to August), to 2 pm in October (to 3 pm on weekends), and closed in winter. Take a pullover: it's chilly down there.

KŘIVOKLÁT

Křivoklát Castle was built in the late 13th century as a royal hunting lodge. In the 15th century Vladislav II gave it its present Gothic face.

There's no hunting anymore: much of the upper Berounka basin, one of Bohemia's most pristine forests, is now the Křivoklát Protected Landscape Region and a Unesco 'biosphere preservation' area.

Half the pleasure of going is getting there, by train up the wooded valley hemmed in by limestone bluffs. On weekdays you'll find none of the crowds associated with places like Karlštejn.

Orientation & Information

Křivoklát is a drowsy village beside the Rakovnický potok, a tributary of the Berounka River. There is said to be a 16th century mill on the stream. From the Hotel Sýkova, climb up the road about 10 minutes to the castle turning. If you're driving, there's a petrol station farther up the hill. Křivoklát's telephone code is 0313.

The Castle

Scarred on the outside by clumsy renovations, the castle's best features are inside. Its **chapel** is one of the country's finest unaltered late-Gothic interiors, full of intricate polychrome carvings. The altar is decorated with angels carrying instruments of torture – perhaps not surprising in view of the castle's 16th century use as a political prison.

Right under the chapel are the **prison** and torture chambers. The **Knights' Hall** features a permanent collection of late-Gothic religious sculpture and painted panels. Across one end of the 1st floor is the 25-metre-long **King's Hall**, the second-biggest non-church Gothic hall in the republic, after Vladislav Hall in Prague Castle.

Křivoklát is open June to August from 9 am to 6 pm, April to May and September/October to 5 pm, and the rest of the year to 4 pm; it's closed Monday.

Walking from Křivoklát to Skryje

If you've got the gear and an extra day or two, consider walking the fine 18-km trail (marked red) south-west up the Berounka valley to Skryje. It starts on the west side of Rakovnický potok near the train stop. Beyond the bridge to Roztoky are the **Nezabudice Cliffs** (Nezabudické skály), part of a state nature reserve, and the village of Nezabudice. Across the river from Týřovice village is **Týrov**, a 13th century French-style castle used for a time as a prison and abandoned in the 16th century. Around this is another nature reserve.

The summer resort of **Skryje** has some old thatched houses. You can also walk down the other side of the valley for a closer look at Týrov Castle. There are local buses down the valley to the train at Roztoky, or on to Beroun.

Places to Stay & Eat

From the castle turning, climb on up the road for about half a km to the plain *Hotel U Černých* (☎ 983 11), with doubles for about US$20. There are *campsites* about three km up the Berounka at Višňová, across the river at Branov (cross at Roztoky), and at Skryje.

The friendly *Hotel Sýkora* (no rooms) in Křivoklát village is a beer hall with cheap pork and dumplings.

Getting There & Away

You can get from Prague to Křivoklát and back on a long day trip, but staying a night at Beroun makes it easier. Rakovník-bound trains leave Beroun every two hours or so; Křivoklát is 50 minutes up the line. There are occasional direct trains to Křivoklát from Prague's Smíchov station.

KARLŠTEJN

Karlštejn was founded by Charles IV in 1348 as a royal hideaway and a treasury for the crown jewels and his holy relics. Perched on a crag above the Berounka River, looking taller than it is wide, it's unquestionably the most photogenic castle in the Prague region – and the most popular, with coachloads of tourists trooping through all day.

Heavily remodelled in the 19th century, it's now in amazingly good shape. But the best views are from the outside, so if the tours are sold out, relax and enjoy a good tramp in the woods (see the following Walks section).

Orientation

It's a 10-minute walk from the station to the village, and another 10 minutes up to the castle along a gauntlet of overpriced restaurants and souvenir shops.

Information

Foreigners are expected to buy a guided tour at 90 Kč, commencing when there are enough people who speak your language. But you can try in your best Czech for a 20-Kč ticket and tag along with a Czech group.

The castle is open year-round (except lunch times, Mondays, 24 December and 1 January) – in July/August from 9 am to 7 pm, May/June and September to 6 pm, April and October to 5 pm, and the rest of the year to 4 pm. Karlštejn's telephone code is 0311.

The Castle

The south-facing palace is where most of the open rooms are, including a handsome **audience hall** and the **imperial bedroom**. You must use your imagination since they have been largely stripped of their furnishings. Several scale models indicate how drastic the 19th century renovation was.

North of the palace is the **Marian Tower** (Marianská věž), with Charles' private quarters and the Church of Our Lady (Kostel Panny Marie), with fragments of its beautiful original frescoes. Charles' private St Catherine Chapel (Kaple sv Kateřiny) is in a corner of the church.

The centre of the complex is the **Great Tower** (Velká věž), where the royal regalia, jewels and relics were kept. At its heart is the lavish Chapel of the Holy Cross (Kaple sv Kříže), furnished in gilt, thousands of semiprecious stones and scores of panels by Master Theodoric, Bohemia's best known painter of the time. But it's closed to the public, and you must settle for photographs and a scale model in the sacristy behind the Church of Our Lady.

Walks

On a red-marked path east from Karlštejn village, it's seven km via Mořinka (not Mořina) village into the **Karlík valley** (Karlícké údolí), a nature reserve where you may find the remains of Charles IV's Karlík Castle, abandoned in the 15th century. Karlík village, one km down the valley, has a 12th century rotunda. A road and a green-marked trail run 1.5 km south-east to Dobřichovice, on the Prague-Beroun railway line.

From Srbsko, one train stop west of Karlštejn, another red trail climbs up the wooded valley of Buboviský potok, eight km to the ridge-top **Monastery of St John Under the Rock** (Klášter sv Jan pod Skálou), allegedly once an StB (secret police) training camp. About 1.5 km farther on a blue-marked trail, just beyond the highway, is Vráž, with buses back to Beroun or to Prague.

Either walk can be done in under three hours.

Places to Stay

Avoid the pricey pensions in Karlštejn village. There's a *campsite* on the north side of the river, half a km west of the bridge, and the *Hotel Mlýn* (☎ 942 08) down the south side of the river, east of the bridge. Mořina, on the road 2.5 km north-east of Karlštejn, has a modest pension, the *Na růžku*. Or take the train 10 minutes on to Beroun.

Getting There & Away

Karlštejn is on the Beroun railway line from Prague's Smíchov station. Local trains depart at least hourly for the 40-minute trip, for 10 Kč; express trains don't stop here. There are return departures from Karlštejn until at least 7 pm.

PRŮHONICE

In this village just outside Prague is a photogenic 13th century chateau, restored at the end of the 19th century in a mix of neo-Gothic and neo-Renaissance styles, fronting onto a 250-hectare landscaped park, one of the finest of its kind in Europe.

The **chateau** is now occupied by the Botanical Institute of the Czech Academy of Sciences and is closed to the public. The little **Church of the Birth of Our Lady** (Kostel Narození Panny Marie) beside the chateau, consecrated in 1187, still has some 14th century frescoes visible. This too is closed, unless you attend 5 pm Sunday Mass.

But the **park**, now a state botanical park, is the main attraction. On weekends it's packed out with Czech families, but on a drizzly weekday morning you could have the exotic gardens, sweet-smelling woods and three artificial lakes literally to yourself. In May, rhododendrons come out in rainbows.

Admission is 10 Kč, and a map of the park, with some English, is available at the entrance.

Průhonice Chateau (JK)

Getting There & Away

On weekdays, buses leave every 30 to 60 minutes all morning from the ČAD (not city bus) stand at Opatov metro station. The 15-minute trip is 6 Kč. On weekends there are more buses (and more visitors).

KONOPIŠTĚ

The French-style castle at Konopiště dates from 1300. It got a neo-Gothic facelift in the 1890s from its best-known owner, Archduke Franz Ferdinand of Austria-Este, heir to the Austro-Hungarian throne, whose 1914 assassination set off WW I.

He was an obsessive hunter, as you will see from a tour through the wood-panelled castle, packed with a grossly over-the-top collection of dead animals and an armoury of hunting weapons. In 25 years he dispatched several hundred thousand creatures on the 225-hectare estate (and kept a tally of them all).

Nowadays the animals are back, and the English-style wooded grounds, dotted with lakes, gardens and statuary, are really the best reason to visit – and an antidote to the heavy tourist scene around the castle.

Orientation & Information

The nearest town is Benešov. Its train and bus stations are opposite one another and less than five minutes on foot from the town square, Masarykovo náměstí (turn left out of the train station, then right at Tyršova). Komercní banka on the square does foreign exchange. Benešov's telephone code is 0301.

The castle is two km away in the opposite direction from town, a fine half-hour walk through the estate. Cross the bridge over the railway, take the first left into Ke stadiónu and the third right down Spartakiádní. Drivers can go straight down Konopišťská from the bridge.

The Castle

The castle is divided into two long tours that are tiresome inventories of every teacup with not a word on the castle's history. For each, you can join a Czech group for 20 Kč, or take a 70 Kč English tour, making it perhaps the most expensive attraction in the Prague region.

Both tours take in the archduke's **trophies**, a forest of mounted heads, antlers, claws and teeth. **Tour I** looks at the stately rooms with their Italian cabinets, Dürer graphics and Meissen porcelain. **Tour II** takes in hunting weapons, the chapel and a plush mens' party room.

If that's not enough, go around the back to see the archduke's St George fetish: scores of paintings, statues and other renderings of the mythical dragon-slayer (and this is only some 10% of the hoard).

The castle is open May to August from 9 am to 6 pm, September to 5 pm, and April and October to 4 pm; it's closed Monday, 13 April, 7 July and during lunch time.

Places to Stay & Eat

The *Hotel Pošta* (☎ 223 55), off Masarykovo náměstí at Tyršova 162, has plain doubles with toilet and shower, overpriced at US$20, and a restaurant that serves breakfast.

Two monstrous motels sit south-west of town at the edge of the Konopiště estate. *Motel Švarc* (☎ 256 11) on Ke stadiónu has doubles with toilet and shower for US$35, plus a restaurant and 24-hour snack bar. The similar *Motel Konopiště* (☎ 227 32) also has a *campsite*.

Adequate cheap eats (main dishes US$2 to US$3) are available at the *U Kovářů* pub in one corner of the square.

Getting There & Away

Benešov is a pleasant train ride, through broadly rolling farmland and forest, from Prague's main station. There are trains every one to 1½ hours, and the trip takes just over an hour. Buses depart from Florenc and from Roztyly metro station about every three hours.

ČESKÝ ŠTERNBERK

This hulking fortress, on a sheer ridge above the Sázava River, dates back to the 13th century. It probably owes its survival not only to its impregnable position, but to its having been in the same family, the Šternberks, for almost its entire life.

It succumbed to heavy Baroque remodelling in the 17th and 18th centuries, and the only remaining traces of its Gothic personality are in the fortifications. Nowadays its most impressive features are the views – up from the river, and out from the castle windows. The scenery on the train journey up the Sázava River valley is itself probably worth the ride.

Orientation

Don't get off at Český Šternberk station, but one stop on at Český Šternberk zastávka, across the river from the castle. A road and a shorter footpath climb around behind the castle.

The Castle

The tedious 45-minute tour reveals an Italian Baroque renovation, very heavy on stucco ornamentation. Highlights include the Rococo **St Sebastian Chapel** (Kaple sv Šebestiána) and the **'Yellow Room'**, with fine views over the countryside. From here you can see trees marking out a 17th century French-style park across the river, the only part of a planned Šternberk chateau that was completed before the money ran out.

Places to Stay & Eat

The friendly *Hotel Tesla* (☎ 0303-551 82) is at a quiet spot on the river, a 25-minute trek downstream on the castle side. The hotel, about US$5 a bed, is booked out all summer with Czech groups, but there are US$2 bunk-beds in spartan quads with no toilet or shower.

The castle has a pricey *vinárna*. The *Hotel pod hradem* (no accommodation) in the hamlet below has cheap eats, and the *Hotel Tesla's* food is good.

Getting There & Away

Change at Čerčany on the railway line towards Benešov (see the earlier Konopiště section). From there, trains lumber up the Sázava valley about every 2½ hours, taking about 1¼ hours to Český Šternberk.

KUTNÁ HORA

It's hard to imagine today, but in its time this was Bohemia's most important town after Prague.

In the late 13th century, silver ore was found in these hills, and a town sprouted. In 1308, Wenceslas II imported a team of Italian minters and established his central Royal Mint here. The town's power grew, splendid churches and palaces rose, and in 1400 Wenceslas IV moved the royal residence here. In less than 150 years Kutná Hora had become one of Europe's biggest, richest towns and Bohemia's economic mainstay.

But in the 16th century the silver began to run out and decline set in, hastened by the Thirty Years' War. A Baroque building boom came to an end with a devastating fire in 1770.

Today Kutná Hora is a fraction of its old self, but still dressed up in a collection of fine architectural monuments. With a pastel-hued square dotted with cafés, medieval alleys with façades from Gothic to Cubist, and a cathedral to rival St Vitus, comparisons with Prague are hard to resist. Kutná Hora is certainly as densely picturesque as Prague, and blessed with warmer people and lower prices.

Don't come on a Monday, when everything is closed.

Orientation

The historical centre is compact enough to see on foot. Most attractions lie between the central square, Palackého náměstí, and the St Barbara Cathedral in the south-west corner of town.

The bus station is a five-minute walk north of the town centre. Although there's a train station here, trains from Prague stop only at Sedlec, three km away to the north-east.

The user-friendly town centre has almost too many signs. Quite a few places accommodate disabled visitors. Chronological (red) house numbers are in more common use than sequential (blue) ones.

Information

Čedok (☎ 2534), Palackého náměstí 330, open weekdays from 8 am to 4 pm, is faintly helpful. Komercní banka is at Tylova 9/390. A good 30-page brochure about the town is available from Čedok and newsagents. Kutná Hora's telephone code is 0327.

Italian Court (Vlašský Dvůr)

The Vlašský dvůr, on Havličkovo náměstí, was built by Wenceslas II as a royal seat and later the Royal Mint. The name in old Czech refers to its original Italian architects. A palace, chapel and tower were added a century later by Wenceslas IV, who made it his home.

When the mint closed in the early 18th century it became the town hall. The 20-Kč guided tour (from 9 am to 5 pm, except Monday) is worth it for a look at the few historical rooms open to the public.

The oldest remaining part, the (now bricked-up) niches in the courtyard, were **minters' workshops**. The original **treasury rooms** now hold an exhibit on coins and minting.

In Wenceslas IV's **Audience Hall** are 19th century murals of two important events that took place here: the 1471 election of Vladislav II Jagiello as king (the angry man in white is Matthias Corvinus, the loser), and an agreement between Wenceslas IV and Jan Hus (then rector of Charles University) to alter the university's German-Czech ratio.

About all that remains of Wenceslas IV's **Chapel of SS Wenceslas & Vladislav** (Kaple sv Václava a Vladislava) is the oriel, best seen from the courtyard – although the 1904 Art-Nouveau interior renovation is very striking.

Plague column in Šultysova ulice, Kutná Hora (JK)

From Vlašský Dvůr to St Barbara

Around the corner from Vlašský dvůr is the huge **St James Church** (Kostel sv Jakuba), begun in 1330 but only completed a century later. Passing south of the church, you come to **Ruthardská ulice**, a very old and photogenic lane running up beside the old town walls. It's named after Rozina Ruthard who, a local legend says, was sealed alive in a closet by her father, a medieval burgher.

At the top of the lane is the **Hrádek** ('Little Castle'), originally part of the town's fortifications. It was rebuilt in the 15th century as the residence of Jan Smíšek, administrator of the royal mines, who grew rich from silver he illegally mined right under the building. It's now a Museum of Mining (open from 9 am to noon and 1 to 5 pm, except Monday); non-claustrophobes can go down into Smíšek's tunnel.

The approach to the cathedral up Barborská ulice is between 13 crumbling **Gothic statues** and the former **Jesuit College** (1700), the biggest after Prague's Klementinum.

Cathedral of St Barbara (Kostel Sv Barbora)

The miners' guilds of Kutná Hora pipped Prague in the cathedral department: their Gothic masterpiece dedicated to the patron saint of miners is one of the finest Gothic churches in Europe.

Work was started in 1380, interrupted during the Hussite Wars and abandoned in 1558 when the silver began to run out. The rear (west) end was completed in neo-Gothic style only at the turn of this century.

Inside, eight **ambulatory chapels** surround the main altar, some with vivid frescoes – including mining scenes – as old as the 15th century. The lofty, bright **ceiling vault** is covered in a tangle of ribs, stars and floral patterns, and the coats of arms of the miners' guilds and local nobility. In the south-west chapel are **murals** of 15th century minters at work. The north-west chapel has an eye-popping mural of the *Vision of St Ignatius*.

The cathedral is open from 8 am to 5 pm in summer, 9 am to noon and 1 to 4 pm in winter, closed Monday. On the hillside below the cathedral is the former **Corpus Christi Chapel** (Kaple Božího těla), built in the 14th century.

Other Attractions

From the Jesuit College, walk through náměstí Národního odboje and left on Husova to see bits of the **old city walls**. Return along Husova to Rejskovo náměstí, with its 1495 Gothic **Stone Fountain** (Kamenná kašna).

Cross via Lierova to Radnická. The Gothic confection at No 183 is the **Stone House** (Kamenný dům), a burgher's house dating from 1490. Pop in to the Museum of Arts & Crafts there, just to see the inside. East and then south is Šultysova, once part of the town's medieval marketplace, lined with handsome townhouses, in particular the **Marble House** (D ům U Mramorů) at No 173. At the bottom of the street is a 1715 **plague column**.

Across Palackého náměstí, walk down Tylova to No 507, the **Birthplace of Josef Tyl**, the 19th century playwright who wrote *Where is My Home?*, later to become part of the Czech national anthem. On the Baroque façade is a statue of three miners.

Cross the square again to Kollárova and turn right on Jiřího z Poděbrad. Two blocks down is the unfinished former **Ursuline Convent** (Klášter Voršilek), with a 1743 chapel by Kilian Dientzenhofer. In the convent is an exhibit of furnishings from various chateaux in central Bohemia.

Places to Stay

Best at the bottom end is the year-round tourist hostel, the *Turistická ubytovna* (☎ 2960) on náměstí Národního odboje, with US$3.50 beds in rooms of six, communal shower and toilet, and a little kitchen. Reception is only open from 8 to 9 am and 5 to 6 pm. Quite a few private homes have *Zimmer frei* ('room for rent') signs.

Two good pensions are in listed 14th century buildings. Quiet *Hotel U Rytířů* (☎ 2256), Rejskovo náměstí 123, has rooms of all kinds at US$7 to US$15 per bed. *Hotel U Hrnčíře* (☎ 2113) at Barborská 24 has plain doubles with shower and toilet for US$12 a bed, with breakfast.

The *Hotel Mědínek* (☎ 2741) on Palackého náměstí has singles/doubles with TV, toilet and bath for about US$30/40, with breakfast, and a few US$30 doubles with shower and shared toilet.

A *campsite* five km south on the River Vrchlice (on the road to Malešov) is useful if you've got a car.

Places to Eat

In addition to daytime cafés, a few restaurants stay open until 10 pm. The *China Restaurant* (☎ 327 41 51), náměstí Národního odboje 48, does respectable Chinese dishes for around US$3, and helpings are generous; it's closed from 2 to 5 pm.

Restaurace U Bakaláře (☎ 2547), Husova 103, has distracted service but delicious chicken dishes (US$1.50 to US$2.50) and pricier venison specials. The *Kavárna v domě u tří pávů* (House of the Three Peacocks), at the east end of Palackého náměstí, has an eclectic menu with main dishes from US$2 to US$3. *U Kamenného domu* at Lierova 4/147 is a cheerful pub with cheap grub.

Getting There & Away

No trains go directly from Prague to Kutná Hora. Three or four go to Sedlec each day from Masarykovo station, taking about an hour. From the Sedlec station there are local buses into Kutná Hora.

Long-distance buses go from Florenc about every hour on weekday afternoons. For a weekend or morning trip, go to the ČAD stand on Počernická (see the Žižkov map). PIS can give you current departure and return times. The 1¼-hour trip is 35 Kč.

By car, the fastest route is Highway 12 via Kolín and Sedlec; the prettiest is road 333 via Kostelec. Kutná Hora is about 65 km east-south-east of Prague.

Getting Around

Local *(městská doprava)* buses on Masarykovo ulice go to/from the train station and Sedlec every 20 to 30 minutes. Buy tickets from the driver.

AROUND KUTNÁ HORA

Sedlec & the Ossuary Chapel of All Saints

Today Sedlec is a suburb of Kutná Hora, but it's been around longer, since the founding of Bohemia's first Cistercian Monastery here in 1142.

After a 13th century abbot brought back some earth from Jerusalem and sprinkled it on the monastery's graveyard, its popularity mushroomed. Demand was augmented by plague epidemics, and within a century there were tens of thousands of graves, and bones began to pile up. The small 14th century All Saints' Chapel (Kaple Všech Svatých) was pressed into service as an ossuary.

When Joseph II abolished the monasteries, the Schwarzenberg family bought this one, and in 1870 a Czech woodcarver named František Rint turned the bones into the ghoulishly artistic attraction you can see in the chapel cellar today. There are bone chalices and bone crosses; the Schwarzenberg coat of arms in bones; and an extraordinary chandelier made from at least one of every bone in the human body. Rint even signed his name in bones, at the foot of the stairs.

The ossuary is open from 8 am to 5 pm in summer, 9 am to noon and 1 to 4 pm in winter; it's open daily in July and August, and daily except Monday the rest of

Ossuary Chapel of All Saints (JK)

the year. Admission is 20 Kč, or 30 Kč if you want to take photos.

Down on the main road is the monastery's **Church of the Ascension of the Virgin** (Kostel Nanebevzetí Panny Marie), renovated at the start of the 18th century by Giovanni Santini in his 'Baroque-Gothic' style, unique to Bohemia. Nearby, the old monastery is now part of a tobacco factory and closed to the public.

Sedlec is two km from Kutná Hora by local bus. Some buses stop by the church, some opposite the ossuary, two blocks up Zámecká from the church.

Žleby Chateau

This beautiful chateau, 18 km south-east of Kutná Hora, dates from at least the 13th century. Its fairy-tale appearance is the result of renovation by Duke Vincent Karl Auersperg in the latter 19th century – a sugary Gothic-Renaissance style meant to conjure up romantic visions of medieval castles.

The Auerspergs lived here until 1945, when they fled to Austria, leaving everything behind. The chateau is therefore in immaculate – and authentic – shape, and offers a glimpse of how the other half was living in Czechoslovakia in this century. (Had they stayed until 1948, the chateau would now, under post-Communist reparations law, be theirs again.)

Inside it's all armour and mounted firearms, wood panelling and leather wallpaper, Rococo flourishes and a treasure trove of old furniture. Highlights include the **Knights' Hall** with a huge Baroque cupboard and rows of Czech and German glass; the **Duchess Study**, with a replica Rubens on the ceiling and a fantastic door of inlaid wood; and the **kitchen**, fitted out with the 19th century's most up-to-date equipment.

The chateau is open May to August from 8 am to 5 pm, September from 9 am, closed Monday and the day following national holidays; in April and October it's open only on weekends from 9 am to 4 pm. There are no crowds here, save the occasional tour bus.

Getting There & Away The chateau is 50 minutes from Kutná Hora by bus, for 15 Kč. There's only one suitable direct connection (leaves about 2.15 pm, returns about 5.30 pm), but a dozen options if you change at Čáslav. Ask for Žleby náměstí, the square at the foot of the chateau. Check return times, as buses peter out soon after 5 pm.

PŘEROV NAD LABEM

In this village east of Prague is the **Labe River Region Ethnographic Museum** (Polabské národopisné muzeum), the Czech Republic's oldest open-air museum of traditional architecture. It was begun in 1895, soon after the first such museum opened in Stockholm (the Swedish word for such a museum, *skansen*, has stuck). Contrived as *skansens* are, they are a unique help in visualising life of an earlier day.

This one was started around a Přerov house that was already here: the 'Old Bohemian Cottage', dressed in herringbone clapboard and carved ornaments. Other exhibits have been brought in piece-wise from around the region: over a dozen houses, as well as belfries, pigsties, decorated beehives and a pigeon house. Staff tend gardens and raise bees with traditional methods.

The museum is open May to October from 9 am to 5 pm, except Monday. Admission is 10 Kč, plus 5 Kč for a detailed English brochure.

Getting There & Away

Prague-Poděbrady buses from Palmovka metro station (about half a dozen during the day) stop at an isolated petrol station about 35 minutes from Prague. From there it's a 20-minute walk north to the village. Give yourself about 1½ hours, including the walk.

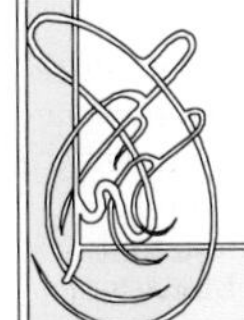

Index

MAP LEGEND

BOUNDARIES

........International	..............Regional

SYMBOLS

..................Bus Station	.........................Parking
..............Camping Area	...................Post Office
.....................Cathedral	.... Railway Station
.........................Church	............Railway Tunnel
.............................Cave	66 ....Route Number
........................Hospital	..................Synagogue
...............Metro Station	...... Tourist Information

ROUTES

.........Major Road	.... Railway
.........Minor Road	...................Metro
...........City Street	.... Bicycle Path
Pedestrian Street	.......Walking Path

HYDROGRAPHIC FEATURES

........River, Creek	....................Lake

OTHER FEATURES

.............................Building	.......................Urban Area
...................Place to Shop	....................Park, Garden
■ .... Place to Stay	.... Cemetery
▼ ....Place to Eat	

Note: not all symbols displayed above appear in this book

Top : Old Town Square (JK)
Bottom : John Lennon Wall (JK)

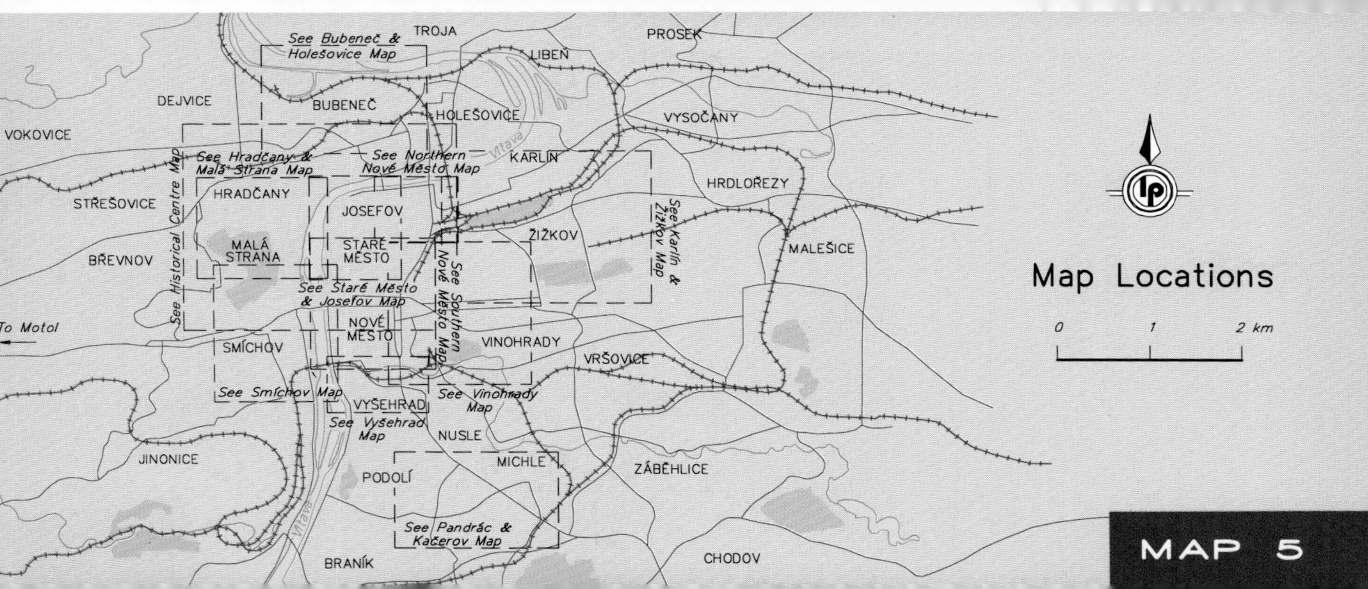
MAP 5
Map Locations
0
1
2 km
TROJA
PROSEK
See Bubeneč & Holešovice Map
LIBEŇ
DEJVICE
BUBENEČ
HOLEŠOVICE
VYSOČANY
VOKOVICE
Vltava
See Hradčany & Malá Strana Map
See Northern Nové Město Map
KARLÍN
HRDLOŘEZY
STŘEŠOVICE
HRADČANY
JOSEFOV
See Historical Centre Map
MALÁ STRANA
STARÉ MĚSTO
ŽIŽKOV
See Karlín & Žižkov Map
MALEŠICE
BŘEVNOV
See Staré Město & Josefov Map
See Southern Nové Město Map
To Motol
NOVÉ MĚSTO
SMÍCHOV
VINOHRADY
VRŠOVICE
See Smíchov Map
VYŠEHRAD
See Vinohrady Map
See Vyšehrad Map
NUSLE
JINONICE
MICHLE
PODOLÍ
ZÁBĚHLICE
See Pandrác & Kačerov Map
BRANÍK
CHODOV

Hradčany & Malá Strana

0 200 400 m

Jelení
Power Bridge Street (U Prašného mostu)
U Brusnice
Hradčany
Nový svět
Černínská
Keplerova
U Kasáren
Hradčanské nám
Loretánské náměstí
Loretánská
Ke Hradu
Castle Steps
Parléřova
Pohořelec
Úvoz
Nerudova
Strahovská zahrada
Vlašská
Lobkovická zahrada
Schönbornská zahrada
Malá Strana
'Hunger Wall'
Seminářská zahrada
Růžový sad
Olympijská
Vaníčkova
Chaloupeckého
Petřínské sady
Kinského zahrada
1 2 16 17 18 19 20 21 22 23 24 25 26 27 28 29 30 31 32 33 34 35 36 37 38 39 40 41 42 43 44 45 50 51 52
113 114 115 116 117 118 119 120

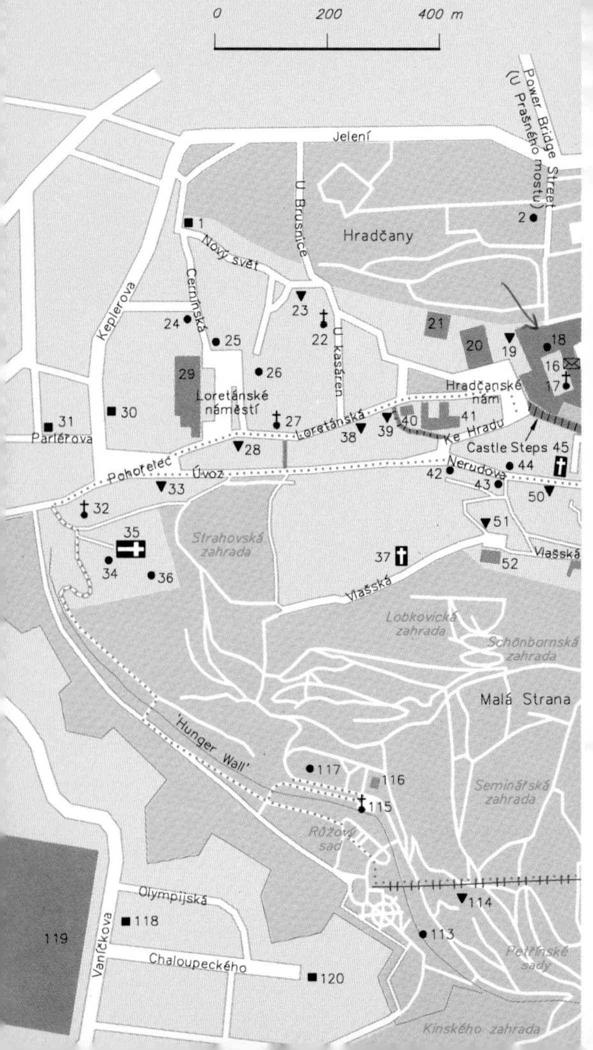

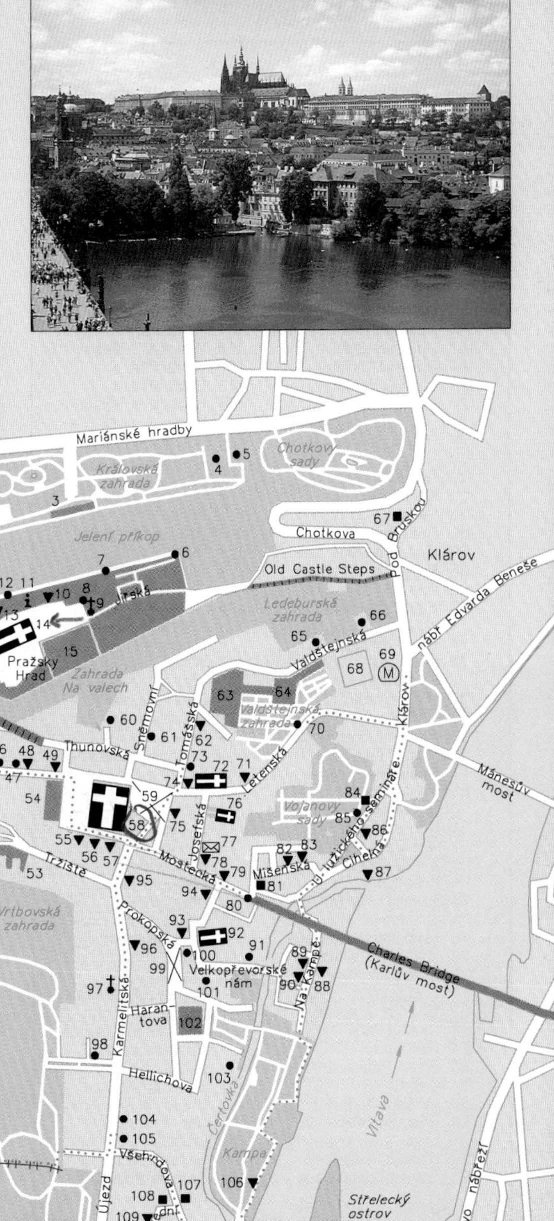
Mariánské hradby
Královská zahrada
Chotkovy sady
Jelení příkop
Chotkova
Pod Bruskou
Klárov
Old Castle Steps
Jiřská
nábř Edvarda Beneše
Ledeburská zahrada
Valdštejnská
Pražský Hrad
Zahrada Na valech
Sněmovní
Tomášská
Valdštejnská zahrada
Thunovská
Letenská
Klárov
Mánesův most
Josefská
Vojanovy sady
U lužického semináře
Cihelná
Mišeňská
Tržiště
Mostecká
Vrtbovská zahrada
Prokopská
Velkopřevorské nám
Na Kampě
Charles Bridge (Karlův most)
Karmelitská
Harantova
Hellichova
Čertovka
Kampa
Vltava
Všehrdova
Újezd
Střelecký ostrov
Besední
Říční
Smetanovo nábřeží
Vítězná
most Legií
3 4 5 6 7 8 9 10 11 12 13 14 15
46 47 48 49 53 54 55 56 57 58 59 60 61 62 63 64 65 66 67 68 69 70
71 72 73 74 75 76 77 78 79 80 81 82 83 84 85 86 87 88 89 90
91 92 93 94 95 96 97 98 99 100 101 102 103 104 105 106 107 108 109 110 111 112

Map 6 Hradčany & Malá Strana

■ PLACES TO STAY

1 Pension U raka
30 Hotel Savoy
31 Kolej JA Komenského Hostel
67 Hotel Hoffmeister
81 U tří pštrosů
84 Hotel U Páva
107 Hotel Kampa
108 Privat U Kiliána
118 ESTEC Hostel
120 Strahov Hostel

▼ PLACES TO EAT

10 Restaurace U Kanovníků
13 Vikárka
19 Café Poet
23 U zlaté hrušky
28 Pivnice U černého vola
33 Sate indonéské speciality
34 Peklo Restaurant
38 Potraviny U Loretánské
39 U staré radnice
48 U tří housliček
49 Hostinec U kocoura
50 U zeleného čaje
51 Restaurant Faros
55 Restaurant U Mecenáše
56 U tří zlatých hvězd
57 Jo's Bar
62 Valdštejnská hospoda
71 Pivnice U sv Tomáše
74 U Schnellů
75 Malostranská beseda
78 U tří bílých jehňátek
79 Mostecká pekárna
81 U tří pštrosů
82 Vinárna Gaudium
83 Charlie Pub
84 Restaurant U Páva
86 Bistro Tkalcovský dvůr
87 Vinárna Čertovka
88 Restaurace Kampa Club
89 U zlatých nůšek
90 Bar Art Club Galerie
93 Mazlova vinárna u malířů
94 U snědeného krámu
95 J+J Mašek & Zemanová Food Shop
96 Grand Restaurant Regent
106 Rybářský klub
107 Restaurant Zbrojnice
108 Snack & U Kiliána
109 Canto Club
112 Steak House
114 Nebozízek Restaurant

OTHER

2 Former Riding School
3 Ball-Game House (Míčovna)
4 Singing Fountain (Zpívajíci Fontána)
5 Summer Palace (Letohrádek)
6 Daliborka
7 White Tower (Bílá věž)
8 National Gallery (Klášter sv Jiří)
9 Basillica of St George (Bazilika sv Jiří)
11 Information Office
12 Mihulka
14 St Vitus Cathedral
15 The Old Royal Palace (Starý královský palác)
16 Post Office
17 Chapel of the Holy Cross (Kaple sv Kříže)
18 Prague Castle Gallery (Obrazárna pražského hradu)
20 Archbishop's Palace (Arcibiskupský palác)
21 Sternberg Palace
22 Church of St John of Nepomuk (Kostel sv Jana Nepomuckého)
24 Gambra Surrealist Gallery

25 Capuchin Monastery
26 Loreta
27 Chapel of St Barbara (Kaple sv Barbory)
29 Černín Palace (Černínský palác)
32 Church of St Roch (Kostel sv Rocha)
34 Strahov Monastery (Strahovský klášter)
35 Church of the Assumption of Oue Lady (Kostel Nanebevzetí Panny Marie)
36 National Literature Museum
37 Church of St Charles Borrome (Kostel sv Karla Boromejského)
40 Church of St Benedict (Kostel sv Benedikta)
41 Military Museum (Schwarzenberg Palace)
42 House of Two Suns (Dům U dvou slunců)
43 Bretfeld Palace
44 House at the Golden Horseshoe (Dům U zlaté podkovy)
45 Kostel P Marie U kajetánů
46 Italian Embassy
47 House of St John of Nepomuk
52 Lobkovic Palace/ German Embassy
53 Schönborn Palace/ US Embassy
54 Liechtenstein Palace
58 St Nicholas Church (Kostel sv Mikuláše)
59 Malostrandské náměstí
60 British Embassy
61 Parliament House (Sněmovna)
63 Komenský Pedagogical Museum
64 Wallenstein Palace
65 Polish Embassy
66 Belgian Consulate
68 Wallenstein Riding School (Valdštejnská Jízdárna)
69 Malostranská Metro Station (Line A)
70 Entrance to Wallenstein Garden (Valdštejnská zahrada)
72 Church of St Thomas (Kostel sv Tomáše)
73 House at the Golden Stag
76 Church of St Joseph (Kostel sv Josefa)
77 Post Office
80 Malá Strana bridge towers (Malostranská mostecká věž)
85 Entrance to Vojan Park (Vojanovy sady)
91 John Lennon Wall
92 Church of our Lady below the Chain (Kostel Panny Marie pod řetězem)
97 Church of our Lady Victorious (Kostel Panny Marie Vítězné) & Infant of Prague
98 Prague Spring (Pražské jaro) Music Festival Box Office
99 Maltézké náměstí
100 Museum of Musical Instruments
101 French Embassy
102 Nostitz Palace/Netherlands Embassy
103 MXM Gallery
104 Sokol Sport Shop
105 Museum of Physical Education & Sport (Muzeum Tělovýchovy a sportu)
110 Church of St John at the Laundry (Kostel sv Jan Na prádle)
111 Borát (or Újezd) Rock Club
113 Štefánik Observatory & Planetarium
115 Church of St Lawrence (Kostel sv Vavřince)
116 The Maze (Bludiště)
117 Petřín Tower (Petřínská rozhledna)
119 Spartakiádní stadion

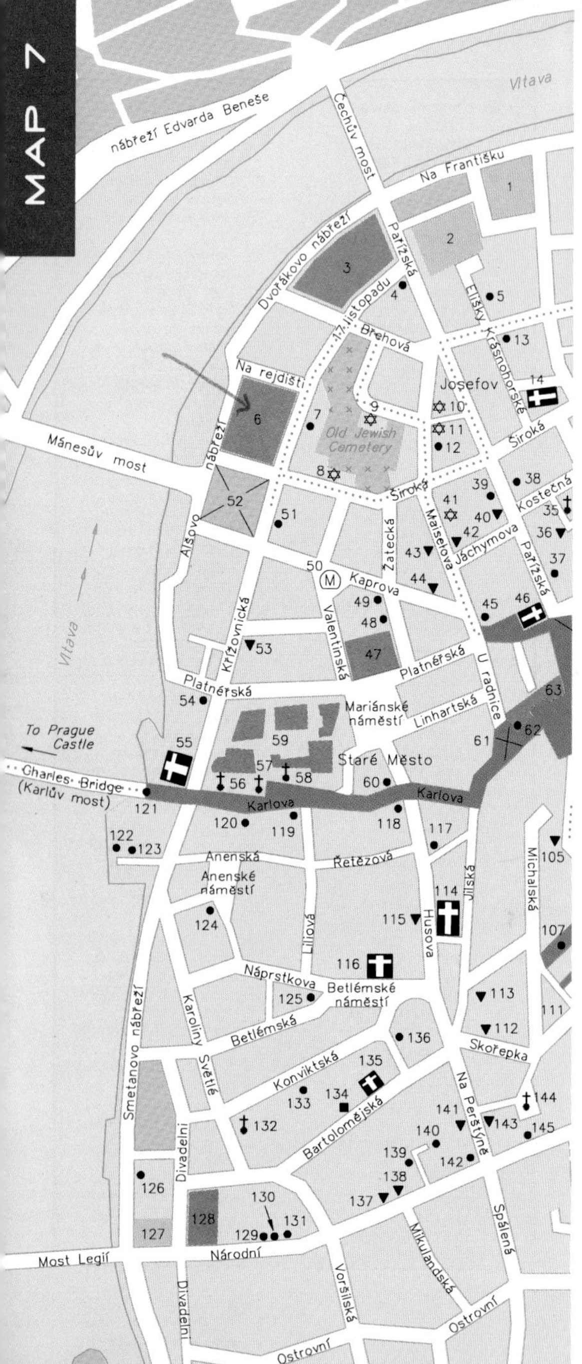
MAP 7
Vltava
nábřeží Edvarda Beneše
Čechův most
Na Františku
Dvořákovo nábřeží
Pařížská
17. listopadu
Břehová
Elišky Krásnohorské
Na rejdišti
Josefov
Old Jewish Cemetery
Mánesův most
nábřeží
Široká
Alšovo
Kostečná
Maiselova
Jáchymova
Žatecká
Kaprova
Valentinská
Křižovnická
Platnéřská
U radnice
Linhartská
Mariánské náměstí
To Prague Castle
Staré Město
Charles Bridge (Karlův most)
Karlova
Anenská
Řetězová
Anenské náměstí
Michalská
Jilská
Husova
Liliová
Náprstkova
Betlémské náměstí
Smetanovo nábřeží
Karoliny Světlé
Betlémská
Konviktská
Skořepka
Bartolomějská
Na Perštýně
Divadelní
Spálená
Mikulandská
Most Legií
Národní
Voršilská
Ostrovní

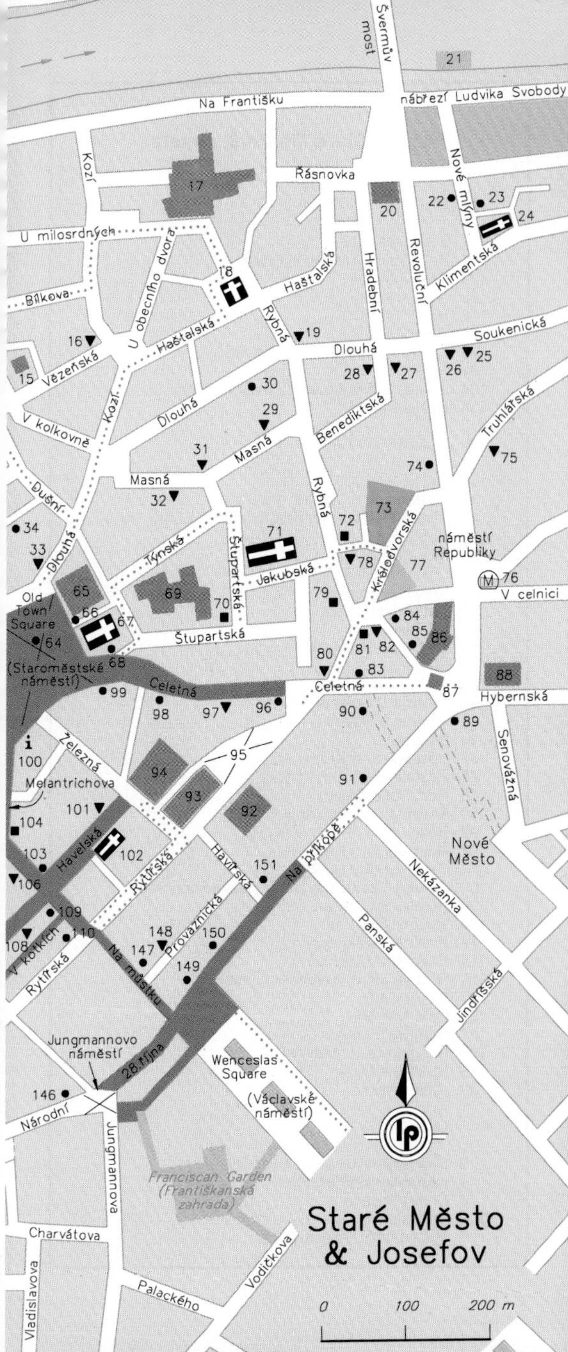

Staré Město
& Josefov
0
100
200 m

Map 7 Staré Město & Josefov

■ PLACES TO STAY

1 President Hotel
2 Hotel Inter-Continental Praha
21 Botel Albatros
70 Hotel Ungelt
72 Hotel Central
77 Hotel Paříž
79 Top Tour Accommodation Agency
81 Hotel Bohemia
104 Prague Suites Accommodation Agency
134 Unitas Penzion

▼ PLACES TO EAT

16 Česká hospoda
19 Restaurace U Dlouhé
25 The White Elephant (Restaurace U Bílého Slona)
26 Café Four
27 Mikuláš Pizzeria
28 U Benediktská
29 Hospoda (Pub)
31 Caffé Zlatá ulička
32 US Burger
33 Michelské pekařství Bakery
36 Kavárna Hogo Fogo
40 Press Club (Klub novinařů)
42 Vinárna U Golema
43 Vinárna U Rudolfa
44 Bakery
53 Restaurace U Křižovníků
75 Restaurace M D Rettigové
78 Red, Hot & Blues
80 Kavárna U zlatých andělů
82 Restaurace U králova dvora
97 Restaurace U supa
101 Club-Bar Que Húóng
105 Country Life Restaurant & Health Food Shop
106 Restaurace Mucha
108 Queenz Grill Bar
112 Pivnice ve Skořepce
113 Hospoda U Vejvodů
115 Restaurace U svatého Huberta
127 Slavia Café
137 Café Národní
138 Café-Bar Evropa
141 Restaurace U medvídků
143 New York Pizza
148 Caffé Antik

OTHER

3 Charles University Law Faculty
4 International Bookstore
5 Cubist Façade
6 Rudolfinum
7 Museum of Decorative Arts

8 Pinkas Synagogue
9 Klaus Synagogue
10 Old-New Synagogue
11 High Synagogue
12 Jewish Town Hall & Shalom Kosher Restaurant
13 Čedok
14 Church of the Holy Spirit (Kostel sv Ducha)
15 Spanish Synagogue
17 Convent of St Agnes (Anežský klášter)
18 St Castulus Church (Kostel sv Haštala)
20 ČSA City Terminal 'Vltava'
22 Petrská Waterworks Tower (Petrská vodárenská věž)
23 Postage Stamp Museum (Muzeum poštovní známky)
24 St Clement Church (Kostel sv Klimenta)
30 Eduard Čapek's Junk Shop
34 BTI Ticket Agency
35 Church of the Holy Saviour (Kostel sv Salvátora)
37 Classic Club
38 Profoto Camera Repair & Film Shop
39 Balnea Spa & Travel Agency
41 Maisel Synagogue
45 Franz Kafka's Birthplace & Exhibition
46 St Nicholas Church (Kostel sv Mikuláše)
47 City Library (Městská lidová knihovna)
48 Marionette Kingdom, or National Marionette Theatre (Divadélko Říše loutek)
49 Fišer Bookshop
50 Staroměstská Metro Station
51 Charles University Philosophy Faculty & Student Bookshop
52 Jan Palach Square
54 V Andrle Antique Shop
55 Church of St Francis Seraphinus (Kostel sv Františka Serafinského)
56 Church of the Holy Saviour (Kostel sv Salvátora)
57 Assumption Chapel (Vlašská kaple Nanebevzetí Panny Marie)
58 St Clement Church (Kostel sv Klimenta)
59 Klementinum
60 Prague House of Photography
61 Little Square (Malé náměstí)
62 Dům U minuty, Kafka's home 1889-96
63 Old Town Hall (Staroměstská radnice) & Astronomical Clock
64 Jan Hus Statue
65 Kinský Palace (Palác Kinských)
66 House at the Stone Bell (Dům U kamenného zvonu)
67 Church of Our Lady Before Týn (Kostel Panny Marie před Týnem)
68 The Three Kings, Kafka's home 1896-1907
69 Týn Court (Týnský dvůr)
71 St James Church (Kostel sv Jakuba)
73 Kotva Department Store
74 ČSA Ticketing Office
76 Náměstí Republiky Metro Station
83 Všeobecná Úverová banka
84 Pragotur Agency
85 FOK Prague Symphony Ticket Agency
86 Municipal House (Obecní dům)
87 Powder Tower (Prašná brána)

Key continued next page

Map 7 key continued

88 Hibernian House (Dům U hybernů)
89 Komerční banka
90 ČD Travel Agency
91 Cizojazyčná Literatura Bookshop
92 Kolowrat Theatre (Kolowrat divadlo)
93 Tyl (or Estates) Theatre (Tylovo divadlo)
94 Karolinum
95 Old Fruit Market (Ovocný trh)
96 House at the Black Madonna (Dům U černé Matky boží)
98 Klub U zoufalců
99 Kafka's Home 1888-89
100 Prague Information Service
102 Church of St Gall (Kostel sv Havla)
103 Bank of Austria
107 Havelská Market
109 Albatros Bookshop
110 Hungarian Cultural Centre
111 Old Coal Market (Uhelný trh)
114 St Giles Church (Kostel sv Jiljí)
116 Bethlehem Chapel (Betlémská kaple)
117 Centrum České Grafiky
118 Central Bohemian & Central European Galleries
119 The Golden Snake (U zlatého hada)
120 BTI Ticket Agency
121 Old Town Bridge Tower (Staroměstská mostecká věž)
122 Bedřich Smetana Museum
123 Opera Mozart Theatre
124 Theatre on the Balustrade (Divadlo Na zábradlí)
125 Náprstek Museum (Náprstkovo muzeum)
126 Hollar Gallery
128 Academy of Science
129 Viola Building
130 Topič Salon Gallery
131 Československý spisovatel Bookshop
132 Chapel of the Holy Cross (Kaple sv Kříže)
133 Police Station (Prague 1)
135 St Bartholomew Church (Kostel sv Bartoloměje)
136 Jednorožec s Harfou Gallery
139 Exodus Club
140 Gag Studio
142 Albatros Bookshop
144 Church of St Martin in the Wall (Kostel sv Martina ve zdi)
145 Western Union (at Sport Turist)
146 Kodak Processing Lab
147 American Hospitality Center
149 Melantrich Bookshop
150 All-Night Pharmacy
151 Dětský dům Department Store

Top : St Nicholas Church, Old Town Square (RN)
Bottom : Sword swallower, Old Town Square (RN)

MAP 8

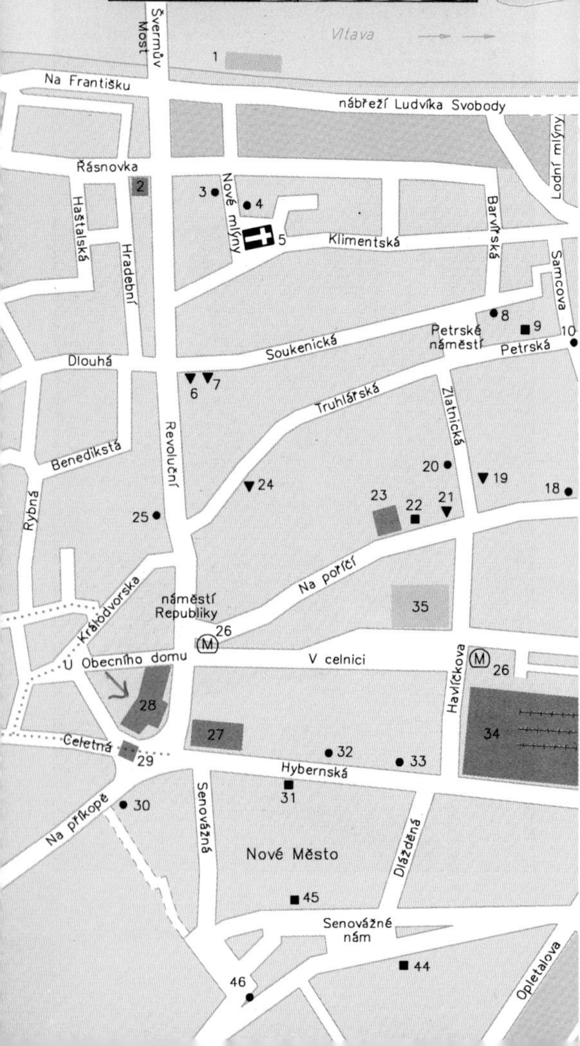

Švermův Most
Vltava
1
Na Františku
nábřeží Ludvíka Svobody
Lodní mlýny
Řásnovka
2
3
Nové mlýny
4
5
Klimentská
Barvířská
Haštalská
Hradební
Samcova
8
9
Petrské náměstí
10
Petrská
Dlouhá
Soukenická
6
7
Truhlářská
Zlatnická
Revoluční
Benedikstá
20
19
24
18
Rybná
23
22
21
25
Na poříčí
Králodvorska
35
náměstí Republiky
26
U Obecního domu
V celnici
Havlíčkova
26
28
27
34
Celetná
29
32
33
Hybernská
31
Na příkopě
30
Senovážná
Nové Město
Dlážděná
45
Senovážné nám
44
46
Opletalova

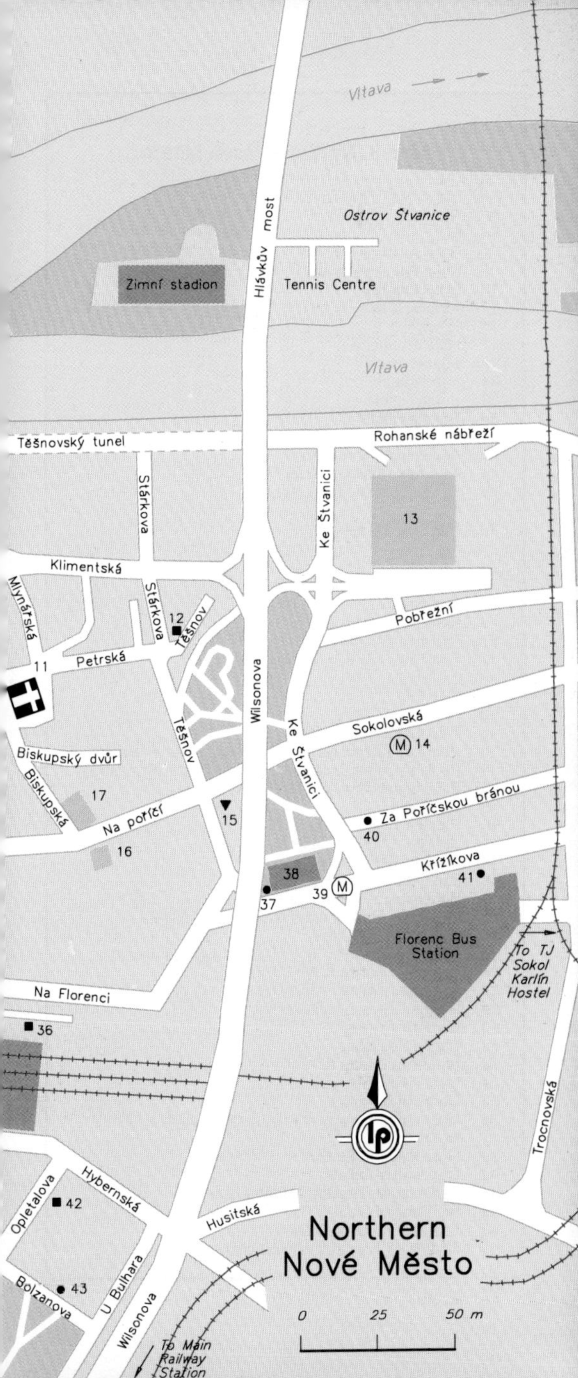

Vltava
Ostrov Štvanice
Hlávkův most
Zimní stadion
Tennis Centre
Vltava
Těšnovský tunel
Rohanské nábřeží
Stárkova
Ke Štvanici
13
Klimentská
Mlynářská
Stárkova
12
Těšnov
Pobřežní
11
Petrská
Wilsonova
Ke Štvanici
Sokolovská
14
Těšnov
Biskupský dvůr
Biskupská
17
Na poříčí
15
Za Poříčskou bránou
40
16
Křížkova
38
41
37
39
Florenc Bus Station
To TJ Sokol Karlín Hostel
Na Florenci
36
Trocnovská
Hybernská
Opletalova
42
Husitská
Northern Nové Město
Bolzanova
43
U Bulhara
Wilsonova
0
25
50 m
To Main Railway Station

Map 8 Northern Nové Město

■ PLACES TO STAY

1 Botel Albatros
9 Kolej Petrská Hostel
12 Hotel Opera
13 Atrium Hotel
16 Hotel Axa
17 Hotel Harmony
22 Atlantic Hotel
31 Hotel Meteor
35 Penta Hotel
36 Raketa Hostel
42 Kolej Jednota Hostel & Universitas Tour Accommodation Agency
44 Tour (also Unitour) Hotel
45 Hello Accommodation Agency

▼ PLACES TO EAT

6 Café Four
7 Restaurace U Bílého slona
15 McDonald's
19 Kobra Dyfo Club & Café
21 Pizzeria Mamma Mia
24 Restaurace M D Rettigové

OTHER

2 ČSA City Terminal 'Vltava'
3 Petrská Waterworks Tower (Petrská vodárenská věž)
4 Postage Stamp Museum (Muzeum poštovní známky)
5 St Clement Church (Kostel sv Klimenta)
8 RC Bunkr
10 Petrská Tower (Petrská věž)
11 St Peter Church (Kostel sv Petra)
14 Florenc Metro Station
18 Bílá Labuť Department Store
20 Bohemiatour Travel Agency
23 Insurance Firm where Kafka worked 1908-22
25 ČSA Ticketing Office
26 Náměstí Republiky Metro Station (two entrances)
27 Hibernian House (Dům U hybernů)
28 Municipal House (Obecní dům)
29 Powder Tower (Prašná brána)
30 Komerční banka
32 Nadas Bookshop
33 American Center for Culture & Commerce
34 Masarykovo Railway Station
37 Ceres Bus Tickets
38 Museum of the City of Prague (Muzeum hlavního města Prahy)
39 Florenc Metro Station
40 Čebus Bus Tickets
41 Karlín Music Theatre (Hudební divadlo)
42 Big Pohoda Club
43 City Lost & Found Office
46 Jindřišská Tower (Jindřišská věž)

Top : Neo-Renaissance sgraffito façade (JK)
Bottom : Façade & sun-worshipper (JK)

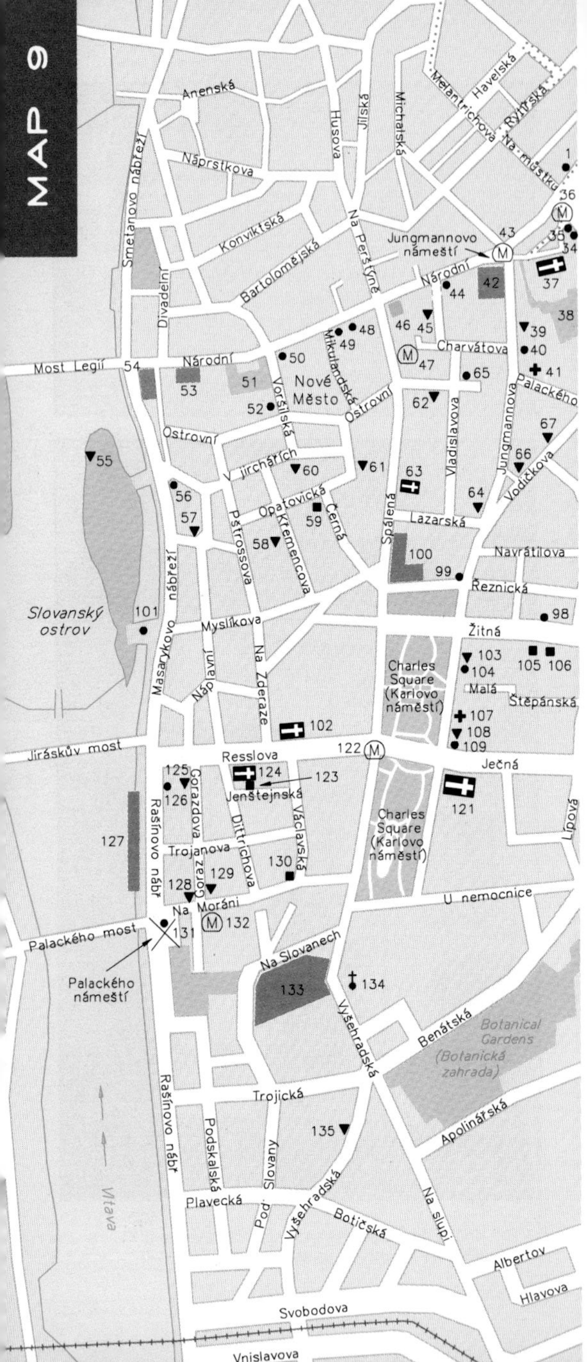

MAP 9
Anenská
Náprstkova
Konviktská
Bartolomějská
Smetanovo nábřeží
Divadelní
Husova
Jilská
Michalská
Melantrichova
Havelská
Rytířská
Na můstku
Na Perštýně
Jungmannovo náměstí
Národní
Charvátova
Most Legií
Nové Město
Mikulandská
Voršilská
Ostrovní
V jirchářích
Opatovická
Černá
Křemencova
Pštrossova
Spálená
Vladislavova
Jungmannova
Palackého
Vodičkova
Lazarská
Navrátilova
Řeznická
Žitná
Slovanský ostrov
Masarykovo nábřeží
Myslíkova
Náplavní
Na Zderaze
Charles Square (Karlovo náměstí)
Malá
Štěpánská
Jiráskův most
Resslova
Ječná
Jenštejnská
Václavská
Gorazdova
Dittrichova
Trojanova
Rašínovo nábř
Lípová
Na Moráni
U nemocnice
Palackého most
Palackého náměstí
Na Slovanech
Vyšehradská
Benátská
Botanical Gardens (Botanická zahrada)
Trojická
Apolinářská
Podskalská
Pod Slovany
Plavecká
Botičská
Na slupi
Vltava
Albertov
Hlavova
Svobodova
Vnislavova
1
34
35
36
37
38
39
40
41
42
43
44
45
46
47
48
49
50
51
52
53
54
55
56
57
58
59
60
61
62
63
64
65
66
67
98
99
100
101
102
103
104
105
106
107
108
109
121
122
123
124
125
126
127
128
129
130
131
132
133
134
135

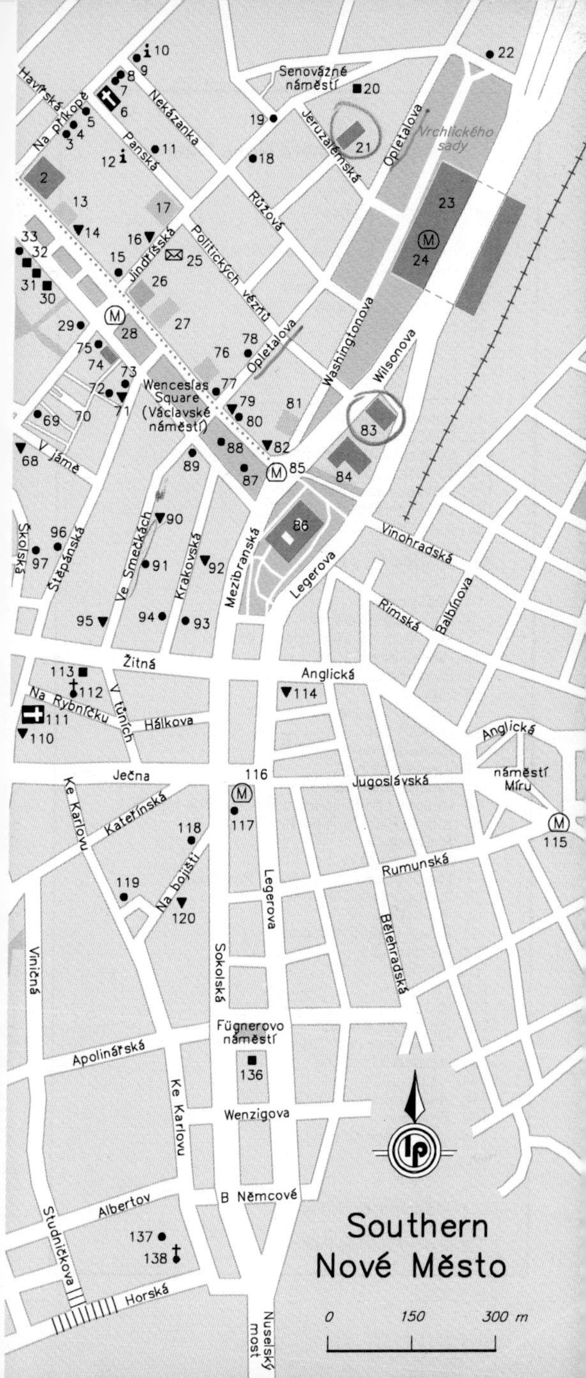

Southern
Nové Město
Senovážné náměstí
Vrchlického sady
Havířská
Na příkopě
Panská
Nekázanka
Jeruzalémská
Opletalova
Růžová
Jindřišská
Politických vězňů
Washingtonova
Wilsonova
Wenceslas Square (Václavské náměstí)
V jámě
Školská
Štěpánská
Ve Smečkách
Krakovská
Mezibranská
Legerova
Vinohradská
Balbínova
Římská
Žitná
Anglická
Na Rybníčku
V tůních
Hálkova
Ječna
Jugoslávská
náměstí Míru
Ke Karlovu
Kateřinská
Na bojišti
Rumunská
Bělehradská
Viničná
Sokolská
Fügnerovo náměstí
Apolinářská
Wenzigova
B Němcové
Albertov
Studničkova
Horská
Nuselský most
0
150
300 m

Map 9 Southern Nové Město

■ PLACES TO STAY

13 Ambassador Hotel & Hotel Zlatá Husa
17 Hotel Palace
20 Tour (also Unitour) Hotel
27 Grand Hotel Evropa
30 Hotel Adria
31 Hotel Juliš
32 Hotel Družba
59 Hotel Koruna
76 Hotel Jalta
81 Hotel Esplanade
105 CKM Juniorhotel
106 CKM Hostel & Accommodation Agency
113 TJ Praha Summer Hostel
123 Hlávkova kolej Hostel
130 City Hotel Morán
136 Hotel Patty

▼ PLACES TO EAT

14 McDonald's
16 Paris-Praha kavárna
17 Delicatesse Buffet (in Hotel Palace)
39 Restaurace U Mázlů
45 Cukrárna U Tety Stejskalový
55 Café
57 Pivnice U zpěváčků
58 U Fleků Beer Hall
60 Pizzeria Kmotra
61 Kavárna Velryba
62 Restaurace Pezinok
64 Country Life Restaurant & Health Food Shop
66 Buffalo Bill's Tex-Mex Bar & Grille
67 McDonald's
68 U Purkmistra
71 Mayur Indický Snack Bar & Restaurant
79 Galaxy mléčné lahůdky
82 Bonal Café
90 Smečky dietní restaurace
92 V Krakovské
95 Pohádka
103 Pizza Taxi
108 U Čížků
110 Ice Cream Parlour
114 Restaurace Zlatý Drak (Chinese)
120 Hostinec U Kalicha
125 Na Rybárně
128 Restaurace U Pomníku
129 Snek Bar
135 U Čínského labužníka

OTHER

1 Melantrich Bookshop
2 Koruna Palace
3 Sylva-Taroucca Palace

4 House at the Black Rose & Moser Glass Shop
5 Česká obchodní banka
6 Church of the Holy Cross (Kostel sv Kříže)
7 BTI Ticket Agency
8 Čedok
9 Živnostenská banka
10 Prague Information Service
11 Čedok Accommodation Office
12 Prague Information Service
15 Former Office of Assicurazioni Generali (Kafka's workplace 1907-08)
18 CKM Accommodation & Travel Agency
19 Jindřišská Tower (Jindřišská věž)
21 Jubilee (Jubilejní) or Great Synagogue (Velká synagóga)
22 City Lost & Found Office
23 Main Railway Station (Praha hlavní nádraží)
24 Hlavní nádraží Metro Station
25 Main Post Office
26 Krone Department Store
28 Můstek Metro Station
29 Future Site of Česká obchodní banka
33 Peterkův dům
34 Baťa Shoe Store
35 Lindt Building
36 Můstek Metro Station
37 Church of Our Lady of the Snows (Kostel Panny Marie Sněžné)
38 Františkanská zahrada (Franciscan Garden)
40 Popron Music Shop
41 All-Night Emergency Medical Clinic
42 Adria Palace & Theatre
43 Můstek Metro Station
44 Václav Špála Gallery
46 Máj Department Store
47 Národní Třída Metro Station
48 Reduta Jazz Club & Rock Café
49 Memorial to students clubbed by police on 17 November 1989
50 British Council
51 Church & Convent of St Ursula (sv Voršila)
52 Nová síň Gallery
53 Nová Scéna (Laterna Magika) Theatre
54 National Theatre (Národní divadlo)
56 Goethe Institute
63 Holy Trinity Church (Kostel Nejsvětější Trojice)
65 All-Night Dental Clinic
69 U Nováků Building
70 Lucerna Palace
72 Lucerna Bar
73 ČAD-Kličov Travel Agency
74 Melantrich Building
75 Wiehl House
77 Thomas Cook
78 Euroclub
80 Polish Embassy & Cultural Centre
83 State Opera House (Statní opera)
84 National Assembly
85 Muzeum Metro Station

Key continued next page

Map 9 key continued

86 National Museum (Národní muzeum)
87 St Wenceslas Statue
88 Memorial to Victims of Communism
89 American Express
91 Dramatic Club (Činoherní Klub)
93 Bulgarian Embassy
94 AghaRTA Jazz Centrum
96 Institut Français de Prague
97 Rent a Bike
98 CKM Travel Agency
99 New Town Hall (Novoměstská radnice)
100 Municipal Courthouse
101 Mánes Gallery
102 Church of SS Cyril & Methodius (Kostel sv Cyrila a Metoděje)
104 Cyklocentrum Bicycle Shop
107 Fakultní poliklinika
109 All-Night Pharmacy
111 St Stephen Church (Kostel sv Štěpána)
112 Rotunda of St Longinus (Rotunda sv Longina)
115 Náměstí Míru Metro Station
116 I P Pavlova Metro Station
117 AVE Accommodation Agency
118 Prague Transport Department (Dopravní podnik)
119 Villa Amerika & Antonín Dvořák Museum
121 St Ignatius Church (Kostel sv Ignáce)
122 Karlovo Náměstí Metro Station
124 Church of St Wenceslas in Zderaz (Kostel sv Václava na Zderaze)
126 President Havel's Flat
127 Central Quay (Vltava Cruise Boats)
131 František Palacký Monument
132 Karlovo Náměstí Metro Station
133 Emmaus (also Na Slovanech) Monastery
134 Church of St John of Nepomuk on the Rock (Kostel sv Jana Nepomuckého na Skalce)
137 Police Museum
138 Church of the Assumption of the Virgin Mary & Charlemagne (Kostel Nanebevzetí Panny Marie a Karla Velikého)

Façade of National Museum (JK)

Wrought-iron shutters (RN)

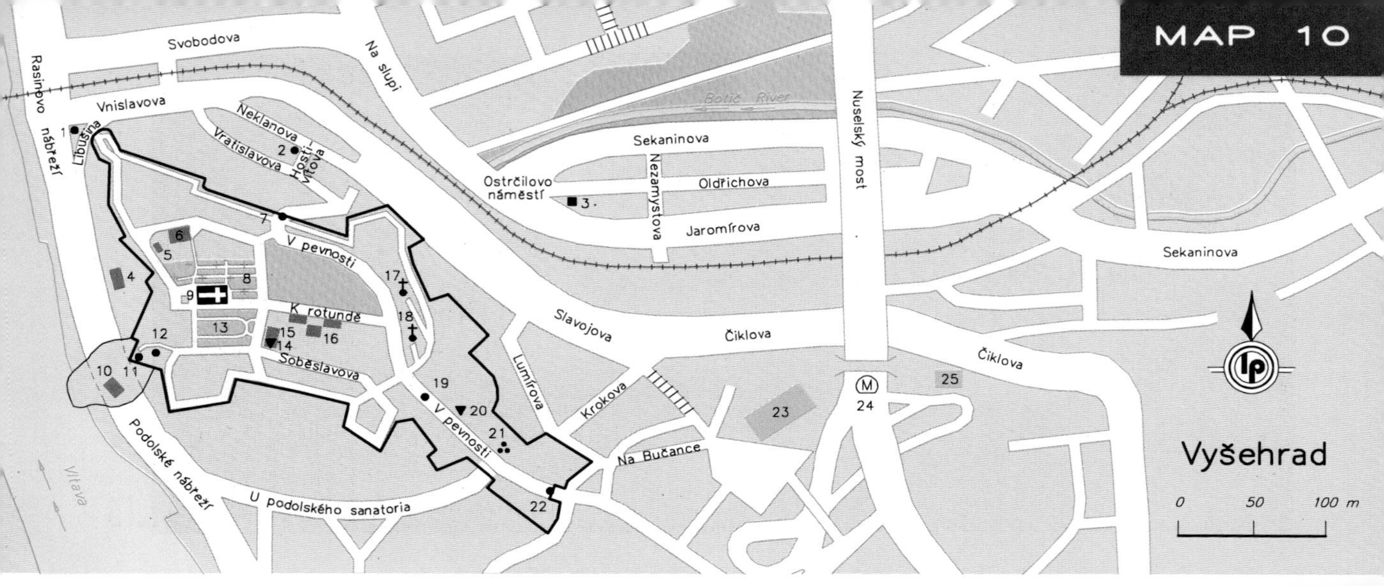
MAP 10
Vyšehrad
0
50
100 m
Svobodova
Na slupi
Rasinovo nábřeží
Vnislavova
Libušina
Neklanova
Vratislavova
Hostivítova
Botič River
Sekaninova
Nezamystova
Oldřichova
Jaromírova
Ostrčilovo náměstí
Nuselský most
V pevnosti
K rotundě
Soběslavova
Slavojova
Čiklova
Lumírova
Krokova
Na Bučance
Podolské nábřeží
U podolského sanatoria
Vltava
1
2
3
4
5
6
7
8
9
10
11
12
13
14
15
16
17
18
19
20
21
22
23
24
25

Map 10 Vyšehrad

■ PLACES TO STAY

3 Hotel Union
25 Hotel Forum

▼ PLACES TO EAT

14 Snack shop in Old Archdeaconry
20 Café

OTHER

1 Cubist House
2 Cubist House
4 Cubist Houses
5 Old Provost's House
6 Cultural Hall (Kulturní síňv), in New Provost's House (Nové proboštsví)
7 Brick Gate (Cihelná brána) & Visitors' Map
8 Vyšehrad Cemetery (Vyšehradský hřbitov) & Slavín Monument
9 Church of SS Peter & Paul (Kostel sv Petra a Pavla)
10 'Libuše's Bath'
11 Galerie Vyšehrad
12 Foundations of Charles IV's palace
13 Vyšehrad Gardens (Vyšehradské sady) & Myslbek statues
14 Foundations of St Lawrence Basilica (Bazilika sv Vavřince)
15 Old Archdeaconry (Staré Děkanství)
16 Vyšehrad Museum, in former New Archdeaconry (Nové Děkanství)
17 St Mary Chapel in the Ramparts (Kaple Panny Marie v hradbách), Plague Pillar & remains of the Church of the Beheading of John the Baptist (Kostel Stětí sv Jana Křtitele)
18 Rotunda of St Martin (Rotunda sv Martina)
19 Leopold Gate (Leopoldova brána)
21 Remains of Špička Gate
22 Tábor Gate (Táborská brána)
23 Palace of Culture (Palác kultury)
24 Vyšehrad Metro Station

MAP 11

Bubeneč & Holešovice

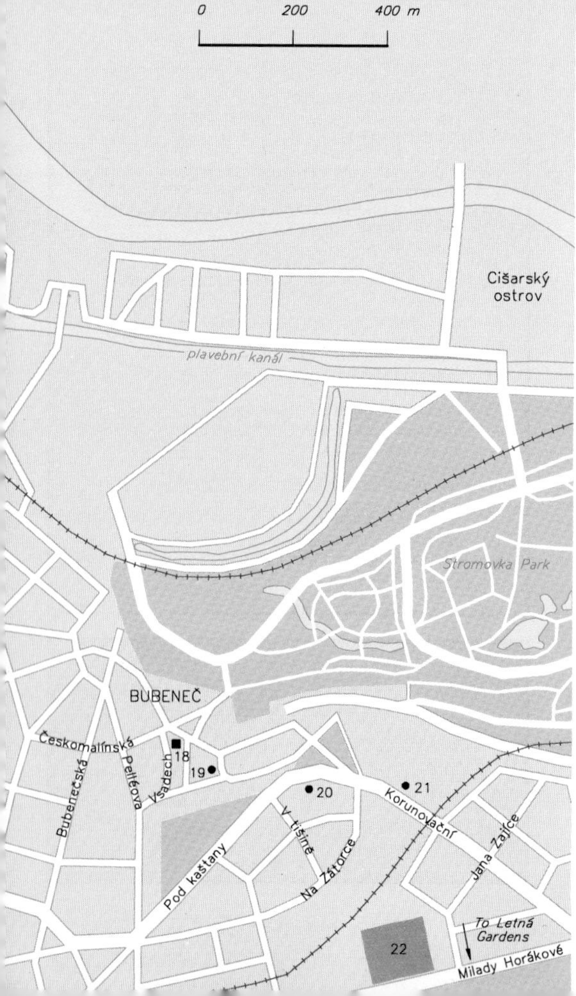

0 200 400 m

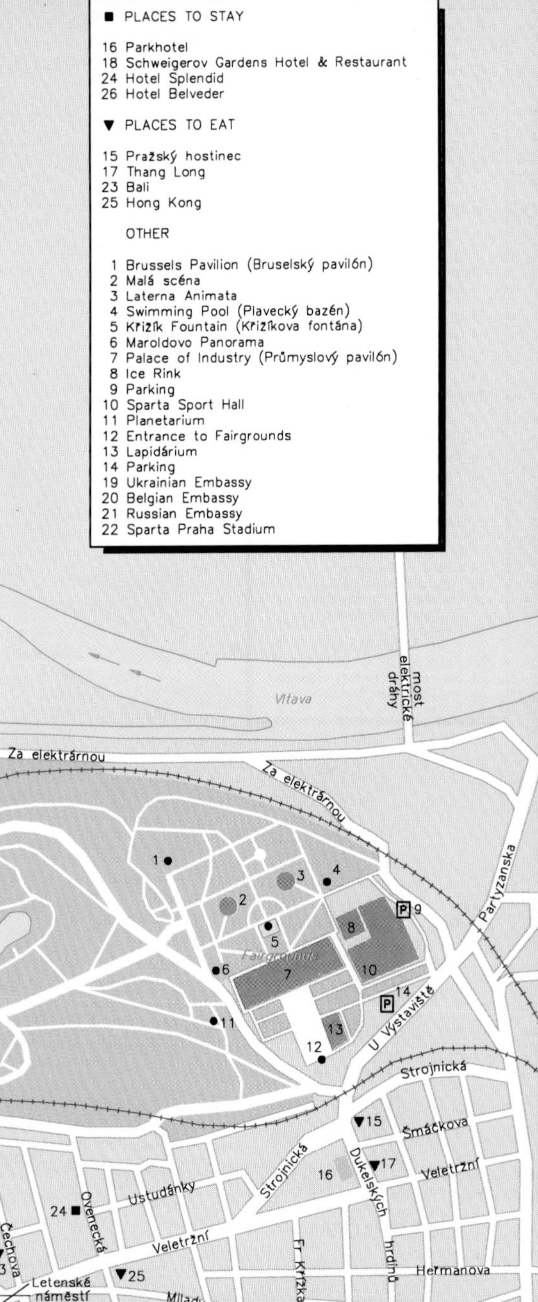
■ PLACES TO STAY
16 Parkhotel
18 Schweigerov Gardens Hotel & Restaurant
24 Hotel Splendid
26 Hotel Belveder
▼ PLACES TO EAT
15 Pražský hostinec
17 Thang Long
23 Bali
25 Hong Kong
OTHER
1 Brussels Pavilion (Bruselský pavilón)
2 Malá scéna
3 Laterna Animata
4 Swimming Pool (Plavecký bazén)
5 Křižík Fountain (Křižíkova fontána)
6 Maroldovo Panorama
7 Palace of Industry (Průmyslový pavilón)
8 Ice Rink
9 Parking
10 Sparta Sport Hall
11 Planetarium
12 Entrance to Fairgrounds
13 Lapidárium
14 Parking
19 Ukrainian Embassy
20 Belgian Embassy
21 Russian Embassy
22 Sparta Praha Stadium
Vltava
most elektrické dráhy
Za elektrárnou
Za elektrárnou
Partyzanská
Fairgrounds
U Výstaviště
Strojnická
Šmáckova
Strojnická
Dukelských hrdinů
Veletržní
Ustudánky
Ovenecká
Čechova
Veletržní
Heřmanova
Fr Křížka
Letenské náměstí
Milady Horákové
Nad Štdou
To National Technology Museum
HOLEŠOVICE

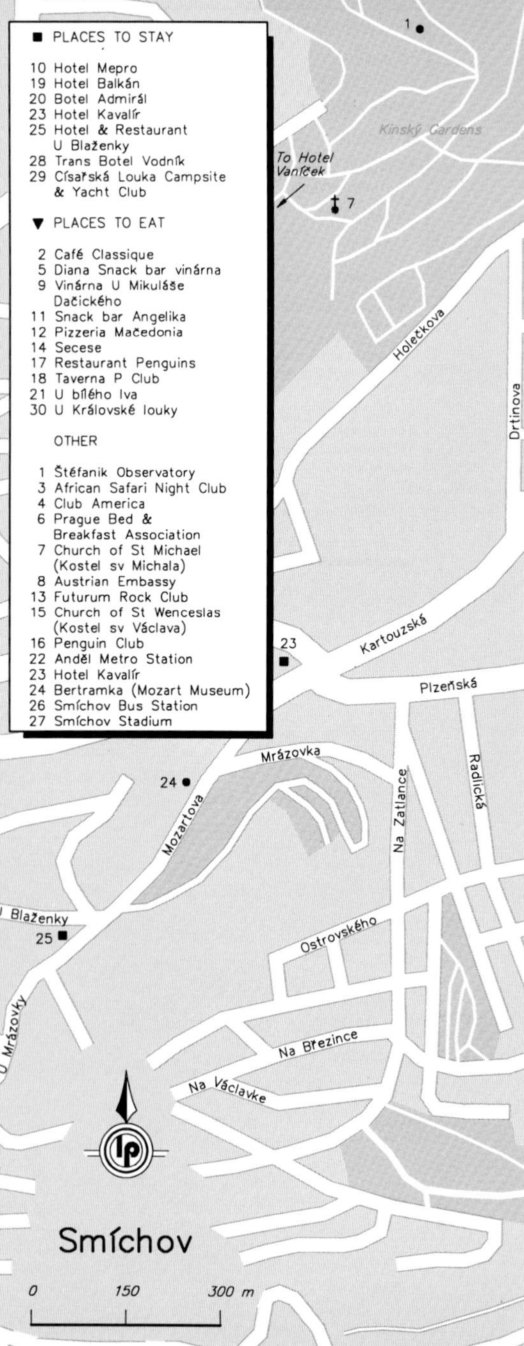
■ PLACES TO STAY
10 Hotel Mepro
19 Hotel Balkán
20 Botel Admirál
23 Hotel Kavalír
25 Hotel & Restaurant U Blaženky
28 Trans Botel Vodník
29 Císařská Louka Campsite & Yacht Club
▼ PLACES TO EAT
2 Café Classique
5 Diana Snack bar vinárna
9 Vinárna U Mikuláše Dačického
11 Snack bar Angelika
12 Pizzeria Mačedonia
14 Secese
17 Restaurant Penguins
18 Taverna P Club
21 U bílého lva
30 U Královské louky
OTHER
1 Štéfanik Observatory
3 African Safari Night Club
4 Club America
6 Prague Bed & Breakfast Association
7 Church of St Michael (Kostel sv Michala)
8 Austrian Embassy
13 Futurum Rock Club
15 Church of St Wenceslas (Kostel sv Václava)
16 Penguin Club
22 Anděl Metro Station
23 Hotel Kavalír
24 Bertramka (Mozart Museum)
26 Smíchov Bus Station
27 Smíchov Stadium
Kinský Gardens
To Hotel Vaníček
Holečkova
Drtinova
Kartouzská
Plzeňská
Mrázovka
Radlická
Na Zatlance
Mozartova
U Blaženky
Ostrovského
U Mrázovky
Na Březince
Na Václavke
Smíchov
0
150
300 m

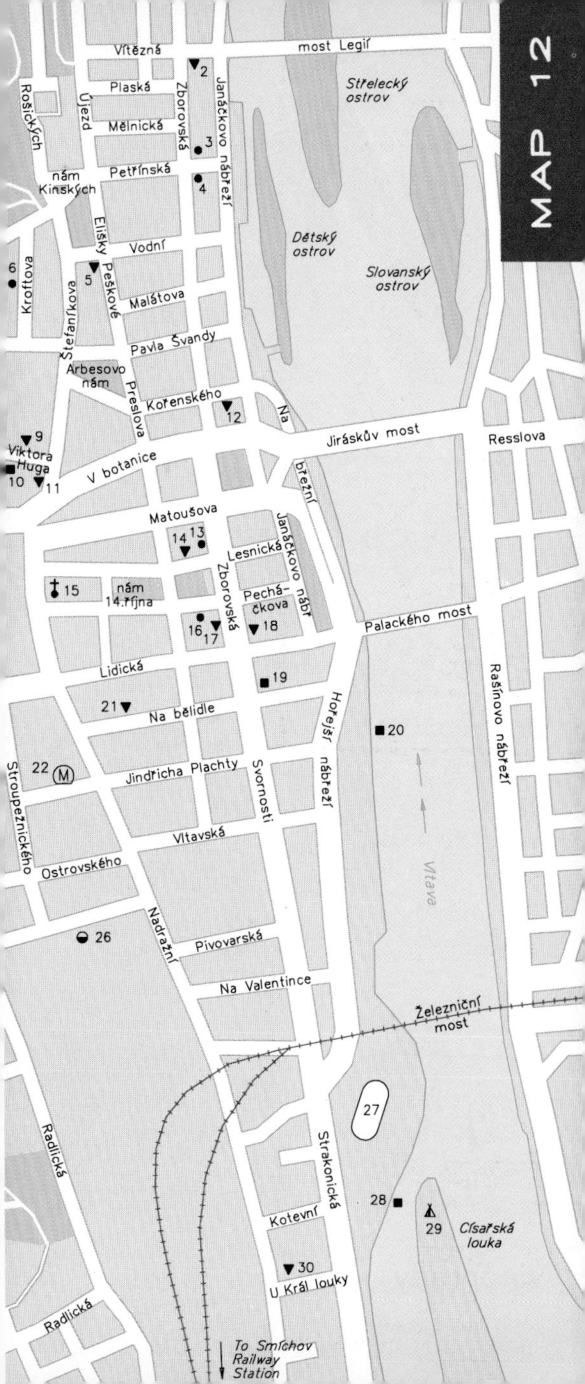
MAP 12
most Legií
Vítězná
Plaská
Mělnická
Petřínská
Vodní
Malátova
Pavla Švandy
Kořenského
Zborovská
Janáčkovo nábřeží
Újezd
Rošických
nám Kinských
Elišky Peškové
Kroftova
Štefánikova
Arbesovo nám
Preslova
Střelecký ostrov
Dětský ostrov
Slovanský ostrov
Na
Jiráskův most
Resslova
Viktora Huga
V botanice
břežní
Matoušova
Lesnická
Janáčkovo nábř
nám 14.října
Pechá-čkova
Palackého most
Lidická
Na bělidle
Hořejší nábřeží
Jindřicha Plachty
Svornosti
Stroupežnického
Vltavská
Ostrovského
Rašínovo nábřeží
Vltava
Nádražní
Pivovarská
Na Valentince
Železniční most
Radlická
Strakonická
Kotevní
U Král louky
Císařská louka
To Smíchov Railway Station
2
3
4
5
6
9
10
11
12
13
14
15
16
17
18
19
20
21
22
26
27
28
29
30

MAP 13

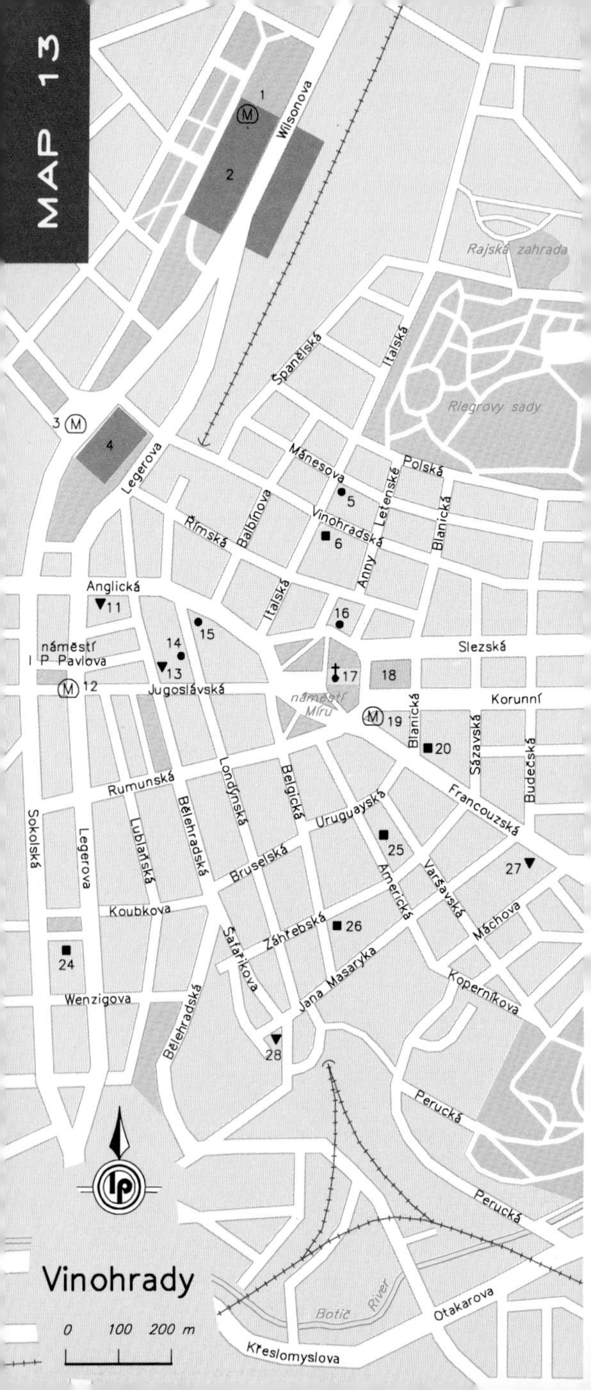

Vinohrady

0 100 200 m

Wilsonova
Rajská zahrada
Riegrovy sady
Španělská
Italská
Legerova
Mánesova
Polská
Vinohradská
Letenské
Blanická
Římská
Balbínova
Anny
Anglická
Italská
Slezská
náměstí I P Pavlova
Jugoslávská
náměstí Míru
Korunní
Blanická
Sázavská
Budečská
Rumunská
Londýnská
Belgická
Francouzská
Uruguayská
Sokolská
Legerova
Lublaňská
Bělehradská
Bruselská
Americká
Varšavská
Koubkova
Máchova
Záhřebská
Šafaříkova
Jana Masaryka
Kopernikova
Wenzigova
Bělehradská
Perucká
Perucká
Botič River
Otakarova
Křeslomyslova

1 M
2
3 M
4
5
6
11
12 M
13
14
15
16
17
18
19 M
20
24
25
26
27
28

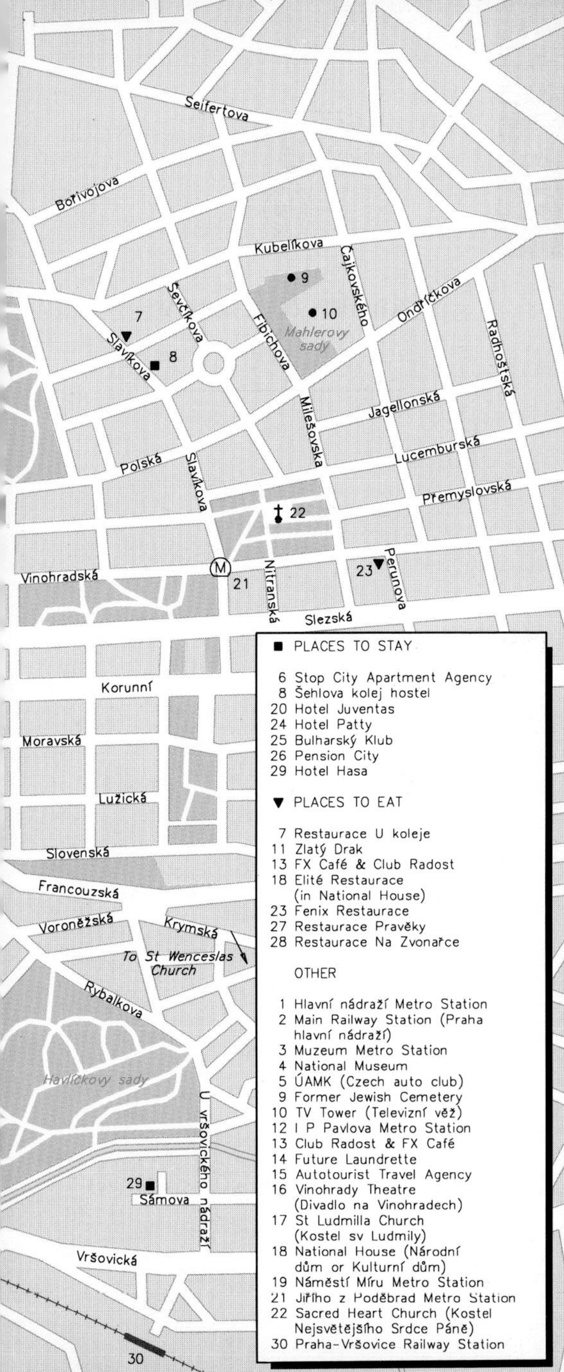

Seifertova
Bořivojova
Kubelíkova
Čajkovského
Ondříčkova
Radhošťská
Ševčíkova
Slavíkova
Fibichova
Mahlerovy sady
Jagellonská
Milešovská
Lucemburská
Polská
Slavíkova
Přemyslovská
Perunova
Vinohradská
Nitranská
Slezská
Korunní
Moravská
Lužická
Slovenská
Francouzská
Voroněžská
Krymská
To St Wenceslas Church
Rybalkova
Havlíčkovy sady
U vršovického nádraží
Sámova
Vršovická
PLACES TO STAY
6 Stop City Apartment Agency
8 Šehlova kolej hostel
20 Hotel Juventas
24 Hotel Patty
25 Bulharský Klub
26 Pension City
29 Hotel Hasa
PLACES TO EAT
7 Restaurace U koleje
11 Zlatý Drak
13 FX Café & Club Radost
18 Elité Restaurace (in National House)
23 Fenix Restaurace
27 Restaurace Pravěky
28 Restaurace Na Zvonařce
OTHER
1 Hlavní nádraží Metro Station
2 Main Railway Station (Praha hlavní nádraží)
3 Muzeum Metro Station
4 National Museum
5 ÚAMK (Czech auto club)
9 Former Jewish Cemetery
10 TV Tower (Televizní věž)
12 I P Pavlova Metro Station
13 Club Radost & FX Café
14 Future Laundrette
15 Autotourist Travel Agency
16 Vinohrady Theatre (Divadlo na Vinohradech)
17 St Ludmilla Church (Kostel sv Ludmily)
18 National House (Národní dům or Kulturní dům)
19 Náměstí Míru Metro Station
21 Jiřího z Poděbrad Metro Station
22 Sacred Heart Church (Kostel Nejsvětějšího Srdce Páně)
30 Praha-Vršovice Railway Station

MAP 14

Karlín & Žižkov

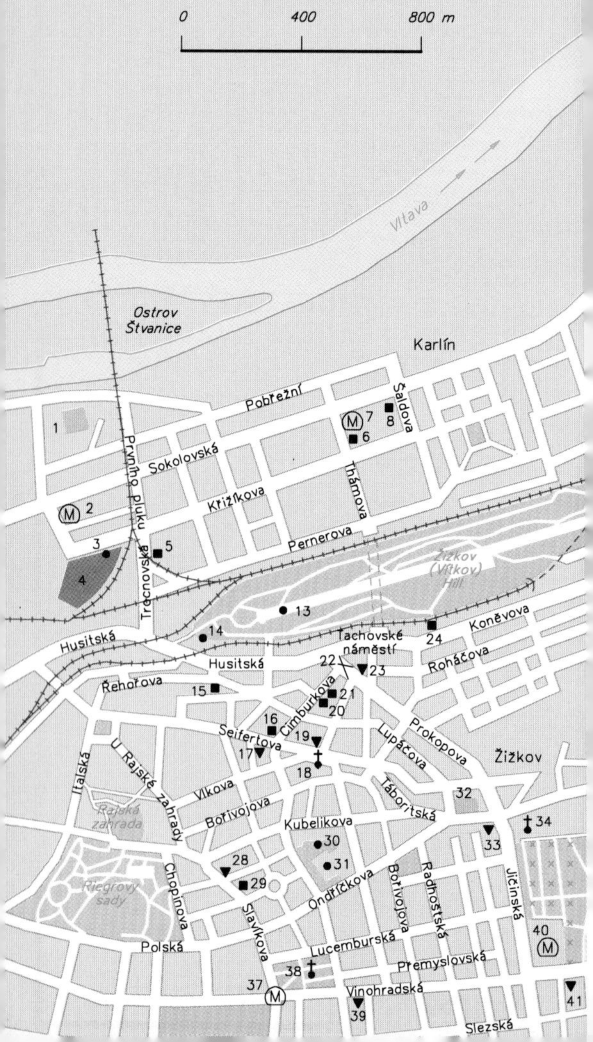

0 400 800 m

Vltava

Ostrov Štvanice

Karlín

Pobřežní

Šaldova

1

M 7

8

6

Sokolovská

Prvního pluku

Thámova

M 2

Křižíkova

3

5

Pernerova

4

Trocnovská

Žižkov (Vítkov) Hill

13

14

Husitská

Tachovské náměstí

24

Koněvova

Husitská

22

23

Roháčova

Řehořova

15

21

20

Cimburkova

16

Seifertova

19

Prokopova

Lupáčova

U Rajské zahrady

17

18

Žižkov

Italská

Vlkova

Táboritská

32

Rajská zahrada

Bořivojova

Kubelíkova

33

34

30

28

31

Chopinova

29

Ondříčkova

Bořivojova

Radhošťská

Jičínská

Riegrovy sady

Slavíkova

40

Polská

Lucemburská

M

38

Přemyslovská

37

M

Vinohradská

41

39

Slezská

■ PLACES TO STAY

1 Atrium Hotel
5 TJ Sokol Karlín Hostel
6 Hotel Brno
8 Hotel Karl-Inn
10 Hotel Olympik
11 Hotel Olympik-II
12 Hotel Čechie
15 Hotel Ostaš
16 Hotel Ariston
20 Hotel Bílý Lev
21 Hotel Kafka
24 TJ Tesla Žižkov (also TJ Sokol Žižkov) Hostel
25 Hotel Vítkov
27 Hotel Jarov
29 Švehlova kolej Hostel
32 Olšanka Hotel & Central European University
36 TJ Kovo Praha Hotel & Hostel

▼ PLACES TO EAT

17 Restaurace Asia
19 Vinárna pod kostelem sv Prokopa
23 Restaurace Viktoria
28 Restaurace U koleje
33 Restaurace Rebecca
39 Fenix Restaurace
41 Restaurace Venezia

OTHER

2 Florenc Metro Station
3 Karlín Music Theatre (Hudební divadlo)
4 Florenc Bus Station
7 Křižíkova Metro Station
9 Invalidovna Metro Station
13 Jan Žižka Monument & National Memorial
14 Military Museum
18 St Procopius Church (Kostel sv Prokopa)
22 Prokopovo náměstí
26 All-night Pharmacy
29 Belmondo Revival Club
30 Former Jewish Cemetery
31 TV Tower (Televizní věž)
34 St Roche Chapel (Kaple sv Rocha)
35 Foreigners' Police & Passport Office
37 Jiřího z Poděbrad Metro Station
38 Sacred Heart Church (Kostel Nejsvětějšího Srdce Páně)
40 Flora Metro Station
42 Želivského Metro Station
43 Želivského Long-Distance Bus Stand

Sokolovská
Pod plynojemem
10
11
M
9
12
U Sluncové
Pod Krejcárkem
Šikmá
27
Koněvova
Na vápence
26
Na hřídce
Jeseniova
V zahrádkách
25
Jana Želivského
Biskupcova
Jeseniova
Na Vackově
Jilmová
Malešická
36
Olšanská
35
Na Třebešíně
New Jewish Cemetery (Židovské hřbitovy)
Nad vodovodem
Olšany Cemetery (Olšanské hřbitovy)
Jana Želivského
M
42
Počernická
43
Vinohradská
Vinohradská

Pankrác & Kačerov

■ PLACES TO STAY

3 Interhotel Panorama
4 Hotel Fasádostav
5 Sky Club Brumlovka
6 Hotel Kačerov
9 Hotel ILF

▼ PLACES TO EAT

2 Dlouhá Zeď
7 Pub & Restaurant

OTHER

1 Pankrác Metro Station
8 Budějovická Metro Station
10 Polyclinic, Prague 4
11 Kačerov Metro Station

PANKRÁC
KAČEROV
Park Družby
Pujmanové
Hvězdova
Na strži
5.května
5.května (E50/65)
Baarova
Telčská
Jemnická
Vyskočilova
Na rolích
Na návrší
Na úlehlí
Michelská
Podle Kačerova
Milevská
Hanusova
Budějovická
Přímětická
Za zelenou liškou
Horáčkova
Olbrachtova
Poláčkova
Jihlavská
Sedlčanská
Hornokrčská
Antala Staška
U krčské vodárny

0 200 400 m

Around Prague

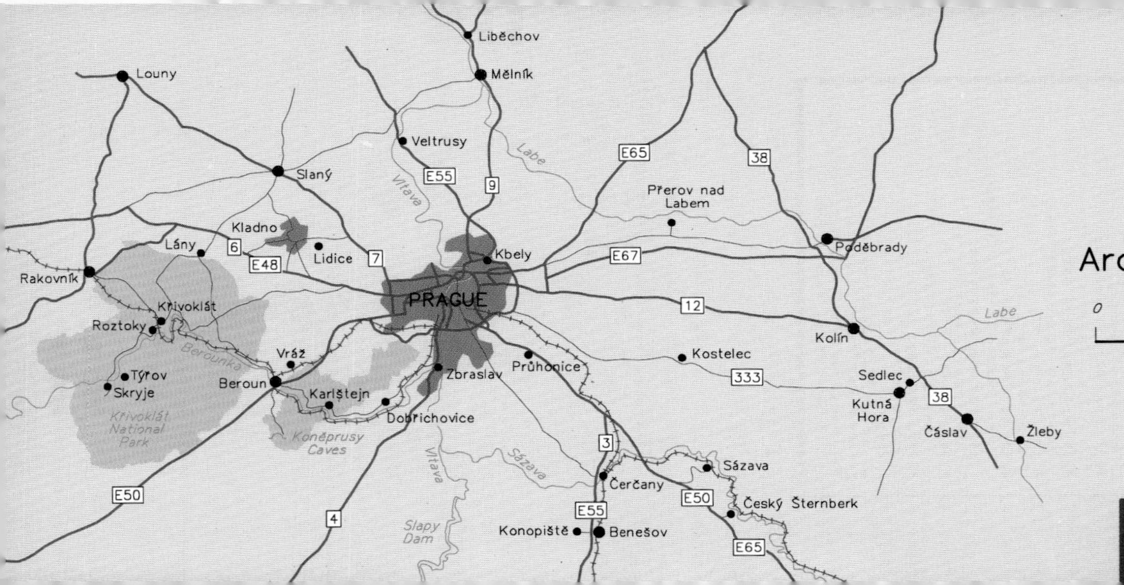

MAP 16

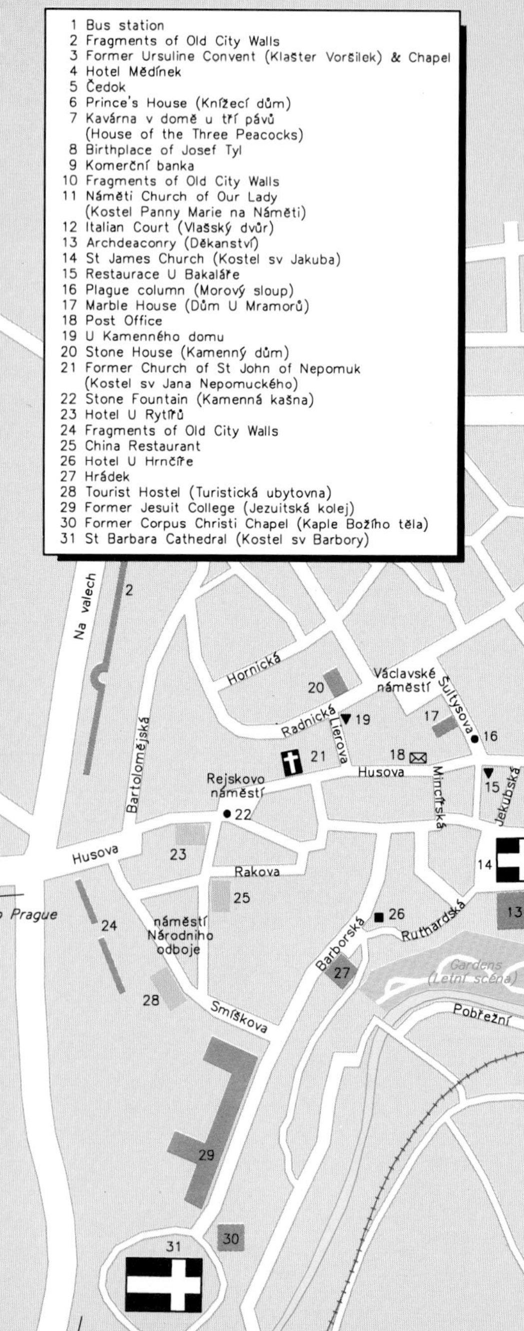

1 Bus station
2 Fragments of Old City Walls
3 Former Ursuline Convent (Klašter Voršilek) & Chapel
4 Hotel Mědínek
5 Čedok
6 Prince's House (Knížecí dům)
7 Kavárna v domě u tří pávů
(House of the Three Peacocks)
8 Birthplace of Josef Tyl
9 Komerční banka
10 Fragments of Old City Walls
11 Náměti Church of Our Lady
(Kostel Panny Marie na Náměti)
12 Italian Court (Vlašský dvůr)
13 Archdeaconry (Děkanství)
14 St James Church (Kostel sv Jakuba)
15 Restaurace U Bakaláře
16 Plague column (Morový sloup)
17 Marble House (Dům U Mramorů)
18 Post Office
19 U Kamenného domu
20 Stone House (Kamenný dům)
21 Former Church of St John of Nepomuk
(Kostel sv Jana Nepomuckého)
22 Stone Fountain (Kamenná kašna)
23 Hotel U Rytířů
24 Fragments of Old City Walls
25 China Restaurant
26 Hotel U Hrnčíře
27 Hrádek
28 Tourist Hostel (Turistická ubytovna)
29 Former Jesuit College (Jezuitská kolej)
30 Former Corpus Christi Chapel (Kaple Božího těla)
31 St Barbara Cathedral (Kostel sv Barbory)
Na valech
Hornická
Václavské náměstí
Šultysova
Radnická
Lierova
Bartolomějská
Rejskovo náměstí
Husova
Mincířská
Jakubská
Rakova
To Prague
náměstí Národního odboje
Barborská
Ruthardská
Gardens (Letní scéna)
Pobřežní
Smíškova
To Campsite

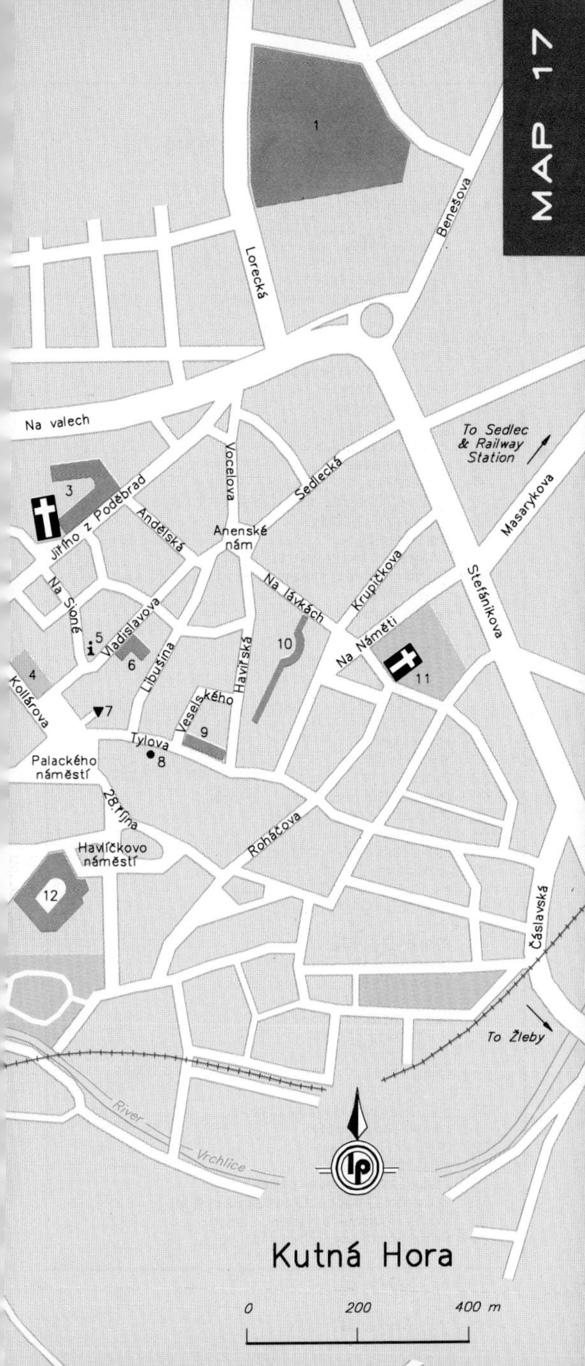
MAP 17
Kutná Hora
1
Lorecká
Benešova
Na valech
To Sedlec & Railway Station
Masarykova
3
Jiřího z Poděbrad
Andělská
Vocelova
Sedlecká
Anenské nám
Na Sioně
5
Vladislavova
6
4
Kollárova
7
Libušina
Havířská
10
Na lávkách
Krupičkova
Na Náměti
11
Štefánikova
Veselského
9
Tylova
8
Palackého náměstí
28.října
Havlíčkovo náměstí
12
Roháčova
Čáslavská
To Žleby
River Vrchlice
0
200
400 m

Map 18 Greater Prague

■ PLACES TO STAY

1 Pension BoB
2 Tour Hotel
4 TJ Hvězda Praha
3 Kemp Džbán & TJ Aritma Hostel
5 Hotel Praha
6 International Hotel
9 Hotel Diplomat
16 TJ Sokol Troja Campsite
17 Autocamp Trojská
18 Hájek Campsite
19 Dana Campsite
21 Youth Hostel B & B
22 Hotel Morávek
24 Hotel Stírka
25 TJ Sokol Kobylisy (also TJ Admira Kobylisy) Hostel
26 Hotelový dům Kobylisy
27 Botel Neptun
30 TJ Motorlet Praga Hostel
31 Siesta Hotel & Campsite
32 Hotel Rhea
46 Hotel Coubertin
47 Hotel Vaza
49 Hotel Pyramida
51 Hotel Golf
52 Caravancamp Motol
53 Hotel Kavalír
55 Hotel Tourist
56 Hotel Viator
60 Slavia Hotel
62 Botel Racek
63 Pension Bohemians
66 Intercamp Kotva Braník
68 Hotel Globus
69 Hotel Opatov & Hotel Sandra
70 Hotel Kupa

▼ PLACES TO EAT

7 Pivnice U Švejka
8 Bar restaurant Harlekin
23 Acapulco Club
28 Góvinda Vegetarian Club
64 Terasy na Barrandově
67 Restaurace Eureka

OTHER

10 Praha-Dejvice Railway Station
11 Ukrainian Embassy
12 Belgian Embassy
13 Russian Embassy
14 Troja Castle (Trojský zámek)
15 Botanical Gardens (Botanická zahrada)
20 Praha-Holešovice Railway Station
29 Praha-Vysočany Railway Station

33 New Jewish Cemetery (Židovské hřbitovy)
34 Olšansky Cemetery (Olšanské hřbitovy)
35 TV Tower (Televizní věž)
36 Žižkov Hill
37 Florenc Bus Station
38 Masarykovo Railway Station
39 Main Railway Station (Praha hlavní nádraží)
40 Wenceslas Square (Václavské náměstí)
41 Charles Square (Karlovo náměstí)
42 Old Town Square (Staroměstské náměstí
43 Charles Bridge (Karlův most)
44 Prague Castle (Pražský Hrad)
45 Spartakiádní Stadión
48 Břevnov Monastery (Břevnovský klášter) & Church of St Margaret (Kostel sv Markéta)
50 Na Homolce Hospital
54 Customs (Celnice) & Post Office
57 Praha-Smíchov Railway Station
58 Vyšehrad
59 Praha-Vršovice Railway Station
61 Plavecký Stadión Sports Complex
65 Barrandov Cliffs

METRO STATIONS

M1 Dejvická
M2 Hradčanská
M3 Malostranská
M4 Staroměstská
M5 Můstek
M6 Muzeum
M7 Náměstí Míru
M8 Jiřího z Poděbrad
M9 Flora
M10 Želivského
M11 Strašnická
M12 Skalka
M13 Nádraží Holešovice
M14 Vltavská
M15 Florenc
M16 Hlavní Nádraží
M17 I P Pavlova
M18 Vyšehrad
M19 Pražského Povstání
M20 Pankrác
M21 Budějovická
M22 Kačerov
M23 Roztyly
M24 Chodov
M25 Opatov
M26 Háje
M27 Českomoravská
M28 Palmovka
M29 Invalidovna
M30 Křižíkova
M31 Náměstí Republiky
M32 Národní Třída
M33 Karlovo Náměstí
M34 Anděl
M35 Smíchovské Nádraží
M36 Radlická
M37 Jinonice
M38 Nové Butovice

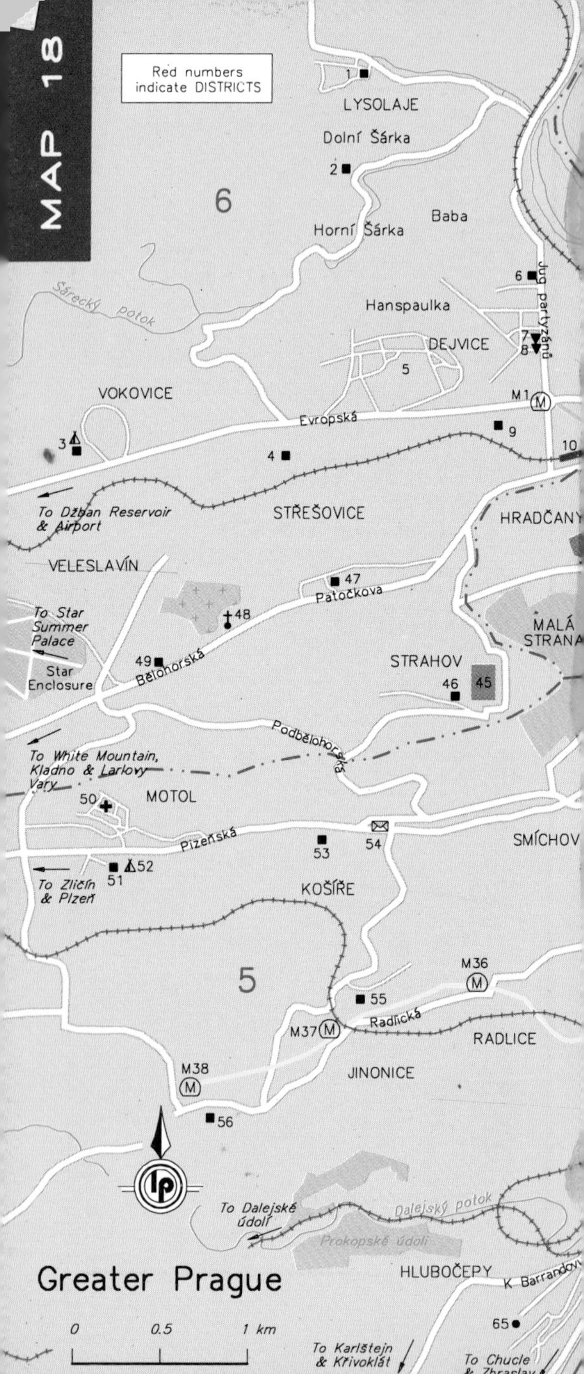

MAP 18
Red numbers indicate DISTRICTS
LYSOLAJE
Dolní Šárka
6
Baba
Horní Šárka
Šárecký potok
Hanspaulka
Jug partyzánů
DEJVICE
5
VOKOVICE
M1
Evropská
To Džban Reservoir & Airport
STŘEŠOVICE
HRADČANY
VELESLAVÍN
Patočkova
To Star Summer Palace
Star Enclosure
Bělohorská
MALÁ STRANA
STRAHOV
Podbělohorská
To White Mountain, Kladno & Karlovy Vary
MOTOL
Plzeňská
SMÍCHOV
To Zličín & Plzeň
KOŠÍŘE
5
M36
M37
Radlická
RADLICE
M38
JINONICE
To Dalejské údolí
Dalejský potok
Prokopské údolí
HLUBOČEPY
K Barrandovu
Greater Prague
0
0.5
1 km
To Karlštejn & Křivoklát
To Chuchle & Zbraslav

Map 1 Historical Centre

■ PLACES TO STAY

1 Hotel Diplomat
20 Hotel Belveder
24 Atrium Hotel
48 ESTEC Hostel
49 Strahov Hostel
50 Hotel Coubertin
51 Hotel Spiritka
52 Hotel Vaníček

▼ PLACES TO EAT

3 U Cedru
4 U zlatého ražně
5 Budvarka
9 Hostinec U vozovny
16 Hanavský pavilón
17 Bali
18 Hong Kong

OTHER

2 Dejvická Metro Station
6 Laundry Kings
7 Praha-Dejvice Railway Station
8 Hradčanská Metro Station
10 Slovak Embassy
11 Hungarian Embassy
12 Písek Gate (Písecká brána)
13 Canadian Embassy
14 Gočár's Cubist House
15 Bílkova Villa
19 National Technology Museum (Národní technické muzeum)
21 Vltavská Metro Station
22 Tennis Centre
23 Winter-Sports Stadium (Zimní stadión)
25 Florenc Metro Station
26 Florenc Bus Station
27 Masarykovo Railway Station
28 Náměstí Republiky Metro Station
29 Municipal House (Obecní dům)
30 ČSA Ticketing Office
31 ČSA City Terminal 'Vltava'
32 Old Jewish Cemetery
33 Rudolfinum
34 Staroměstská Metro Station
35 Klementinum
36 Malostranská Metro Station
37 Belgian Consulate
38 Prague Castle (Pražský Hrad)
39 British Embassy
40 St Nicholas Church (Kostel sv Mikuláše)
41 American Embassy
42 German Embassy
43 The Loreta
44 Strahov Monastery (Strahovský klášter)
45 Petřín Tower (Petřínská rozhledna)
46 French Embassy
47 Nostický Palác & Netherlands Embassy
53 Austrian Embassy
54 Police Station (for Prague 1)
55 National Theatre (Národní divadlo)
56 Národní Třída Metro Station
57 Main Post Office
58 Můstek Metro Station
59 Hlavní nádraží Metro Station
60 Main Railway Station (Praha hlavní nádraží)
61 Muzeum Metro Station
62 National Museum (Národní muzeum)
63 Bulgarian Embassy
64 Karlovo náměstí Metro Station
65 Central Quay (Vltava Cruise Boats)
66 I P Pavlova Metro Station
67 Náměstí Míru Metro Station

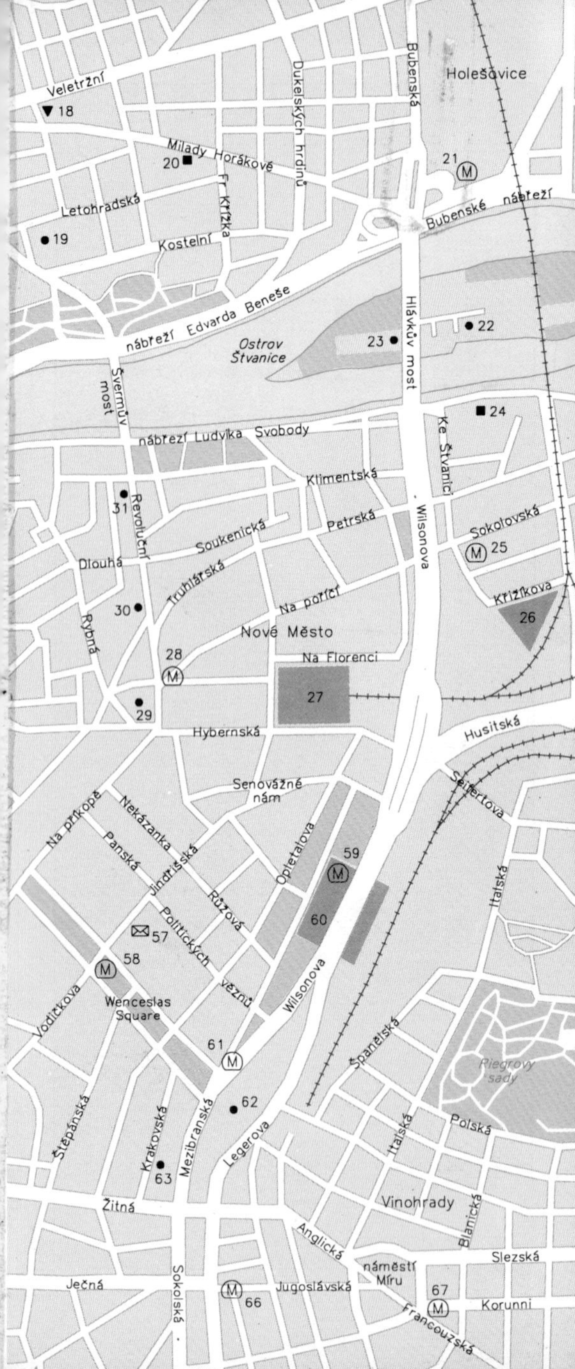

Veletržní
18
Dukelských hrdinů
Bubenská
Holešovice
Milady Horákové
20
21
Fr. Křížka
Letohradská
Bubenské nábřeží
19
Kostelní
nábřeží Edvarda Beneše
22
23
Ostrov Štvanice
Hlávkův most
Švermův most
24
nábřeží Ludvíka Svobody
Ke Štvanici
Klimentská
31
Revoluční
Wilsonova
Petrská
Sokolovská
Soukenická
25
Dlouhá
Truhlářská
Křižíkova
Na poříčí
26
30
Rybná
Nové Město
28
Na Florenci
27
29
Hybernská
Husitská
Seifertova
Senovážné nám
Na příkopě
Nekázanka
Panská
Jindřišská
Opletalova
59
Italská
Růžová
60
57
Politických vězňů
58
Wilsonova
Vodičkova
Wenceslas Square
61
Španělská
Riegrovy sady
Štěpánská
62
Krakovská
Mezibranská
Polská
Legerova
Italská
63
Vinohrady
Žitná
Blanická
Anglická
Slezská
náměstí Míru
Ječná
Sokolská
Jugoslávská
67
66
Korunní
Francouzská